Arthur Prickard

Aristotle on the art of poetry: a lecture with two appendices

Arthur Prickard

Aristotle on the art of poetry: a lecture with two appendices

ISBN/EAN: 9783743376175

Manufactured in Europe, USA, Canada, Australia, Japa

Cover: Foto ©Thomas Meinert / pixelio.de

Manufactured and distributed by brebook publishing software (www.brebook.com)

Arthur Prickard

Aristotle on the art of poetry: a lecture with two appendices

ARISTOTLE

ON THE

ART OF POETRY

ARISTOTLE

ON THE

ART OF POETRY

A LECTURE WITH TWO APPENDICES

A. O. PRICKARD, M.A.,

FELLOW OF NEW COLLEGE, OXFORD

" Homo qui erranti comiter monstrat viam
Quasi lumen de suo lumine accendat facit ;
Nihilominus ipsi lucet, quum illi accenderit."—ENNIUS.

London

MACMILLAN AND CO.

AND NEW YORK

1891

PREFATORY NOTE

THIS lecture was prepared in compliance
with an invitation from the Alexandrian
and Philosophical Clubs of the University
of Glasgow, which reached me through
my friend Professor Ramsay ; and was
read to them (with some omissions) on
12th December 1890. It is printed,
partly because the writer has from time
to time been engaged upon the *Poetics*
in the ordinary course of Oxford work,
and is glad of an opportunity of giving
a more general treatment to some of its
points, partly in the hope that where he

is at fault in fact or inference he may
be corrected by some who are more
familiar with Aristotle. He has attempted to give a plain account of the
chief judgments passed by a very clear
thinker upon the considerable body of
poetical literature accessible to him ; and
also to indicate some among them which
seem to be, in pre - eminent degree,
of lasting value and application. In
Appendix A are added references to
passages from Greek and Latin authors,
and notes on one or two questions which
called for more detailed examination. In
Appendix B is a list, doubtless incomplete, of the principal editions of and
commentaries upon the *Poetics*. The
great literary merit of the edition of
Twining, and the penetrating scholarship

of that of Tyrwhitt, call for a special recognition.

The numerical references in the text of the lecture are to notes in Appendix A ; the marginal references are to chapters of the *Poetics*.

ARISTOTLE ON THE ART OF POETRY

Felix qui potuit rerum cognoscere causas—

. . . . . .

Fortunatus et ille, deos qui novit agrestes.

.

THE short treatise on the Art of Poetry
known to us as the *Poetics*[1] comes
into our hands recommended, even before
we open the volume, by several different
considerations. It is the work of no ordinary man of letters (though Aristotle
was a lover of books, and perhaps the first
who ever formed a library), but of a man
who might have said of himself, as only
one or two could say in the history of our
race, that he had "taken all knowledge
for his province"; who, while dealing[2]

B

with the problems of the physical world, and with those of abstract and applied thought, and with the conditions of human nature, in the individual and in the body-politic, found his survey incomplete unless it included those Arts which ensure to us the gifts of ordered and beautiful speech—Rhetoric and her sister Poetry. Again, this is the earliest attempt to treat deliberately, and in set form, the subject of literature. The ground had been prepared by the teaching of the rhetoricians, by the Middle Comedy, above all by the speculations of Plato, so lofty and so penetrating, yet often ironical and sometimes bewildering ; but here for the first time questions as to the nature and office of Poetry are asked directly and are answered with authority. And, once more, over what a noble field of existing poetry did the gaze of the philosopher travel : Homer, the whole of Greek Tragedy,—for in Aristotle's time Tragedy, for all creative purposes, was a thing of the past,[3]—the whole of the Old Comedy, the whole of Greek Lyric. The poetry of the world, as we now know it, is doubtless a fuller as well as a more complex whole than this. Many languages, new civilisations, intellectual forces unknown to the Greek, a widening of the affections [4] inconceivable to the ancient world, have renovated and enriched the material which is still poured into poetic moulds. Yet something is gained to the critic whose effort is concentrated on a single language ; and what single volume of national poetry can compare in brilliance with that which was open to Aristotle—what in life and in life-giving power ? And, lastly, how much of the literary criticism of later time has been avowedly based on the results obtained by him. Often his words have been misunderstood, and his authority claimed for doctrines which he never contemplated. Yet how many has his method impelled to true inquiry ; how often has he been a guide to reasonable and fruitful judgments ; how many of his conclusions, faithfully worked out in the field of his own observation, remain literally true for the wider regions in which the modern critic moves.

I ask you to-day, first, to look into the substance and content of the *Poetics*, in the form in which the book has come down to us ; and afterwards to examine some of the leading thoughts which are, as you will see, successively brought under our notice in it.

In approaching the book itself two cautions are not unnecessary. First, let us not be disappointed if we fail to find much which we may have expected to be there. The treatment (let us at once allow it) is severe and scientific ; there is not a very large addition to our knowledge of facts about Greek poetry ; there are few judgments about particular poets and their works. And, secondly, let us be content with what is written, not asking to read into the words of the Greek writer our own thoughts, formed among surroundings and traditions other than his, and, in some points, essentially different.

We will now take the opening sentence, and consider the plan of treatment which the Author, with care and close definition, proposes to himself.

" My design is to treat of Poetry in C. 1. general and of its several species—to inquire, what is the proper effect of each —what construction of a fable or plan is essential to a good Poem—of what and how many parts each species consists ; with whatever else belongs to the same subject : and I shall begin, as Nature directs, with first principles." [5]

The several species of poetry here mentioned are explained to be Tragedy, Epic, Comedy, and Lyric ; the other matters belonging to the same inquiry

are those connected with the other Fine
Arts, and especially with Music and
Dancing, or Pantomime: the first principle, which is enunciated in the next
sentence, is that of Imitation.

How is this undertaking fulfilled in the
book before us? Partially, it must be
answered, and too shortly. Of one of
the species, Tragedy, we have a full examination. There is a carefully drawn
definition of Tragedy, which tells us what
it is and what it does; it is analysed into
six constituent parts or elements, which
are considered in order; and practical
rules are laid down for the management
of Plot, to which special prominence
had been already given in the opening
sentence. Yet even here we shall see
that there are gaps in important parts of
the argument; as is clear, not only to the
sense of the reader, but also from the
terms in which the Author refers to the
Poetics in his other works; there some-

times seems to have been misplacement
of material ; on the other hand some
chapters have appeared to scholars to be
the work of a later hand, of a grammarian
rather than a philosopher. Epic poetry
is treated far more shortly, yet perhaps
not inadequately, when it is remembered
that Aristotle considered Tragedy to have
in a sense superseded Epic, as the more
complex and manifold organism supersedes
that which is simpler ; so that the results
obtained for Tragedy are up to a certain
point capable of being transferred to
Epic ; and the inquiry need not begin
over again, or be conducted independently. The notice of Comedy is ex-
tremely slight ; of Lyric there is hardly a
word. About Poetry itself, the whole Art
as contrasted with its own species, there
is little except what arises incidentally in
the discussion of Tragedy. One chapter,
indeed, of great interest and value, traces
the Art from its earliest beginnings, and its

development under its several heads, until
its full and final proportions were reached
in the forms of Tragedy and Comedy.
But we have no definition of the nature
and office of Poetry; little about poets
and their claims upon our hearing.

After making allowance for the supreme
importance attached to Tragedy, and the
probability that the treatment of the other
species would be slighter, and that Poetry
itself would be approached through Tragedy
and not independently, we cannot fail to
conclude that the work as we have it is
fragmentary.   And, in fact, external evidence bears out this presumption.   In the
lists of Aristotle's works framed in the
second century A.D.[6] we find mention made
of a work entitled *Enquiry into Poetic Art*
in two books, of another *Concerning Poets*
in three books ; another is called *Didas-
caliæ*, another *Difficulties in Homer*.   It
seems reasonable to suppose that the first
of these works is represented to us by the

Poetics : the existence of the others, now lost, not only testifies to the interest taken by Aristotle in literature and its problems, but also explains why we ought not to look for much statement of facts in the extant book. Just as Bacon placed his *Historia Naturalis* before his theoretic work ; just as Aristotle himself collected accounts of the constitutions of a hundred and fifty-eight states before he wrote the *Politics* ; so in the case of Poetry the book *Concerning Poets* and the others contained the historical material : that which is in part preserved to us embodies his philosophical judgments upon the facts so brought together.

Happily, in spite of such gaps as I have indicated, and although we do not know how the work was put into its present form, the general argument is clear and satisfactory. I take up the account of its contents from the opening sentence. The C. 1. general principle that all Poetry rests on

Imitation having been laid down, the various kinds of Poetry, with the arts most nearly akin to it, are next compared with one another in respect of this principle. This is done under three heads, treated in three successive chapters ; the instruments or means of the imitation, its object, and its manner being taken separately. The process of comparison may appear somewhat mechanical ; it is supplemented by

C. 4. the historical chapter, to which I have already referred, one very weighty and luminous, and by one on the special history of Comedy ; and the results are then stated

C. 6. for Tragedy in the famous Definition :—

" Tragedy is an imitation of some action that is important, entire, and of a proper magnitude, by language embellished and rendered pleasurable—the different kinds of embellishment being kept separate in the different parts—in the way, not of narrative, but of action ; effecting through Pity and Terror the purgation of such passions or tendencies." An explanation follows :—" By pleasurable language I mean a language that has the embellishments of rhythm, melody, and metre. And I add ' by different means in different parts,' because in some parts metre alone is employed, in others melody."

You will observe that this Definition is in two parts. In the first we are told what Tragedy *is*, in the second what it *does*.[1] The first part states the "genus" and "differentia" of Tragedy : by genus it is, according to the first principle laid down on the first page, a form of Imitation ; the differentia is stated in the clauses which gather up the results of the first three chapters, and contrast Tragedy successively with the various kindred arts, under the three heads of comparison already mentioned. The second part states the effect or office of Tragedy ; namely, to work upon the feelings of Pity and Fear in a particular manner, which has not so far been explained, and which in fact is not explained in any part of the *Poetics*. The first part takes its significance from the word *Mimesis*, or Imitation; the second from the word *Katharsis*, or Purgation. It is not too much to say that in these two words, rightly understood, lies the whole of Aristotle's teaching on Tragedy, so far, at least, as it is theoretical. We will return to them presently for a more particular examination.

C. 6. The inquiry starts afresh from this point, and the six constituent "parts" of Tragedy are determined. This is done by a process something like chemical analysis; or, if we may vary the figure, like that by which the sections of the cone are derived from the solid figure, viewed under different aspects. On the first view of Tragedy you see that it is a performance given before the eyes of spectators : therefore *Spectacle* (in which term is included all that meets the eye—scenery, grouping of persons on the stage, and the like) is its most obvious element. Ask next by what means these performers effect their imitation, and you find that they use words and music : therefore *musical composition* and *verbal diction* are also elements of Tragedy. Ask further what it is which these performers seek thus to imitate, and the answer is that they reproduce the actions of men, or men engaged in action ; men who have each a moral character, and each an intellectual habit or faculty, which are the two determinants of all that is done or said. Hence the poet must reproduce *Character* and *Thought* (conventionally translated Sentiment), and he must further and above all reproduce the story or *Plot*, which is in fact the action itself ; and these are three additional parts, or elements, of Tragedy. The six parts must be present in all Tragedy, though the relative importance attached to each may vary with different poets, and in different plays.

But the order of derivation is not the order
of intrinsic worth.   Plot stands far above
the rest ; and for this judgment, which is
highly characteristic of Aristotle, but which
must not be accepted without reserve, a
series of reasons is given.   Character is
second, since men are only less interesting
than men's actions.   Thought and Language follow.   Music and Spectacle are
dismissed ; because, though of great practical importance, they have little to do
with the Art of Poetry considered apart
from that which is subsidiary to it, and
they do not concern the critic or theorist.
The other four are treated in order.   In
connection with Plot the following ques-
C. 7. tions are discussed — How long should
C. 8. a play be?   What standard of Unity is
C. 9. required?   Must the incidents be true in
the same sense as the facts of the his-
torian?   What is the place, to use a
modern phrase, of " poetical justice "?
C. 10. At this point, Plot is itself analysed into

four constituents : Peripeteia (or Evolution) and Recognition, which together are
the distinguishing signs of a complex plot ;
Character, and Suffering, which, if unsup-
ported by the other two, belong to the
simple plot. This second analysis, valuable as it is, may be found confusing, the
more so as Character figures twice over,
once as an independent part of Tragedy,
once as a part of Plot. The actions which
may possibly be treated in a tragedy are
then considered with special reference to
their power of working upon Pity and
Fear. Recognition receives a very full C. 16.
examination, cases found in actual plays
being considered and classified.

Under the head of Character four points
are noted. The characters must be *good*, C. 15.
that is, must not fall below a certain level
of worthiness and elevation ; they must be
suitable to conditions of age, sex, or station,
like the characters found in Nature or in
literature, and lastly *uniform* ; and again

illustrations are given from Greek plays. It is interesting to notice in passing that Aristotle's four rules for Character, or at any rate three of them, will be found in the *Ars Poetica* of Horace, a work perhaps deriving much of its detail, though not directly, from the *Poetics* ; and certainly written from an assured conviction that a Roman poet, writing for a grave Roman public, must above all things study Character.[8]

The third element of Tragedy, Thought, is only treated by reference to the

C. 19. Rhetoric.   For the stage speaker and the speaker of real life must draw upon the same faculty, to ensure that what they say shall be adapted to the circumstances under which they speak.   Thus Ajax about to fall upon his sword, or Clytemnestra exulting over her accomplished deed of blood, go to the same storehouse of thought as a real speaker in a great crisis of affairs ; and what Ajax or

Clytemnestra says the poet must conceive ; so that the faculty of thought which he appears to copy is in fact part of his own equipment.

The fourth element, Diction, is also CC. 19-22. common to Rhetoric, but is treated independently. The various deviations from plain or literal speech which may make words and expressions poetical are carefully explained; the treatment of Metaphor, both simple and compound, being especially lucid.

The account of Tragedy is now com- CC. 23, 24. plete, and we pass to Epic Poetry, to which the results obtained for Tragedy are, so far as the conditions admit, applied. For Tragedy is, as we saw, the more complex organism, and of its six parts two (Music and Spectacle) have no place in Epic. Some interesting criticism of the *Iliad* and *Odyssey*, and of other so-called Homeric poems, is given ; but the treatment is intentionally slight. A long and C. 25.

difficult chapter follows, in which difficulties currently alleged against poets,
especially Homer, are stated, and methods
C. 26. of solution offered.   In the last chapter
of the book Epic Poetry and Tragedy
are compared in point of excellence, and
the palm is, on the whole, awarded to
Tragedy.

It will be seen that the treatise is far
fuller on Tragedy than on any of the
other branches of Poetry ; also that it is
partly speculative, where the phenomena
of poetry are examined, and its nature
and office determined ; in part critical,
embodying rules for writing a good
play, and for judging . those which are
already in our hands.   Let us look first
at Aristotle's theory of Tragedy, in which
much of his theory of Poetry is involved.

C. 6.   "All Tragedy is a *Mimesis*, and it
effects a *Katharsis*."   We will take the
two terms in order.

In a certain superficial sense it is at

once plain that dramatic poetry is imitative, because it copies, or mimics, the doings of men. In another sense, also superficial, we can understand how some descriptive poetry is called imitative, the word being here borrowed from the art of Painting. But that neither of these will satisfy Aristotle's meaning we shall readily see if we consider the groups into which he arranges the various Fine Arts. Poetry in its several forms, Music in most of its forms, are all imitative arts. To the group thus formed he presently adds Dancing, or Pantomime; which, it need hardly be said, was so practised among the Greeks, and among other Southern European peoples, as to attain the dignity of a Fine Art.[9] Painting and Sculpture are also, no doubt, arts of imitation; but they belong to another group, and are always mentioned by way of illustration only.[10] Can we then so far attain to Aristotle's point of view as to see how

Poetry, Music, and Dancing cohere, and form a homogeneous group?

You will remember that, after laying down the general principle of Imitation, Aristotle proceeded to consider the different members of this group; taking three points in the imitation—its instruments, its object, and its manner—which he used as so many criteria for distinguishing the several arts, and in particular for comparing Tragedy with each of the others. Let us take the same three points, and ask under each head what the arts of our group have in common with one another, but not with Painting or Sculpture. First, by what means, or instruments, do they all imitate? Aristotle gives the answer: by rhythm, melody, and language; or some one, or some combination of these. Now by what do Painting and Sculpture imitate? Again let him answer: by colours and outlines. Secondly, what is it which our arts have to imitate? The

actions, characters, and passions of men.
But does not the painter also imitate
these? Yes, says Aristotle, in another
work,[11] but not immediately. The painter
imitates the outward embodiment or sign
of the passion, say, of anger, or of the
action of an angry man ; the musician or
poet imitates the very passion itself.
Thirdly, what is the manner, or process, of
imitation? The answer to this question is
not given by Aristotle, but may be readily
supplied. Poetry, Music, and Dancing
all suppose performers—one or many, and
an audience or body of spectators. Painting and Sculpture work by a permanent
representation of the thing intended. So
Poetry is, like Music, but unlike Painting,
an audible, direct, momentary presentment
of the actions and feelings of men.

Again, the unity and common basis of
these arts may be seen in another way,
if we remember that all were developed
out of a single elementary art. The

minstrel of early days sang and played, and the performance was helped out by gesticulation or dance.[12]   Song, says Plato,[13] has three elements, rhythm, melody, language—the very same three used by our arts ; which have in fact come into being by the expansion, on different sides, of the simple original performance of the minstrel.

Let us now try to understand what this principle of imitation is which we have seen to be shared by Poetry and Music. C. 4. We will turn to the fourth chapter, where a historical sketch is given of the evolution of Poetry.

Poetry, regarded as a whole, owes its being to two causes, both natural.   First, there is the instinct of imitation — the desire to copy the actions and gestures of others ; which is shared to some extent by the other animals, but is characteristic of man from his cradle.   This it is which sets the infant to delight in his mimic

creations ; a picture familiar to us from
Wordsworth's lines :

> See, at his feet, some little plan or chart,
> Some fragment from his dream of human life,
> Shaped by himself with newly-learned art ;
>> A wedding or a festival,
>> A mourning or a funeral ;
>>> And this hath now his heart,
>> And unto this he frames his song :
>>> Then will he fit his tongue
> To dialogues of business, love, or strife ;
>> But it will not be long
>> Ere this be thrown aside,
>> And with new joy and pride
> The little Actor cons another part ;
> Filling from time to time his "humorous stage"
> With all the Persons, down to palsied Age,
> That Life brings with her in her equipage ;
>> As if his whole vocation
>> Were endless imitation.

Next, it is also an instinct of man's
nature to take pleasure in recognising
things imitated by others. Whether
Aristotle intended this to be his second
natural cause is not quite clear : it may
well, perhaps better, be regarded as the ob-
verse or subjective side of the instinct first

mentioned.[14]   In any case, the pleasure
seems to be derived through a process
of the intellect : you look at a picture, or
other work of imitation, and you recognise,
by a sudden flash of thought, that this is
such - and - such a person or landscape.
This gratifies that universal desire of add-
ing to our knowledge which Aristotle,
" Master of those who know," imputes
without reserve to every member of the
human family.[15]   The pleasure is pro-
portionate to the speed and sureness of
the process of thought, just as a word
or metaphor which bears in upon us a
thought more quickly than its prosaic
equivalent, is always a vehicle of delight.[16]
But the desire of imitation, and the pleasure which we take in discerning imitation,
are not all.   There is a further physical
cause special to Poetry, or shared by it
with Music ; and this is what we understand by ear—the charms of melody and
rhythm, and especially of that branch of

rhythm known as metre. Here then are
two factors in our nature, distinct and
independent of one another — first, the
imitative instinct; secondly, the delicate
perceptions of ear: and Poetry is, if we
may borrow a mathematical word, a function or outcome of these two. Let us
watch the process at work. In the earliest
and rudest times there were those who
felt, more than their fellows, an impulse
which stirred them to reproduce, to themselves or to those about them, the feelings
by which they had been moved. But as
they did so, they found that their rude
improvisations took an added charm when
they fell into rhythmical words and movements and sounds. By degrees the
imitation became more refined and subtle,
and association gave fuller shades of
meaning to what at first was mere
mimicry; while, at the same time, the
other element, that of rhythm and cadence,
was beautified and enlarged; and at last,

after several such stages were passed, there was no longer a rude extemporaneous utterance, but—a poem. But the original motive had taken two different directions : some of the early inhabitants of the world whose feelings overflowed thus readily were of the graver sort, others of the lighter. Hence hymns to gods and panegyrics of heroes on the one hand ; hence rough abuse of a neighbour on the other. The growth of poetry still went on, and both tendencies met in Homer, the grander exemplified by his *Iliad* and *Odyssey*, the more ignoble in the *Margites*, a curious poem of so-called Homeric authorship, in which mere abuse had made way for that raillery directed at another's weakness or clumsiness which is in essence humorous. And still poetry grew : Tragedy, with its fuller organism, was the outcome of Epic ; Comedy displaced its simpler predecessors. And each grew on its own ground ; and in particular, those stories of mythology which were great enough to bear the weight of Tragedy lived down those which were slighter. And now, says Aristotle, though the full resources of Tragedy, in all its branches, may not have been exhausted, and future poets may yet make it stronger in particular directions ; yet the process of natural growth is over, the organism, as we know it, is complete.

In this paraphrase of Aristotle's words I have not read into them anything which is not there ; at least it has been my endeavour not to do so : more likely I have failed to render many particulars in his account, and some qualifications. But the theory itself is so strikingly and beautifully set out by Shelley in his *Defence of Poetry* (whether consciously or by coincidence of idea I do not know [17]), that, at the risk of some repetition, I must ask you to listen to a few of his sentences.

" A child at play by itself will express its delight by its voice and motions ; and every inflexion of tone and every gesture will bear exact relation to a corresponding antitype in the pleasurable impressions which awakened it ; it will be the reflected image of that impression ; and as the lyre trembles and sounds after the wind has died away, so the child seeks, by prolonging in its voice and motions the duration of the effect, to prolong also a consciousness of the cause.   In relation to the objects which delight a child, these expressions are what poetry is to higher objects.   The savage (for the savage is to ages what the child is to years) expresses the emotions produced in him by surrounding objects in a similar manner ; and language and gesture, together with plastic or pictorial imitation, become the image of the combined effects of those objects, and of his apprehension of them. Man in society, with all his passions and his pleasures, next becomes the object of the passions and pleasures of man ; an additional class of emotions produce an augmented treasure of expressions ; and language, gesture, and the imitative arts become at once the representation and the medium, the pencil and the picture, the chisel and the statue, the chord and the harmony."

And again :

" In the youth of the world men dance and sing, and imitate natural objects, observing in these actions, as in all others, a certain rhythm or order. And although all men observe a similar, they observe not the same order in the motions of the dance, in the melody of the song, in the combinations of language, in the series of their imitation of natural objects. For there is a certain order or rhythm belonging to each of these classes of mimetic representation, from which the hearer and the spectator receive an intenser and purer pleasure than from any other. The sense of an approximation to this order has been called taste by modern writers."

To recapitulate : in laying the foundation of poetry in imitation, Aristotle asserts the identity of its operation with music ; since in both arts men, obeying an imperious instinct, reproduce, for themselves or for those about them, the feelings which they have themselves experienced. It would seem to follow that, upon this view, taken in its full strictness, lyric poetry should be the most imitative of all the kinds; more imitative than Tragedy, except so far as Tragedy, according to Greek usage, incorporates Lyric with itself. But there is another and more obvious sense of the word, in which the drama, mimicking directly the details of human action, is most imitative ; and the two senses cannot always be kept apart. The distinction is finely laid down by De Quincey in a paper on *The Antigone of Sophocles*. He writes :

"In this argument" (one directed against oratorio or lyrical drama) "lies an ignorance of the very first principle concerned in *every* Fine Art. In all alike, more or less directly, the object is to reproduce in the mind some great effect, through the agency of *idem in alio*. The *idem*, the same impression, is to be restored, but *in alio*, in a different material—by means of some different instrument."

And again :

"If a man, taking a hint from the Roman *saltatio* (*saltavit Andromachen*), should say that he would ' whistle Water-loo,'—that is, by whistling connected with pantomime, would express the passion and the charges of Waterloo,—it would be monstrous to refuse him his postulate on the pretence that people did not whistle at Waterloo. . . . It is the very worst objection in the world to say that the strife of Waterloo did not reveal itself through whistling. Undoubtedly it did not ; but that is the very ground of the man's art. He will reproduce the fury and the movement as to the only point which concerns you, viz. the effect upon your own sympathies, through a language that seems without any relation to it : he will set before you that which *was* at Waterloo through that which was *not* at Waterloo—whereas any direct factual imitation, resting upon painted figures dressed up in regimentals, and worked by watchwork through the whole movements of the battle, would have been no art whatever in the sense of a Fine Art, but a base *mechanic* mimicry."

We are now led to a point at which a new aspect of the Imitation theory comes in. The word was not first applied to poetry by Aristotle ; on the contrary, it was much in Plato's mouth, and is one of the two supports which bear up his attack upon Poetry. For Plato, poet though he was, and lover of poets, could

yet find room for none in his ideal State;
and one-half of his case against them is
summed up in the word Imitation. You
will find the charge set out in the third
book of the *Republic.* Life, in Plato's
State, was divided into sections, like the
squares upon a chessboard; and justice,
the characteristic virtue of his community,
was to move on your own squares, and
never trespass upon your neighbour's.
But the poet is a trespasser.[18] He may
know little of leading an army, or steering
a ship, or mixing a posset; yet he pro-
fesses to be equally at home in all these
functions, and expects a hearing when he
speaks about them. Also, it is unworthy
of a man to be always speaking in the
person of others. Even Homer does it:
yes, he is the captain of the company of
tragedians, and, as often as not, speaks in
a part. Open the *Iliad.* For sixteen
lines Homer speaks, while he invokes the
Muses, and expounds the causes of the

Wrath. But at the seventeenth it is no longer Homer but the priest Chryses who speaks. Perhaps what he says and imprecates might be thrown into narrative form, and Plato gives a sample, and perhaps this might pass. But then it would no longer be Homer!

The attack on Imitation is resumed in the tenth book from a different side, in connection with Plato's so-called " Ideas." The world, with the things which we see, is but a counterpart or imitation of the world and things which really are. What then of the Painter and Poet? The Painter copies what he thinks he sees in the world : not the things which are, nor even the things which seem to be, but his own notion of those appearances. And so of the Poet. So each is three degrees removed from truth and reality.

To this attack Aristotle does not refer. Yet in basing all Poetry upon Imitation, he takes up, surely with conscious purpose,

an impregnable position against it. Poetry
is, not accidentally but essentially, imitative ; it is so because of an instinct
which lies deep in our nature. Tragedy,
which is in the most obvious sense imitative, is also the highest branch of Poetry ;
and Homer is excellent because he knows
how to keep himself in the background,
and, after a word of prelude, introduces
a man or a woman—always one whose
character is distinct and individual. Yet
Aristotle allows for the possible abuse of
the mimetic impulse. The tragedian must
not overdo his part, or the charge of vul-
garity lies ; and a good play must stand
the test of being read at home, not depend-
ing for its success upon the incidents of
its public performance.

We pass on to the concluding words of
the Definition of Tragedy. Tragedy deals C. 6.
with the feelings of Pity and Fear, and
its operation is defined by the word

Katharsis, which we must now endeavour to understand.   In the first place, I will ask you to observe that Plato's case against Poetry has another and a stronger side than we have yet seen; and this is precisely that which is concerned with Pity and Fear.   Homer, or one of the tragedians, exhibits a suffering hero, who makes a long utterance about his woes, or even weeps, or beats his breast; and the spectator's heart goes out to such a sufferer. Thus the emotional part of our nature, which a strong man restrains within himself, and a wise lawgiver will wish to see starved in others, is fed to satiety; our sympathy is elicited in such a way that it seems a virtue to give it; and that nobler part of the soul, which should watch over its mere impulses, is enfeebled and lulled into a false security.   It will be seen that, along with much that is whimsical, there is a very solid groundwork here.   " Passive impressions," says Butler, in well-known

words, " by being repeated, grow weaker " :
and so, in a sense, the more generous the
emotions upon which the tragic poet plays,
the more disastrous is the paralysis of moral
being which follows. How does Aristotle
meet the difficulty ?

First, just as we saw him doing with
Mimesis, he directly confronts Plato.
Tragedy, not by an incidental operation
which needs apology, but in its own
proper function, raises Pity and Fear.
Fear is defined [19] to be the pain or dis-
tress felt in view of a considerable evil,
nearly impending over oneself or some one
like oneself. And Pity is much akin to
this ; only the person to be affected by
the evil must be, on the whole, undeserv-
ing of what befalls him. Thus the death
or danger which in a play threatens the
hero, affects us, the spectators, with Pity
and Fear. Now let us carry our thoughts
back to the poet of the early world—the
savage, as we called him. He has an

impression of fear or pity fresh upon
him, and he wishes to reproduce it, and
to make clear to others what he felt.
Then he will go through in pantomime
some deed of horror, probably a murder;
gesticulating and droning a wild dirge;
and a thrill of horror or sympathy will
pass through his hearers. Thus he has, in
the strictest sense of the word, imitated
those elementary feelings—in this case,
those of Pity and Fear — which had
moved him. The Arts unfold themselves.
Tragedy, with all its appliances,— stage,
actors, musicians,—does in effect just what
the savage did ; it copies a deed of horror,
and communicates to the poet's audience
the thrill which the poet first felt in himself. Music, in its developed power, does
the same ; it reproduces, or imitates, the
same elementary feeling. Only Music
deals with a more varied field of emotions,
and does not confine itself to Pity and
Fear. Tragedy deals only, or mainly,

with those feelings : this is possibly to narrow its scope too much ; for other feelings—Admiration, for example, or Hope—are legitimate motives for serious drama. But in the conventional and historical[20] use of the word, which Aristotle accepts, suffering is essential. Tragedy then only exists in order to awaken Pity and Fear ; but how can it be held innocent in so doing ?

The answer lies in the word Katharsis. Tragedy effects a Katharsis of the feelings of Pity and Fear, or more strictly of the tendencies to those feelings, and it does so through Pity and Fear. No word of explanation is added in the *Poetics*. But in the *Politics*,[21] where the place of Music in education is under discussion, we find the key.

Certain kinds of Music, those namely which are exciting, should be listened to by the young rather than performed by them, since a passive attitude is necessary.

For all of us are susceptible, in different degrees, to the power of such Music. Watch a person of a specially susceptible temperament when the "sacred" melodies are played, and you will see him first excited, then calmed. The reason is that the nature was before overcharged with susceptibility : now the excitement has been called to the surface, and worked out of the system, which is left clearer and more healthy for its absence ; in fact, the man has been restored to his true and natural habit. And so it is with all according to the several degrees of their susceptibility to musical impressions. And so too with the tendency to any feeling, Pity and Fear being specially named : you may call up the feeling by an artificial process, and so get rid of it. Notice, first, that the metaphor is medical ; and, secondly, that the result is in all cases a *pleasurable* relief.[22] "Such," says Aristotle, "is Katharsis in outline : hereafter I will deal with the subject more exactly in my treatise on Poetry." So far as the work in our hands goes, this promise is unredeemed ; but we can have no doubt what the main features of the explanation were. Only it seems right to assume that we should not have a mere repetition of the crude medical metaphor : it is essential, according to all Aristotle's teaching about Tragedy, that the purging should be effected by a tale of great passions and of a noble sufferer, that the feelings should be elevated as well as relieved.

Though the explanation of Katharsis in connection with the passage in the *Politics* is given with sufficient exactness in a note to Twining's edition,[23] yet much misconception has prevailed about it, and a vast amount of criticism, often valuable in itself, has been based upon erroneous views of Aristotle's meaning.[24] Indeed, I believe that I am correct in saying that the question has only been put upon a

certain basis in recent times by Jacob
Bernays.[25]   It is then remarkable to find
that our own Milton, who was a diligent
student of the *Poetics* and of its Italian
commentators, has expressed so much of
the true sense in his preface to *Samson
Agonistes* :

   " Tragedy, as it was anciently composed,
hath been ever held the gravest, moralest,
and most profitable of all other poems :
therefore said by Aristotle to be of power,
by raising pity and fear, or terrour, to purge
the mind of those and such-like passions ;
that is, to temper or reduce them to just
measure with a kind of delight, stirred
up by reading or seeing those passages
well imitated.   Nor is Nature herself wanting in her own efforts to make good his
assertion : for so, in physick, things of
melancholick hue and quality are used
against melancholy, sour against sour, salt
to remove salt humours."

   Look again at the closing lines :

His servants he, with new acquist
Of true experience, from this great event
With peace and consolation hath dismissed,
And **calm** of mind, all passion spent.

If the words of the preface seemed to
sketch out the merely physical view of
the purgative power of Tragedy which we
found in the *Politics*, these lines supply
that requirement of greatness and nobility
in the sufferings, which can never have
been wanting in Milton's thought.   But
this side of the operation of Greek Tragedy
is even more directly set out by a modern
poet :

What hinders that we treat this tragic theme
As the Three taught when either woke some woe
—How Klutaimnestra hated, what the pride
Of Jokasté, why Medeia clove
Nature asunder—small rebuked by large,
We felt our puny hates refine to air,
Our prides as poor prevent the humbling hand,
Our petty passion purify its tide.[26]

We saw that Plato's case against Poetry
rested upon two points—its imitative character, its appeal to feeling.   We have

now seen that Aristotle, without naming his master, yet probably in direct answer to a challenge given in the *Republic*,[27] not only admits the truth of the two allegations, but makes them the foundation of his own theory. Poetry is in essence an Imitation ; it works on and through Pity and Fear, and purges those feelings. Of the sufficiency of the answer we are not now called to judge. But Plato, in his later and more prosaic work on the *Laws*, had returned to the attack. When the tragic and comic poets come forward and ask for sufferance in the State, this is the answer which they receive from the lawgiver : " Excellent sirs, we are ourselves composers of a tragedy,—so far as in us lies, the noblest and the best. All our state is framed to be an imitation of the noblest and best life, and that is indeed, as we hold, the truest tragedy." [28] An imitation of the noblest and best life. The words seem, but only, I think, seem, to supply something which is not in Aristotle, and to give a deeper and more noble conception of Tragedy than his. However this may be, the fact remains that Plato's last word to the poets is— "Go." And Aristotle's word is of welcome. We will trust you, he says in effect, and we will trust human nature. Our citizens have wholesome human appetites, and if you were to offer them garbage they would not consent to feed upon it. Their digestion is vigorous, and man's common food will be good enough to nourish them. Here we notice Aristotle's faith in human nature, and also his generous desire to include in his scheme all which can enrich life and make it beautiful.[29] We see too his strong common sense, as he distinguishes between the thing and its abuse, and will not use the knife when only regulation is needed.

We have so far spoken at some length of the cardinal points in Aristotle's theory of Tragedy ; and of Poetry, so far as it is therein involved. Let us turn from his speculation to his criticism, and observe how he deals with actual Greek plays. We will take the most concrete application of his principles ; and ask at once which are his favourite tragedies, and upon what grounds. The answer comes quite clearly back. The *Œdipus Tyrannus* of Sophocles, and the *Iphigenia in Tauris* of Euripides, are with him standards of excellence, to which appeal is constantly made. Both are plays of high and manifold merit, the former, of course, being the more famous. And why are they selected ?   Largely, but not entirely, for the interest and ingenuity of the plot. Take the *Iphigenia*. Instead of being really sacrificed at Aulis, she has been rescued by Artemis, and made her priestess in the land of the Tauri, now the Crimea, where it is part of the duties of her office to prepare, with

a certain ceremonial, all strangers for the
death to which a barbarous custom
doomed them. Hither comes Orestes in
the course of the wanderings appointed
by Apollo in expiation for a mother's
murder, and with him his faithful Pylades.
It is clear that a double recognition is C. 11.
now necessary ; for neither does brother
know sister, nor sister brother ; and this,
on one side at least, is managed with
extreme cleverness, and with much beauty C. 16.
of detail, and is highly praised by Aristotle. Again, this is a case where one C. 14.
person is about to do a dreadful thing
upon another in ignorance of their near-
ness in blood, and makes the discovery in
time to stay her hand ; and this is the
most effective combination possible. And
further, the poet has shown good judgment C. 17.
in distinguishing between what came
within the story proper, and what was
to be introduced by way of episode. One
very curious feature in the play has not

been noticed by Aristotle, but illustrates
more than one of his principles.   Orestes
and his sister get down to their ship, and
are making their escape (a messenger tells
us) from the barbarous country, and the
action might be thought to be complete.
But a wind gets up,[30] his narrative goes
on, which carries them back to shore, and
they are again at the mercy of Thoas.
Thus the knot is again tied ; and it is
only loosed by the appearance of Athena,
not otherwise a person in the play, *ex
machina*, who announces that they are to
go in safety, and that Thoas must not
detain them.   Now why is this recom-
plication introduced ?   Aristotle lays it
down that the best plays end unhappily ;
since when all leave the stage with friendly
words, and a happy marriage is arranged,
C. 13. the spirit of comedy comes in.   Now if
the fugitives had simply escaped, snap-
ping their fingers at Thoas, the ending
would have been essentially comic : per-

haps, after the grave and pathetic scenes which have gone before, we should rather call it burlesque. But the appearance of the *deus ex machina*, a device not itself to C. 15. be praised, enables the piece to be finished after all with dignity and elevation of feeling.

In the *Œdipus* most of the same merits are found. But Aristotle also, and specially, praises the skill with which the catastrophe is reserved ; it happens coincidently with the recognition of the hero's parentage, and so gains in power ; C. 10. and during a large part of the play the action is masked, so that every step which seems to bring Œdipus towards happiness and relief really leads him nearer to the abyss. Then the character is most happily chosen ; the greatness and generosity of Œdipus, taken with his obvious faults of obstinacy and self- C. 13. will, making him the ideal tragic hero. Aristotle censures a certain element of

E

absurdity in the plot, namely, where we are asked to believe that Œdipus had raised no questions about the death of his pre-

C. 15. decessor on the throne ; but this, as he
C. 24. says, lies not within the play, but among the antecedent circumstances, and therefore is excused.

Another play which deeply interested Aristotle was the *Philoctetes* of Sophocles. It is hardly mentioned in the *Poetics* ; but in the *Ethics* [31] the author twice remarks upon the character of Neoptolemus, so generous that he could not abide by the lie to which Odysseus had schooled him, but gave in to the noble pleasure of telling the truth. Now the *Philoctetes* of Sophocles is a play where the plot is highly ingenious, but is itself worked out of, and through, the characters, and mainly through that of Neoptolemus. It is therefore a play where plot and character are both conspicuous ; it was composed by Sophocles late in life, and when he had before him a play by Euripides on the same story, as well as one by Æschylus.

The *Choephoræ* of Æschylus is also mentioned, with praise, in respect of the particular form of Recognition which it C. 16. illustrates. From the great beauty of the recognition - scene in this play, and the offence which some of its details apparently gave, we could wish that the critic's judgment had been more fully expressed, and, it must be added, less ambiguous.[32]

From the selection of these plays, Aristotle's leading principle in dramatic criticism is now apparent. It is the supreme importance of Plot. This is pointed out by a great English writer, lately taken from us. In an early essay on " Poetry, with reference to Aristotle's *Poetics*," Cardinal Newman writes :—

" Aristotle considers the excellence of a tragedy to depend upon its plot — and

since a tragedy, as such, is obviously the
exhibition of an action, no one can deny
his statement to be abstractedly true.
Accordingly, he directs his principal attention to the economy of the fable ;
determines its range of subjects, delineates
its proportions, traces its progress from a
complication of incidents to their just and
satisfactory settlement, investigates the
means of making a train of events striking or affecting, and shows how the
exhibition of character may be made sub-
servient to the purpose of the action.
His treatise is throughout interesting and
valuable.   It is one thing, however, to
form the *beau ideal* of a tragedy on scientific principles ; another to point out the
actual beauty of a particular school of
dramatic composition.   The Greek tragedians are not generally felicitous in the
construction of their plots.   Aristotle,
then, rather tells us what Tragedy should
be than what Greek Tragedy really was."

The writer proceeds to examine three
plays of acknowledged excellence, one by
each tragedian : the *Agamemnon*, the
Œdipus Tyrannus, and the *Bacchæ* ; showing that the interest of the play does not
in fact vary directly with the elaborateness
of the plot, since in only one of the three
can the plot be said to be elaborate at all.
And he instances the *Œdipus Coloneus* as
one of the two most beautiful plays of
Sophocles, yet one in which the plot is
not striking.

We must first admit that Aristotle
fully and deliberately adopts the opinion
imputed to him : Plot is brought into
prominence in the opening words of the
book, reasons are afterwards carefully
stated for placing it first among the six
constituent parts of Tragedy, and the
discussion of the features of Plot is much
more exhaustive than that bestowed upon
any of the other parts. And in taking
this view Aristotle is at one with him-

self, and his whole method coheres.
Poetry is, in its operation, an appeal to
the feelings ; therefore Tragedy, which
makes this appeal with most strength and
condensation, is higher than the other
kinds of poetry ; therefore plot, which
embodies the appeal in its most immediate
form, is higher than the other parts of
Tragedy.   Let us, however, observe that
Aristotle does not really undervalue character so much as his words may seem
to convey.   He condemns several plays
because the characters are faulty, judged
by his own rules.   He does not name
any play for censure because it is weak in
plot.   It is true that he condemns all
which are episodic ; that is, where
incidents are strung together without
necessary or probable connection.   But
then it is just in such a play that the
characters, however admirable, are presented with least force and directness.   Is
not the *Œdipus Coloneus* itself an illustra-

tion ; since in that play, so entirely re-
deemed by the grandeur and tenderness
of its closing scenes, the reader is somewhat distracted, often perhaps offended,
by the number of the persons, and the
unconnected way in which in the middle
part of the play they enter and leave the
stage ? And Aristotle, though preferring
the elaborate plot, where the successive
scenes involve, so to say, ascending and
descending powers of happiness and misery
in symmetrical sequence, yet finds room for
that which is simple, and which interests
us merely by the character or the
suffering. He tells us that Character is
to be introduced for the sake of Plot, in
order, that is, to colour and vivify Plot.
Yet it is hardly a paradox to say, on the
whole view, that he values Plot so highly
for the sake of Character, as being the
vehicle and mode of its presentment.

Is it possible that we are inclined to
feel dissatisfied with Aristotle's scheme as

narrow and unreal, partly because it may
seem to leave little room for the one
Greek play which we probably know best,
and feel to have more modern and abid-
ing interest than any other—the *Prometheus* of Æschylus?   But in truth the
Prometheus is not faulty in plot, for it
has no plot : it holds us from opening
to close with unquestioned charm ; yet no
advance is made in the action.   Indeed,
the *Prometheus* is an exceptional play,
and proves, that is, puts to the trial, more
than one of the accepted rules of drama.

Passing from plays to poets, we find a
C. 13. few important judgments in the *Poetics.*
Euripides is the " most tragic " of poets ;
that is, by not refusing to have recourse
to the most obvious appeals to feeling, he
practically best succeeds in working upon
pity and fear, as it is the office of Tragedy
to do.   But this is true with reservations ;
in his management of the Chorus he is
unfavourably contrasted with Sophocles ;

and the practice of introducing choral
odes which are unconnected with the
action — mere lyrical interludes — is con-
demned in Agathon, and, by implication, C. 18.
in Euripides. The saying of Sophocles
that "he drew men himself as they ought
to be, Euripides as they are" is quoted ; C. 25.
the context showing [33] that Sophocles
describes his own aim as ideal ; and
Aristotle appears to endorse the statement. Agathon is mentioned as having
attempted a novelty by writing a tragedy
with fanciful names, like a Comedy ;
this Aristotle neither praises nor blames, C. 9.
though he points out the advantage to
the tragedian of the old practice of writing
on an accepted mythological foundation.
Few later poets are named, one Theo- C. 11.
dectes, a contemporary and friend of Aris- C. 17.
totle, being perhaps the most interesting.

We have spoken thus far of Tragedy,
because it is the subject of far the largest

part of Aristotle's work ; and even now we must leave untouched his actual canons of the drama ; a wide and interesting field of inquiry, in which Aristotle is followed by such great critics as Corneille, as Dryden, above all, as Lessing. We must speak even more summarily of the other kinds of poetry. As to their definition, one half of it—that which tells us what each is—will be derived from the definition of Tragedy, by making the suitable variations in the clauses which limit, in each case, the imitation. Thus Comedy will be the imitation of a trivial or ludicrous c. 5. action (and Aristotle provides us with an excellent definition of the ludicrous), but will in other respects conform to the nature of Tragedy ; Epic will proceed by way of narrative, pure or mixed, and not through persons acting ; and so forth. But the definition will be incomplete unless we can make clear what the office or function of each kind is, as the office of

Tragedy was to purge certain feelings.
Aristotle expressly mentions a special
kind of pleasure as arising out of each
kind of poetry, and never to be confounded
with that arising out of other kinds. The
pleasure of Comedy is realised when the
piece ends with smiles, and the bitterest
enemies walk out arm in arm. The C. 13.
pleasure which the Epic poet effects he
does not explain ; but Sir Philip Sidney
will tell us :—

" And with a tale, forsooth, he cometh
unto you, with a tale which holdeth
children from play, and old men from the
chimney corner, and pretending no more,
doth intend the winning of the mind from
wickedness to virtue."

And so of Lyric.

What does Aristotle contribute to our
knowledge about Poetry as a whole?
He ventures on no formal definition. It
is clear that Poetry is, on his view, an
Imitation of a certain kind, producing a

certain pleasurable effect upon the feelings. But how to fill in the epithets left in blank? The most pressing question is whether Metre shall or shall not be made essential. The requirement is omitted in such a well-known definition as that of Mill [34] : " Poetry is thought tinged by feeling, and overheard "; or in Shelley's, " Poetry is the record of the best and happiest moments of the happiest and best minds "; or in Bacon's, " Historiæ imitatio ad placitum conficta "; it is left ambiguous in Coleridge's, "the best words in the best order." [35]   How does Aristotle help us here?   I should say that his answer is clear : metre is not the most essential characteristic of Poetry, yet it would be a misuse of language to call anything a poem which is not metrical in form.   I am aware that, in a passage in

C. 1. the first chapter of the *Poetics*, he has been thought to say the reverse. But I believe that neither the words which he uses, nor the instances which he quotes, in any degree settle the point against the view of his meaning given above,[36] and this although such examples of poetical prose as the Myth in the *Phædrus* and parts of the first book of Herodotus were under his eye. Conversely, indeed, it is true that all which is metrical is not poetry. You might put Herodotus into metre, and the result would be history of a sort, not poetry. The speculations of Empedocles on the physical world remain physics and nothing else, though in hexameters. But elsewhere, Plato and Aristotle invariably assume that only what is metrical is to be called poetry; nay, that metrical writing and poetry are, for the common purposes of language, convertible terms. " In metre, as a Poet," says Plato,[37] " or without metre, as a layman." " A good sentence," says Aristotle,[38] "should have rhythm, but not metre ; if it have metre, it will be a poem."

But though we have no definition of Poetry, yet both Plato and Aristotle lay down distinctions which will help us to clear our view. "Give me an example," says a speaker in Plato's *Banquet* [39] (of a word which has a general and also a restricted use). "Poetry," is the answer; "which is a general name signifying every cause whereby anything proceeds from that which is not into that which is, so that the exercise of every inventive art is poetry, and all such artists poets. Yet they are not called poets, but distinguished by other names; and one portion or species of poetry, that which has relation to music and rhythm, is divided from all others, and known by the name belonging to all. For this is alone properly called poetry, and those who exercise the art of this species of poetry, poets." "The poet," says Aristotle, is a "poet in respect of his imitation." "The poet should be a maker of myths, not a maker of metres." May I

add another distinction laid down by a
modern writer? "Poetry," says Coleridge,[40] "is not the proper antithesis to
prose, but to science. Poetry is opposed to
science, and prose to metre." Somewhere
among these three sayings has not the last
word been spoken on the subject, or shall
we ever be nearer to a formal definition?

Perhaps none of Aristotle's contributions to our general understanding of
Poetry is more fruitful than his profound
saying that "Poetry is more serious and C. 9.
more philosophical than History, because
it deals with universal truth, not with that
which lies in details." Here we must
notice that the conception of history is
somewhat a narrow one, as it is identified
with annals or chronicles; and also that
Poetry is not to be held really to work by
any dull process of abstraction or generalisation, but by the quick insight which
sees the permanent or typical truth under-
lying the casual and individual instance.

The substance of the remark is well given by an old English writer (I believe unconsciously) :—

"Truth, narrative, and past," says Davenant,[41] "is the idol of historians, who worship a dead thing ; and Truth operative, and by her effects continually alive, is the mistress of Poets, who hath not her existence in matter, but in reason."

Then we have an excellent account of Metaphor, followed out in detail, with examples from the poets, of metaphor both simple and compound. Power of metaphor, he holds, is the surest mark of the poet ; for it cannot be learnt or got from without, and is, in fact, the ability to see those finer shades of likeness which underlie nature, and which Bacon calls " una eademque naturæ vestigia aut signacula diversis materiis et subjectis impressa." Poetry is the province of the man of enthusiastic temper, or the man of ready genius : the former is readily fired, and soon touched to

fine issues; the latter penetrates those delicate degrees of likeness which others miss.

But, after all, it is in Aristotle's teaching
about the imitative character of poetry,
and its power of stirring the feelings, that
we must look for the essential part of his
theory. From what we have said above,
it will be clear that what it is and what it
does, the imitation and the feeling, are
closely connected ; and also that when he
says that Poetry is Imitation, Aristotle
is asserting its power to set forth a special
and an elevated kind of truth ; and is
answering the objection, dating from
before Plato's time,[12] that it was nothing
but a glorified falsehood. Let us verify
the meaning of Imitation as applied to
Epic. After allowing for the power which
lies in mere eloquence and rhythm, and
for the subtler charm of association, is it
not still the simple elementary feelings
upon which the epic poet plays, reproduc-
ing and imitating them ? Take the most

F

familiar instances from the Latin Epic,
understanding the word in Aristotle's
enlarged sense. Read the story of the
fall of Troy, or of the deaths of Turnus
and Camilla, for pity and for fear. Read
the burst of feeling in the second *Georgic*
for the passion of pride of country. Or
take those single lines,[43] which have a
power beyond their mere words to repre-
sent a whole mood of feeling ; the passion
of pity in—

Sunt lacrimæ rerum, et mentem mortalia
tangunt ; [44]

the passion of despair in—

Arma amens capio, nec sat rationis in armis ; [45]

the passion of panic and indignation which
breathes beneath the " drums and tramp-
lings " heard in—

Ad confligendum venientibus undique Poenis ; [46]

the passion of the strength which stands
unaided—

Inconcussa tenens dubio vestigia mundo ; [47]

the passion of a great and generous failure—

Quem si non tenuit, magnis tamen excidit ausis.[48]

Every mood of passion, and not the sterner ones only, do the poets call up and, in Aristotle's sense, imitate ; and where this imitation fails, however wise the thought or eloquent its expression, I think we shall find that we withhold or grudge the name of poetry. Many lines and passages there will be, perhaps even in the great poems, which will not bear the test. Aristotle allows for dull reaches of Epic verse, where elaborate diction may properly make up for the absence of other charm. But on the whole view, and in his general work, the poet will be found to imitate feeling : he holds up the mirror to Nature, but it is a magic mirror, one which reflects the deep springs of action as well as the action lying before our eyes ; not only the world of phenomena

C. 24.

(if we may turn Plato's words against himself), but the phenomena as they appear to the eye of genius ; that is, the realities which genius apprehends and can alone interpret.

I cannot hope that I have made Aristotle's conception of Poetry stand out clearly and completely, for the subject is difficult and our review must be summary. But I have endeavoured to touch upon most of the salient points, and to show where his guiding hand has helped those who have come after him. I have freely used the words of modern writers, not for the sake of ornament only, but that we might feel how modern, rather how true for all time, much of our author's thought remains. And as I began by stating reasons which made it likely beforehand that the book would concern us all, as being the first effort of criticism, as coming from a mind so comprehensive and so acute, as based upon the brilliant poetical literature of Greece, so I will now appeal to authority, and ask you to hear Milton's estimate of the place and value of a study of the *Poetics*. You will find it in his treatise *On Education* :—

" When all these employments are well conquered, then will the choice Histories, Heroic Poems, and Attic Tragedies of stateliest and most regal argument, with all the famous Political Orations, offer themselves ; which, if they were not only read, but some of them got by memory and solemnly pronounced with right accent and grace, as might be taught, would endue them with the spirit of Demosthenes or Cicero, Euripides or Sophocles. And now, lastly, will be the time to read with them those organic arts which enable them to discourse and write perspicuously and elegantly, and according to the fittest style of lofty, mean, or lowly. Logic therefore, so much as is useful, is to be repressed

to this due place, with all her well-couched
Heads or Topics, until it be time to open
her contracted palm into a graceful and
ornate rhetoric taught out of the rule
of Plato, Aristotle, Phalereus, Cicero,
Hermogenes, Longinus. To which Poetry
would be made subsequent, or indeed
rather precedent, as being less subtle and
fine, but more simple, sensuous, and
passionate. I mean not here the pro-
sody of a verse, which they could not
but have hit on before among the rudiments of grammar, but that sublime Art
which in Aristotle's *Poetics*, in Horace,
and the Italian commentaries of Castelvetro, Tasso, Mazzoni, and others, teaches
what the laws are of a true Epic Poem,
what of a Dramatic, what of a Lyric,
what Decorum is, which is the grand
masterpiece to observe.

" This would make them soon perceive
what despicable creatures our common
Rimers and Play-writers be, and show

them what religious, what glorious and magnificent use might be made of Poetry both in divine and human things. From hence, and not till now, will be the right season of forming them to be able Writers and Composers in every excellent matter, when they shall be thus fraught with an universal insight into things. Or whether they be to speak in Parliament or Council, honour and attention would be waiting on their lips. Then would there also appear in pulpits other visages, other gestures, and stuff otherwise wrought than what we now sit under ofttimes to as great a trial of our patience as any other that they preach unto us. These are the studies wherein our noble and our gentle youths ought to bestow their time in a disciplinary way from twelve to one-and-twenty ; unless they rely more upon their ancestors dead than upon themselves living."

Such, and so highly praised, is the edifice of poetical criticism which Aristotle

reared. It is simple in its lines, and has
suffered from the ravages, as well as from
the accretions, of ages ; but the hand of the
Master is unmistakeable. If I may be
bold to pursue the metaphor, I would
liken this work, not to the lofty and intri-
cate buildings of lands richly favoured by
Nature, but to such a homely structure as
you may see in latitudes more northerly
than these, among the great Scandinavian
forest tracts, where Aristotle's ancestors
and our own, the learned tell us, once
lived and multiplied as a single race. The
house owes nothing to the quarry, nothing
to the mason, and but little to the plane
or chisel of the carpenter. But every one
of the timbers has been proved by the
wise old builder, and found fit for his use :
when the parent tree grew in the forest,
it had been fed by an iron soil, and trained
by storms, and strengthened by sunshine.
The open beams of the roof are beautiful,
as well as strong ; for they are round and

shapely in all their length, and, being
richly coloured by air and by vital juices
from within, can return the deep glow of
the firelight. The tree was matured
through the lifetime of generations of men,
and the building may hold together as
long, perhaps, as Time himself. Enter, if
you have opportunity : the doorway is
narrow, but noble guests assemble, and
the entertainment satisfies ; the welcome
prepared for all is unfailing ; *and here too
there are gods.*

APPENDIX A

[1] *Title of the " Poetics."*—Aristotle himself refers
to the work as τὰ περὶ ποιητικῆς, sc. τέχνης. See
Politics, 8, 7 (1341 *b*. 39); *Rhetoric*, 1, 11 (1372ᵃ2),
etc. This title precisely corresponds to that of
the *Rhetoric* (*Poet.* c. 19). As there was no
English word " Poetic," and the familiar Latin
title " Poetica " was ambiguous, English writers
early coined the word " Poetics," following the
analogy of " Ethics," " Politics," etc. A word
used by Milton (see above, p. 70) and by Bentley
is plainly classical.

[2] *Order of Aristotle's Works.*—The expression
in the text is purposely vague, because we have
little knowledge as to the order of composition of
the various works of Aristotle ; nor is it very
material, since the oral lectures on the various
subjects with which he dealt need not have
followed any such order. It is probable that
after writing the logical treatises and the first
two books of the *Rhetoric*, he passed to the
Ethics and *Politics*, that the *Poetics* and the

third book of the *Rhetoric* followed, and that the physical works and the *Metaphysics* were later.

See "Aristotle," by Sir Alexander Grant, in Blackwood's series, and the article "Aristotle" in the *Encyclopædia Britannica.*

[3] Aristotle was born in B.C. 384, and died in 322. Sophocles and Euripides had died in 406, and there are no later dates of much importance to be noted in the history of Tragedy. Aristophanes, who had outlived the Old Comedy, died early in the fourth century; on the other hand, Menander, the great name of the New Comedy, was not born till 342.

[4] See "Christianity and the Latin Races," a lecture by the late Dean of St. Paul's.

[5] The translations are in the main adapted from that of Twining.

[6] περὶ ποιητῶν α′β′γ′, πραγματεῖαι τέχνης ποιητικῆς α′β′, ἀπορήματα Ὁμηρικὰ σ′, περὶ τραγῳδιῶν α′, διδασκαλίαι α′.—Diog. Laert. Bk. 5.

[7] The Definition of Tragedy will be more fully understood if it is compared with other definitions drawn by Aristotle, such as those of εὐδαιμονία or ἀρετή in the *Ethics*, or this of πόλις, which is a κοινωνία of a particular kind, existing for a particular purpose :—

ἡ δ′ ἐκ πλειόνων κωμῶν κοινωνία τέλειος πόλις ἤδη, πάσης ἔχουσα πέρας τῆς αὐταρκείας ὡς ἔπος εἰπεῖν, γινομένη μὲν οὖν τοῦ ζῆν ἕνεκεν, οὖσα δὲ τοῦ εὖ ζῆν.—*Politics*, I, I (1252 b).

It is also interesting to compare Dryden's definition of a play, which ought to be—

"A just and lively image of human nature, representing its passions and humours, and the changes of fortune to which it is subject, for the delight and instruction of mankind."—*Essay of Dramatic Poesy*.

(This definition is put into the mouth of Lisideius (Sir Charles Sedley), but it was "well received" by the persons who are supposed to take part in the discussion, after some demur on the ground "that it was only *a genere et fine*," *i.e.* that it contained no *differentia*.)

8 See Horace, *A. P.* 113-127, 153-178, 309-322.

9 τῆς ὀρχήσεως δὲ ἄλλη μὲν Μουσῶν λέξιν μιμουμένων, τό τε μεγαλοπρεπὲς φυλάττοντες ἅμα καὶ ἐλεύθερον· ἄλλη δὲ εὐεξίας ἐλαφρότητός τε ἕνεκα καὶ κάλλους τῶν τοῦ σώματος αὐτοῦ μελῶν καὶ μερῶν.—Plato, *Laws*, 7, p. 795.

οὕτως ἦν τεχνίτης (ὁ Τελέστης), ὥστε ἐν τῷ ὀρχεῖσθαι τοὺς Ἑπτὰ ἐπὶ Θήβας, φανερὰ ποιεῖσθαι τὰ πράγματα δι' ὀρχήσεως.—Athenæus, 1, 39.

"I can deeply sympathise in imagination with the Greeks in this favourite part of their theatrical exhibitions, when I call to mind the pleasure I felt in beholding the combat of the Horatii and Curiatii most exquisitely danced in Italy to the music of Cimarosa."—Coleridge, *Lectures on Shakespeare*, etc., 2, 13.

10 This practice of illustrating Poetry from Painting, and *vice versa*, is habitual in all lan-

guages.   Its limitations are laid down in Lessing's
Laocoön.   The following passages illustrate the
general tendency :—

πλὴν ὁ Σιμωνίδης τὴν μὲν ζωγραφίαν ποίησιν
σιωπῶσαν προσαγορεύει, τὴν δὲ ποίησιν ζωγραφίαν
λαλοῦσαν.—Plutarch, *De Gloria Atheniensium,* c. 3.

"Milton wrote in bronze.   I am sure Virgil
polished off his *Georgics* in marble—sweet calm
shapes ! exquisite harmonies of line !   As for the
Æneid, that, sir, I consider to be so many bas-
reliefs, mural ornaments, which affect me not
much."—Thackeray, *The Newcomes,* c. 35.

" I replied, 'That he confounded the operations
of the pencil and the pen : that the serene and
silent art, as painting has been called by one of
our first living poets, necessarily appealed to the
eye, because it had not the organs for addressing
the ear ; whereas poetry, or that species of composition which approached to it, lay under the
necessity of doing absolutely the reverse, and
addressed itself to the ear, for the purpose of
exciting that interest which it could not attain
through the medium of the eye.'

" Dick was not a whit staggered by my argument, which he contended was founded on mis-
representation.

" 'Description,' he said, 'was to the author
of a romance exactly what drawing and tinting
were to a painter, words were his colours, and,
if properly employed, they could not fail to place
the scene, which he wished to conjure up, as

effectually before the mind's eye as the tablet or canvas presents it to the bodily organ.' "—Scott, Introduction to the *Bride of Lammermoor*.

[11] συμβέβηκε δὲ τῶν αἰσθητῶν ἐν μὲν τοῖς ἄλλοις μηθὲν ὑπάρχειν ὁμοίωμα τοῖς ἤθεσιν, οἷον ἐν τοῖς ἁπτοῖς καὶ τοῖς γευστοῖς, ἀλλ' ἐν τοῖς ὁρατοῖς ἠρέμα· σχήματα γάρ ἐστι τοιαῦτα, ἀλλ' ἐπὶ μικρόν, καὶ πάντες τῆς τοιαύτης αἰσθήσεως κοινωνοῦσιν—ἔτι δὲ οὐκ ἔστι ταῦτα ὁμοιώματα τῶν ἠθῶν, ἀλλὰ σημεῖα μᾶλλον τὰ γιγνόμενα σχήματα καὶ χρώματα τῶν ἠθῶν . . . ἐν δὲ τοῖς μέλεσιν αὐτοῖς ἐστι μιμήματα τῶν ἠθῶν, καὶ τοῦτ' ἐστὶ φανερόν· εὐθὺς γὰρ ἡ τῶν ἁρμονιῶν διέστηκε φύσις ὥστε ἀκούοντας ἄλλως διατίθεσθαι, κ.τ.λ.— *Politics*, 8, 5 (1340ᵃ33).

[12] τοῖσιν δ' ἐν μέσσοισι πάις φόρμιγγι λιγείῃ
ἱμερόεν κιθάριζε, Λίνον δ' ὑπὸ καλὸν ἄειδε
λεπταλέῃ φωνῇ· τοὶ δὲ ῥήσσοντες ἁμαρτῇ
μολπῇ τ' ἰυγμῷ τε, ποσὶ σκαίροντες ἕποντο.

Iliad, 18, 569-572.

Compare *Odyssey*, 8, 256, etc.

[13] τὸ μέλος ἐκ τριῶν ἐστι συγκείμενον, λόγου τε καὶ ἁρμονίας καὶ ῥυθμοῦ.—*Republic*, 3, p. 398.

[14] This view as to the two physical causes is taken in the version of Avicenna :—

"Causae genetrices carminis in humano ingenio duae sunt. Altera delectatio imitationis et usus inde a pueris. . . . Altera causa natura insitus homini amor compositionis aequabilis et numerorum ; quum metra harmoniis natura propinqua essent, propensi in ea animi protulerunt."—

"Poetica Avicennæ," c. 3 in *Analecta Orientalia*, edited by Professor Margoliouth, pp. 85, 86.

It is also taken by Vahlen (*Beiträge*, p. 11).

[15] πάντες ἄνθρωποι φύσει ὀρέγονται τοῦ εἰδέναι. —Opening words of the *Metaphysics*

[16] τὸ γὰρ μανθάνειν ῥᾳδίως ἡδὺ φύσει πᾶσίν ἐστι· τὰ δὲ ὀνόματα σημαίνει τι· ὥστε ὅσα τῶν ὀνομάτων ποιεῖ ἡμῖν μάθησιν ἥδιστα. . . . ἀνάγκη δή, καὶ λέξιν καὶ ἐνθυμήματα ταῦτα εἶναι ἀστεῖα, ὅσα ποιεῖ ἡμῖν μάθησιν ταχεῖαν.—*Rhet.* 3, 10 (1410 *b*. 10).

[17] Shelley's *Defence of Poetry* was written in the year 1821, being an answer to Peacock's *Four Ages of Poetry*. It was not published till some years after the author's death

[18] "'But the knowledge of nature is only half the task of a poet; he must be acquainted likewise with all the modes of life. His character requires that he estimate the happiness and misery of every condition; observe the power of all the passions in all their combinations, and trace the changes of the human mind as they are modified by various institutions and accidental influences of climate or custom, from the sprightliness of infancy to the despondence of decrepitude. He must divest himself of the prejudices of his age or country; he must consider right and wrong in their abstracted and invariable state; he must disregard present laws and opinions, and rise to general and transcendental truths, which will alway be the same; he must therefore content himself with the slow

progress of his name ; contemn the applause of his own time, and commit his claim to the justice of posterity. He must write as the interpreter of nature, and the legislator of mankind, and consider himself as presiding over the thoughts and manners of future generations ; as a being superior to time and place.

"'His labour is not yet at an end : he must know many languages and many sciences ; and that his style may be worthy of his thoughts, must, by incessant practice, familiarise to himself every delicacy of speech and grace of harmony.'

"Imlac now felt the enthusiastic fit, and was proceeding to aggrandise his own profession, when the prince cried out, 'Enough ! thou hast convinced me that no human being can ever be a poet.'"—Johnson, *Rasselas*, chaps. 10, 11.

[19] *Rhet.* 2, 5 (1382ᵃ21).

[20] Φρυνίχου καὶ Αἰσχύλου τὴν τραγῳδίαν εἰς μύθους καὶ πάθη προαγόντων.—Plutarch, *Quæst. Symp.* 1, 5.

"Chaucer's Monk had the true Aristotelic idea of Tragedy :—

> *Tragedie* is to sayn a certain storie,
> As old bookes maken us memorie,
> Of *him that stood in gret prosperitee*
> And is *yfallen out of high degree*
> *In to miserie,* and *endeth wretchedly.*

But the Knight and the Host were among the θεαταὶ ΑΣΘΕΝΕΙΣ.

> Ho ! quod the knight, good sire, no more of this :
> That ye have said is right *ynough* ywis,

And mochel more ; for litel hevinesse
Is right enough to mochel folk, I gesse.
I say for me, it is a gret disese [uneasiness]
Wher as men have ben in gret welth and ese,
To heren of hir soden fall, alas !
And the contrary is joye and gret solas,
As whan a man hath ben in powre estat,
And climbeth, and wexeth fortunat,
And ther abideth in prosperitee :
Swiche thin is gladsom, as it thinketh me,
And of swiche thing were goodly for to telle."

From Twining's note 100. (The italics, etc.,
are his.)

[21] *Politics*, 8, 7 (1341^b39).

[22] καὶ πᾶσι γίγνεσθαί τινα κάθαρσιν καὶ
κουφίζεσθαι μεθ' ἡδονῆς· ὁμοίως δὲ καὶ τὰ μέλη τὰ
καθαρτικὰ παρέχει χαρὰν ἀβλαβῆ τοῖς ἀνθρώποις.
—*Politics*, l.c.

[23] Twining, note 45. He quotes and carefully
examines the passage of the *Politics*, remarking that
the Abbé Batteux is the only commentator known
to himself who had paid a proper attention to this
passage. The note is unfortunately too long to be
given here, and cannot fairly be represented by an
extract. He does not in this passage, though
he does elsewhere, mention the excellent Commentary of Robortelli (published in 1547), the
importance of which was pointed out to me by
Professor Veitch. Robortelli refers to the passage
of the *Politics*, in speaking of the κάθαρσις effected
by Tragedy ; but he goes on to explain the term
of a certain training and direction of the feelings of
pity and fear, and of a fortitude shown under

actual misfortunes, when those who suffer have
been accustomed to see that worse things have
befallen others. He quotes from the Comic poet
Timocles the lines (found in Athenæus, Bk. 5) :—

ὦ τᾶν, ἄκουσον εἴ τί σοι μέλλω λέγειν.
ἄνθρωπός ἐστι ζῷον ἐπίπονον φύσει,
καὶ πολλὰ λυπήρ' ὁ βίος ἐν ἑαυτῷ φέρει.
παραψυχὰς οὖν φροντίδων ἀνεύρατο
ταύτας· ὁ γὰρ νοῦς τῶν ἰδίων λήθην λαβὼν
πρὸς ἀλλοτρίῳ τε ψυχαγωγηθεὶς πάθει,
μεθ' ἡδονῆς ἀπῆλθε παιδευθεὶς ἅμα.
τοὺς γὰρ τραγῳδοὺς πρῶτον, εἰ βούλει, σκόπει,
ὡς ὠφελοῦσι πάντας. ὁ μὲν ὢν γὰρ πένης
πτωχότερον αὑτοῦ καταμαθὼν τὸν Τήλεφον
γενόμενον ἤδη τὴν πενίαν ῥᾷον φέρει.
ὁ νοσῶν τι μανικὸν 'Αλκμέων' ἐσκέψατο.
ὀφθαλμιᾷ τις, εἰσὶ Φινεῖδαι τυφλοί.
τέθνηκέ τῳ παῖς, ἡ Νιόβη κεκούφικεν.
χωλός τίς ἐστι, τὸν Φιλοκτήτην ὁρᾷ.
γέρων τις ἀτυχεῖ, κατέμαθεν τὸν Οἰνέα.
ἅπαντα γὰρ τὰ μείζον' ἢ πέπονθέ τις
ἀτυχήματ' ἄλλοις γεγονότ' ἐννοούμενος
τὰς αὑτὸς αὑτοῦ συμφορὰς ἧττον στένει.

(See Professor Mahaffy's *History of Greek
Literature*, 13, p. 405, note 1.)

The thought recurs in the *Thoughts* of Marcus
Aurelius :

" At first tragedies were brought on the stage as
means of reminding men of the things which
happen to them, and that it is according to nature
for things to happen so, and that, if you are

delighted with what is shown on the stage, you
should not be troubled with that which takes place
on the larger stage.   For you see that these things
must be acomplished thus, and that even they bear
them who cry out ' O Cithaeron ! ' "—11, 6, Long's
translation.

[24] Thus Dr. Johnson, while touching upon Aristotle's point in his own vigorous explanation, goes
on to assume that *all* the passions, and not pity
and fear only, are to be purified by *admixture with*
pity and fear.

" I introduced Aristotle's doctrine, in his *Art of
Poetry*, of κάθαρσις τῶν παθημάτων, the purging
of the passions as the purpose of tragedy.   ' But
how are the passions to be purged by terror and
pity ?' said I, with an assumed air of ignorance.
. . . JOHNSON, ' Why, Sir, you are to consider
what is the meaning of purging in the original
sense.   It is to expel impurities from the human
body.   The mind is subject to the same imper-
fection.   The passions are the great movers
of human actions ; but they are mixed with such
impurities, that it is necessary they should be
purged or refined by means of terror and pity.
For instance, ambition is a noble passion, but by
seeing upon the stage, that a man who is so
excessively ambitious as to raise himself by in-
justice is punished, we are terrified at the fatal con-
sequences of such a passion.   In the same manner
a certain degree of resentment is necessary ; but
if we see that a man carries it too far, we pity the

object of it, and are taught to moderate that passion."—Boswell's *Life*, ann. 1776.

Lessing (*Dramaturgie*, No. 48) explains the purgation of pity and fear to mean the reduction of the extreme of either feeling, whether in excess or in defect, to the mean. He found a "but" (ἀλλὰ) in his text, introducing the last clause of the definition, and is at pains to explain this by a special antithesis between narrative and dramatic poetry, the latter alone being sufficiently vivid to affect the passion in the desired manner.

Goethe (*Nachlese zu Aristoteles Poetik*, 1826) refuses to allow any *moral* import to the term κάθαρσις, which he explains of the compensation made, in a tragedy regarded as a work of art, by the hero's sufferings at its close. Referring to the passage of the *Politics*, he understands two kinds of music to be there intended, one which excites, another which tranquillises.

²⁵ *Grundzüge der verlorenen Abhandlung des Aristoteles über Wirkung der Tragödie*, 1857. (See Appendix B.)

Bernays did not discover the bearing of the *Politics* passage upon the κάθαρσις of Tragedy; for, as has been shown, this was understood by Robortelli in the sixteenth century, and also by the Abbé Batteux and by Twining. Bernays points out that the passage was known to Lessing and to Goethe, though turned to little account by either. Of the intrinsic value of Goethe's remarks he makes fitting recognition. He mentions with satisfaction Milton's appreciation of Aristotle's meaning, and excuses the poet's rendering of κάθαρσις by "lustratio," as being probably the work of a secretary. The main points in Bernays' view, as contained in his paper of 1857 and his letter to L. Spengel of 1859, may be thus summarised :—

(1) κάθαρσις, in its æsthetic use, is a term coined by Aristotle, and bears a specific sense.

(2) The key to this sense is to be sought chiefly in the passage of the *Politics*, where the κάθαρσις effected by certain kinds of music is defined.

(3) The object of Aristotle in that passage is not *moral* improvement ; for he expressly finds room for the lower kinds of music which Plato rejects.

(4) The specific meaning which he intended for κάθαρσις is (not sacrificial or expiatory, but) medical or pathological.

(5) The *patients* are men, not feelings : πάθημα being the condition of the παθητικός, the person who has a tendency towards any πάθος. (It is not certain that this distinction between πάθη and παθήματα can be maintained.)

(6) τοιούτων, in the Definition of Tragedy, means τοιούτων, not τούτων καὶ τοιούτων.

(7) Later Greek literature, and especially the works of the Neoplatonists, shows that κάθαρσις, as an Aristotelian term, was accepted in the pathological sense.

Not the least interesting feature in Bernays'

study is his confidence that the complete *Poetics* will some day be restored to us. When that day comes, we may be sure that Aristotle's doctrine will be approved as no mere phrase, but a well-reasoned and responsible judgment; and only less sure that the correctness of Bernays' reading of it will be established.

26 R. Browning, *Aristophanes' Apology*, p. 10.

27 οὐκοῦν δικαία ἐστὶν οὕτω κατιέναι, ἀπολο-γησαμένη ἢ ἐν μέλει ἤ τινι ἄλλῳ μέτρῳ; πάνυ μὲν οὖν. δοῖμεν δέ γέ που ἂν καὶ τοῖς προστάταις αὐτῆς, ὅσοι μὴ ποιητικοί, φιλοποιηταὶ δέ, ἄνευ μέτρου λόγον ὑπὲρ αὐτῆς εἰπεῖν, ὡς οὐ μόνον ἡδεῖα ἀλλὰ καὶ ὠφελίμη πρὸς τὰς πολιτείας καὶ τὸν βίον τὸν ἀνθρώπινόν ἐστι· καὶ εὐμενῶς ἀκουσόμεθα.—*Rep.* 10, p. 608.

This reference I owe to the kindness of Professor Murray, who pointed out the direct relevancy of the passage. The earnestness of Plato's language cannot be mistaken; and Aristotle's answer is conceived under an equal sense of responsibility.

28 ὦ ἄριστοι τῶν ξένων, ἡμεῖς ἐσμεν τραγῳδίας αὐτοὶ ποιηταὶ κατὰ δύναμιν ὅτι καλλίστης ἅμα καὶ ἀρίστης· πᾶσα οὖν ἡμῖν ἡ πολιτεία ξυνέστηκε μίμησις τοῦ καλλίστου καὶ ἀρίστου βίου, ὃ δή φαμεν ἡμεῖς γε ὄντως εἶναι τραγῳδίαν τὴν ἀληθεστάτην.—*Laws*, 7, p. 816.

29 "Aristotle desires to give music, as he also desires to give tragedy, and even comedy, its full natural verge and scope. He is more careful than Plato had been not to impoverish the life of

his State, or to curtail its opportunities of making a rational use of leisure ; he wishes its enjoyment of the goods of civilised existence to be full and complete."—W. L. Newman's *Politics*, vol. 1, p. 369.

[30] *Iphigenia in Tauris*, l. 1394 *sq.*

[31] *Ethics*, 8, 3 and 10 ($1146^a 19$ and $1151^b 18$).

[32] *The Recognition-Scene in the "Choephorœ" of Æschylus.*—In classifying the various kinds of recognition, Aristotle assigns the first place to plays where the recognition is brought about in the natural unfolding of the incidents ; as Œdipus is made known in the *Œdipus Tyrannus*, or Iphigenia in the *Iphigenia in Tauris* ; the second to those where a " process of inference " is introduced. Of the latter sort he gives two instances. One is a play on the Iphigenia story by an author otherwise almost unknown : here the process was exhibited as taking place in the mind of Orestes, who reasoned thus :

> My sister was sacrificed in Aulis.
> Such things run in families :
> Therefore it is natural that I should be sacrificed also.

This was overheard and he was recognised.

The other case is that in the *Choephorœ*, where Electra recognises her brother by inference. The two cases are not identical, since in the latter it is the person who recognises another, in the former the object of the recognition, who so reasons. But it is with the " syllogism " of Electra itself

that we are concerned.   According to Aristotle
Electra argues thus :

> Some one *like* has come.
> No one is *like* except Orestes
> Therefore Orestes has come.

All interpreters agree to complete the premisses
thus :

> Some one *like me* has come.
> No one is *like me* except Orestes.

If Aristotle really meant this (which is possible
on the words), he is imputing to Electra, that is,
to Æschylus, a fatuity which is not only not intended
by the poet, but which none of those who criti-
cised the details of the scene had found there.
The passage in Æschylus is 165-182.   I quote
the analysis given in Conington's edition, itali-
cising some lines for convenience :—

" *Electra.* Now that the libation is over I see
      something new.

Chorus. What is it ?   How I tremble !

El. A lock of hair on the tomb.

Chor. Whose ?

El. One may easily guess.

Chor. Tell me.

El. There is no one here but me who would think
      of honouring my father.

Chor. No ; for his other kinsmen are his enemies.

El. The lock itself resembles——

Chor. Whose hair ?

El. My own.

Chor. Can it then come from Orestes ?
El. The hair is most like his."
The reasoning is surely clear :—

> Here is a lock of hair put in honour of my father.
> No one would have put it but Orestes :
> Therefore Orestes has come.

But Electra does not choose to name Orestes, and so expose her feminine readiness to believe what she hopes, and find reasons for what she believes ; and in fact she makes the chorus name him. She parries their point-blank question by saying, " I am the only person to make such an offering," and, " Why, the hair is just like mine ! " but her own train of thought is never interrupted, and when Orestes has been once named, she lets out the conclusion at which she has long arrived : " The hair is most like his."

The reasoning is continued at 183. " I too am all perturbed, and know not what to think. *The offering cannot have come from any Argive— still less from my mother.— Yet how to fix it on Orestes ?* Oh, that it could speak and tell us ! May the gods look on our troubles ! they can aid us even now. See, here are footprints, just the size of mine—more and more anguish and perplexity."

The argument from the footprints is of course a sophism ; but it is the sophism of a loving and despairing sister, and when it is uttered the speaker breaks down under her feelings. What could possibly be more true to nature ? Now

Orestes comes forward and tells his sister that her prayers are at last answered, and that he is before her. By a natural reaction of feeling she refuses to believe. Then gravely and gently he rallies her on this incredulity. "Now when I stand before thee thou doubtest, though the colour of my hair and the measure of my footprints seemed proof enough to thee a moment since. *See the place from which the hair was cut.*" In other words, "Your original thought—call it intuition or inference—was right. It *was* Orestes' hair."

This credulity, dear to a woman's mind, is often marked by Æschylus : see *Agam.* 264-316, 483, 484 ; *Prom.* 509, 510.

Now in this scene it would seem easy for an Athenian audience, so easily offended by anything irrational or melodramatic, to find fault with the identification of the lock of hair or of the footprints. But only malice or the exaggerated spirit of burlesque could so confuse the subsidiary proofs with the main reasoning as to make Electra say :

> Some one with hair and feet like mine has come.
> There is no such person but Orestes :
> Therefore Orestes has come.

And in fact Euripides, who has travestied the details of the scene, has not made this mistake.

In his *Electra* (l. 502) the old servant comes in excitedly. He has seen a sacrificed sheep on Agamemnon's tomb and a lock of yellow hair. "And I wondered," he says, "what man was he

who dared come to the tomb ; for it was certainly
no Argive : nay, but perhaps your brother is come
secretly." Here the reasoning suggested is :

> Some one has had the courage and piety to place this
>   offering on the tomb.
> No one but Orestes would do this :
> Therefore Orestes has come.

He goes on to suggest the tests of the hair, and
the footprints, and the garment ; absurd enough
when stated in cold blood, and rightly rejected by
Electra. Finally the recognition is effected in
the orthodox way, by a scar, a σημεῖον used
πίστεως ἕνεκα, which, if serious criticism were in
place, would, on Aristotle's principles, be con-
demned as frigid.

Let us turn to the *Electra* of Sophocles.
Sophocles is aware of the criticism which the
scene in Æschylus had provided, and is to show
his skill in avoiding it. Accordingly the argument
is put into the mouth of Chrysothemis, the less
heroic sister. She enters full of news. " Orestes
is come," she says. " Orestes is dead," answers
Electra ; " but give your proof." " I saw offerings on the tomb," says Chrysothemis, " and a
lock of hair, which I am sure was Orestes'. *For
no one else would have placed one there, I know* ;
not you, not our mother—so it was Orestes." " I
am really sorry," says Electra, "that you are so
foolish. Orestes is dead, and (in answer to a
question) these offerings were perhaps put there

in mourning for him. So leave these imaginings and be practical."

Here again we have the reasoning :

> Some one like Orestes has come.
> No one is like him but himself :
> Therefore Orestes has come.

But it is entrusted to the weaker sister, and rejected by the stronger.

Aristophanes, in the *Clouds* (l. 531), says that his play has come to look for its sister-comedy, " for 'twill know its brother's lock if it see it," *i.e.* it will be as ready with its intuitive recognition as was Electra in Æschylus—" *The hair is most like his.*"

Can there be any reason for not supposing that Aristotle meant what Æschylus meant, and what Sophocles, Euripides, and Aristophanes understood him to mean ?—

> Some one *like Orestes* has come.
> No one is like him but Orestes :
> Therefore Orestes has come.

With regard to the particular fault which the audience, echoed by Euripides, found in the appeal to the hair and the footprints, there is something to be said. It was clearly a mistake— one of the same kind as that noticed by Aristotle in the *Amphiaraus* of Carcinus—to put these details before so quick-witted an audience ; and if the play had to be acted again to the same audience, it would be wise to omit them. And a dramatic author should not write what cannot be acted. But Æschylus knew that he did not in all things satisfy his generation ; and in memorable words, where bombast is out of the question, dedicated his works " to Time." And surely to the reader— who, says Aristotle again and again, has also his verdict to pronounce—there is nothing in this scene but the very truth of nature ; that delicacy of character - drawing which the earliest poets (*Poetics*, c. 6) best attained, before rhetoric and elaboration of plot were made the supreme end. It is to be remembered that this is not the only case where Æschylus might have appealed from contemporary critics. " The silence of Æschylus " passed into a phrase ; that is, his habit of allowing a Cassandra, an Atossa, a Prometheus, to be exhibited in silence for some time, and only at last to find words. Now this offended the audience, but there were competent dissenters from its judgment : ἐγὼ δ' ἔχαιρον τῇ σιωπῇ καί με τοῦτ' ἔτερπεν says Dionysus in Aristophanes (*Frogs*, 916). And Longinus (c. 9), speaking of the eloquence of silence, not with special reference to Æschylus, may be taken to confirm the favourable judgment.

[33] πρὸς δὲ τούτοις ἐὰν ἐπιτιμᾶται ὅτι οὐκ ἀληθῆ, ἀλλ' ἴσως δεῖ, οἷον καὶ Σοφοκλῆς ἔφη αὐτὸς μὲν οἴους δεῖ ποιεῖν, Εὐριπίδην δὲ οἷοι εἰσί, ταύτῃ λυτέον.

> ·· 'Tis a speech
> That by a language of familiar lowness
> Enhances what of more heroic vein
> Is next to follow. But one fault it hath ;

It fits too close to life's realities,
In truth to Nature missing truth to Art ;
For Art commends not counterparts and copies,
But from our life a nobler life would shape,
Bodies celestial from terrestrial raise,
And teach us not jejunely what we are,
But what we may be, when the Parian block
Yields to the hand of Phidias."

Sir H. TAYLOR—*A Sicilian Summer.*

The view expressed in these lines is probably that which Sophocles intended to convey ; it is certainly that which Aristotle had in mind when he recalled the anecdote ; as is clear from the immediate context, and from the language which he always holds about idealisation in character-drawing (see, for example, c. 2 and c. 15). It is thus tersely put by Dacier :—

" Sophocle tâchoit de rendre ses imitations parfaites, en suivant toujours bien plus qu'une belle nature etoit *capable* de faire, que ce qu'elle faisoit. Au lieu qu'Euripide ne travailloit qu'à les rendre semblables, en consultant davantage ce que cette même nature faisoit, que ce qu'elle etoit *capable* de faire." (Dacier's words form the text of an admirable note by Twining.)

Bishop Hurd, in his Notes on the *Art of Poetry* (of Horace), quotes these words of Aristotle (on l. 317) and gives another interpretation. He writes :—

" The meaning of which is, Sophocles, from his more extended commerce with mankind, had enlarged and widened the narrow, partial conception,

arising from the contemplation of *particular* characters, into a complete comprehension of the *kind.*
Whereas the philosophic Euripides, having been
mostly conversant in the Academy, when he came
to look into life, keeping his eye too intent on
single, really existing personages, sunk the *kind*
in the *individual* ; and so painted his characters
naturally indeed, and *truly*, with regard to the
objects in view, but sometimes without that
general and universally striking likeness, which is
demanded to the full exhibition of poetical truth."

He illustrates his meaning from the character
of Electra, who in Euripides carries her desire to
revenge herself upon her mother into unnatural
detail, while in Sophocles her expressions are
more general.   In point of fact, Euripides is writing with Æschylus before him, and is following
Æschylus in bringing into prominence the murder
of Clytemnestra ; whereas Sophocles, very possibly writing later than Euripides, made Ægisthus,
as in Homer, the chief criminal, the first object
of vengeance (see Jebb's *Electra* of Sophocles,
Introduction).   Euripides shows up the weak
points in Æschylus ; and his own treatment of the
character is narrow and "academic," very different
from that of the Electra in his *Orestes.*

Bishop Hurd's view is quoted by Lessing
(*Dramaturgie*, note 51) with emphatic approval,
on the ground that the high *moral* perfection suggested by that of Dacier is a matter of the individual, not of the type.   Lessing's criticism is

contained in a note, and is avowedly not worked out.

After all, we must remember that we are dealing with an *anecdote*, perhaps fact, perhaps well invented, perhaps, as has, I think, been suggested, adapted from a passage in some comedy ; not with the weighed words of a philosopher.

[34] " Every truth which a human being can enunciate, every thought, even every outward impression, which can enter into his consciousness, may become poetry when shown through any impassioned medium, when invested with the colouring of joy, or grief, or pity, or affection, or admiration, or reverence, or awe, or even hatred or terror : and, unless so coloured, nothing, be it as interesting as it may, is poetry. But both these definitions fail to discriminate between poetry and eloquence. Eloquence, as well as poetry, is thoughts coloured by the feelings. . . .

" Poetry and eloquence are both alike the expression or utterance of feeling. But, if we may be excused the antithesis, we should say that eloquence is *heard*, poetry is *over*heard. Eloquence supposes an audience ; the peculiarity of poetry appears to us to lie in the poet's utter unconsciousness of a listener."—Mill, *Dissertations and Discussions*, vol. i. pp. 70, 71.

[35] Coleridge's more formal definition should be recorded here :—

" Poetry is that species of composition which is opposed to works of science by proposing for its *immediate* object pleasure, not truth ; and from all other species—having this object in common with it—it is discriminated by proposing to itself such delight from the *whole* as is compatible with a distinct gratification from each component *part.*" —*Biog. Lit.*

[36] Aristotle includes among works for which a place has to be found in a proper classification of the kinds of poetry, the Mimes of Sophron and Xenarchus, and "the Socratic Dialogues." If by the Socratic Dialogues is meant those written by Plato, Xenophon, Aristotle, *cadit quæstio.* But there is reason to think that he is referring to the dialogues written by a particular author ; which, in a fragment preserved from another work, are named in company with the Mimes of Sophron and Xenarchus, the point under discussion being precisely this, whether all those works are to be considered metrical or nonmetrical. The passage, the actual rendering of which is difficult, is as follows :—

Ἀριστοτέλης δὲ ἐν τῷ περὶ ποιητῶν οὕτως γράφει· οὐκοῦν οὐδὲ ἐμμέτρους τοὺς καλουμένους Σώφρονος καὶ Ξενάρχου μίμους μὴ φῶμεν εἶναι λόγους καὶ μιμήσεις, ἢ τοὺς Ἀλεξαμένου τοῦ Τηΐου, τοὺς πρώτους γραφέντας τῶν Σωκρατικῶν διαλόγων.—Athenæus (11, 505).

Now we do not know much as to the form of the Mimes of Sophron ; but we are told that a certain hymn of Gregory Nazianzene was composed after the models of Sophron, being not

metrical in the classical sense, but semimetrical.
The hymn begins—

Παρθένε, νύμφη Χρίστου,
δόξαζέ σου τὸν νύμφιον.

And the scholiast writes :

ἐν τούτῳ τῷ λόγῳ τὸν Συρακούσιον Σωφρόνα
μιμεῖται · οὗτος γὰρ μόνος ποιητῶν ῥυθμοῖς τισι
καὶ κώλοις ἐχρήσατο, ποιητικῆς ἀναλογίας κατα-
φρονήσας.

The inference would seem to be that all the
poems which Aristotle thinks might be left outside
altogether by a faulty classification resting on
distinctions of metre only, are metrical at least
in this limited sense.

The words in which this kind of poetry is
defined are these :

ἡ δὲ ἐποποιία μόνον τοῖς λόγοις ψιλοῖς ἢ τοῖς
μέτροις· καὶ τούτοις εἴτε μιγνῦσα μετ' ἀλλήλων,
εἴθ' ἑνὶ τινὶ γένει χρωμένη τῶν μέτρων τυγχάνουσι
τῶν νῦν.

Ueberweg has proposed to omit ἐποποιία, and
Bernays to introduce ἀνώνυμος before τυγχάνουσι.
The latter change has been approved by Vahlen,
who stated that the Oriental versions would be
found to support it.   In point of fact, the Arabic
version gives support to both changes (see
Margoliouth's *Analecta Orientalia*, pp. 47, 48).
But if we introduce both, the general sense is
unaltered : only in place of a new and extended
class under the old name of ἐποποιία, we have a

new class hitherto unnamed. This class effects
its imitation by language unaided ($\psi\iota\lambda o\hat{\iota}s$), *that is,*
by metrical language. The word "unaided" seems
to be fairly taken of the absence of aid from
music : compare the use of $\psi\iota\lambda o\mu\epsilon\tau\rho\iota\alpha$ in the next
chapter, and Plato's $\pi o\iota\eta\sigma\iota\nu$ $\psi\iota\lambda\dot{\eta}\nu$ $\ddot{\eta}$ $\dot{\epsilon}\nu$ $\dot{\omega}\delta\hat{\eta}$
(*Phædrus*, p. 278); and the sense given to $\ddot{\eta}$
seems fair enough. Had Aristotle wished to express an alternative between prose and verse, he
would surely have written $\tau o\hat{\iota}s$ $\psi\iota\lambda o\hat{\iota}s$ $\lambda\acute{o}\gamma o\iota s$ $\ddot{\eta}$ $\tau o\hat{\iota}s$
$\mu\acute{\epsilon}\tau\rho o\iota s$ (not $\tau o\hat{\iota}s$ $\lambda\acute{o}\gamma o\iota s$ $\psi\iota\lambda o\hat{\iota}s$).

This note is in the main reproduced from that
of Tyrwhitt's edition. Metastasio (1782) speaks
of the view taken here of the meaning being that
of the majority of interpreters ; and he supports
it against Dacier, who had wished to claim
Aristotle's authority for a prose epic, by the
opinion of Vettori, Castelvetro, and others. But
among modern interpreters, Tyrwhitt seems to
stand nearly alone, with MM. Egger and St.
Hilaire. Metastasio himself seems to misrepre-
sent part of Aristotle's argument ($o\dot{v}\delta\dot{\epsilon}\nu$ $\gamma\dot{\alpha}\rho$
$\ddot{\epsilon}\chi o\iota\mu\epsilon\nu$ $\kappa.\tau.\lambda.$), as do the two French writers.

[37] *Phædrus,* 258 D.

[38] *Rhet.* 3, 8 (p. 1408^{b}31).

[39] *Banquet,* p. 205 (Shelley's translation).

[40] *Lectures on Shakespeare,* etc. Wordsworth (in
a note to the Appendix to his poems) also writes :—

" Much confusion has been introduced into
criticism by the contradistinction of Poetry and
Prose ; instead of the more philosophical one of

Poetry and Matter-of-fact, or Science. The only strict antithesis to Prose is Metre."

[41] Preface to *Gondibert*. So "Peindre sous l'homme momentané l'homme éternel" (Victor Hugo, *Quatre-vingt treize*).

[42] "Solon . . . went to see Thespis himself, as the ancient custom was, act; and after the play was done, he addressed him, and asked him if he was not ashamed to tell so many lies before such a number of people; and Thespis replying that it was no harm to say or do so in play, Solon vehemently struck his staff against the ground: "Ay," said he, "if we honour and commend such play as this, we shall find it some day in our business."—Plutarch's *Life of Solon* (" Dryden's " translation, ed. Clough).

Compare the saying of Gorgias :—

τὴν τραγῳδίαν εἶπεν ἀπάτην ἦν ὁ ἀπατήσας δικαιότερος τοῦ μὴ ἀπατήσαντος, καὶ ὁ ἀπατηθεὶς σοφώτερος τοῦ μὴ ἀπατηθέντος. — Plutarch, *De audiendis poetis*, p. 26.

[43] See Sellar's *Virgil*, end of chap. 11 (on the style of the *Æneid*).

[44] *Æn.* 1, 462.

[45] *Æn.* 2, 314.

[46] Lucr. 3, 845.

[47] Lucan, 2, 248.

[48] Ovid, *Metam.* 2, 328.

These passages and lines have been purposely selected from Latin poetry, as being slightly more modern, certainly more continuous with our own literature, than the Greek, and therefore well suited to an experimental and limited extension of Aristotle's principles. To follow out the attempt into the field of modern poetry would be beyond the scope of these notes. In the following extracts from a Review of Lockhart's *Life of Scott*, by the late Mr. Keble, a wider application is given to principles identical with those of Aristotle on the subject of poetical Imitation ; and the well-known doctrines of the *Prælectiones* will be recognised in English words. I owe my own knowledge of the paper to the kindness of the Rev. W. Lock.

" The idea, then, of poetry in the abstract is something like what follows : *Poetry is the indirect expression in words, most appropriately in metrical words, of some overpowering emotion, or ruling taste, or feeling, the direct indulgence whereof is somehow repressed. . . .*

" As far as these instances go, it would seem that the analogical applications of the word Poetry coincide well enough with Aristotle's notion of it, as consisting chiefly in Imitation or Expression, provided we understand that term with the two following qualifications : 1. That the thing to be imitated or expressed is some object of desire or regret, or some other imaginative feeling, the direct indulgence whereof is impeded. 2. That the mode of imitation or expression is *indirect*, the instruments of it being, for the most part, associations more or less accidental.

" It would seem also that most of the leading

phenomena of poetry may be solved by this account of its nature. To take first that which is most obvious, its connection with metre and music. Setting aside all mysterious natural aptitude, such as universal experience appears to attest, in certain combinations and orders of sounds, as compared with certain passions and moods of mind in ourselves, the very task of metrical arrangement will fall in with the poetical instinct, such as has been above described, in two respects. On the one hand, it shapes out a sort of channel for wild and tumultuous feelings to vent themselves by; feelings whose very excess and violence would seem to make the utterance of them almost impossible, for the throng of thoughts and words, crowding all at once to demand expression. On the other hand, the like rules may be no less useful in throwing a kind of veil over those strong or deep emotions which need relief, but cannot endure publicity. The very circumstance of their being expressed in verse draws off attention from the violence of the feelings themselves, and enables people to say things which they could not venture on in prose, much in the same way as the musical accompaniment gives meaning to the gestures of the dance, and hinders them from appearing to the bystanders merely fantastic. This effect of metre seems quite obvious as far as regards the sympathies of others. Emotions which in their unrestrained expression would appear too keen and outrageous to kindle fellow - feeling in any one, are mitigated, and

become comparatively tolerable, not to say interesting to us, when we find them so far under
control as to leave those who feel them at liberty
to pay attention to measure and rhyme, and the
other expedients of metrical composition.

"But over and above the effect on others, we
apprehend that even in a writer's own mind there
commonly exists a sort of instinctive delicacy, which
finds its account in the work of arranging lines
and syllables, and is content to utter, by their aid,
what it would have shrunk from setting down in
the language of conversation : the metrical form
thus furnishing, at the same time, a vent for eager
feelings, and a veil of reason to draw over them.
All this, if it may be said without irreverence,
would seem to be exemplified in perfection in the
Psalms, and in those other portions of the inspired
writings which take the form of impassioned poetry.
From their perfect parallelism they are the most
artificial of all compositions, yet none were so apt
to relieve the deepest and most overflowing minds ;
exhibiting therefore, by their very form, as compared with their matter, the perfection of that self-
control which must itself be the perfection of a
mixed creature such as man—'thoughts that
breathe and words that burn,' exactly obeying a
certain high law, and shaped by it into perfect
order.

"This notion of the uses of metre as subsidiary
to the end we attribute to poetry, may seem to be
confirmed by reference to those compositions to

which the term Poetry is applied without any sort
of metre. Something will always be discoverable
in them which answers the purpose just now
assigned to numbers: of regulating, and thereby
mitigating, the expression of feeling, and so recon-
ciling to it both the writer and the reader. Thus,
in the prose romances of Sir Walter Scott, and in
all others which would be justly considered poetical,
it will be found, we believe, that the story is in
fact interposed, as a kind of transparent veil,
between the listener and the narrator's real drift
and feelings. The history of Waverley, or Henry
Morton, or Ivanhoe, is but a pretext for the
author's employing himself on those scenes, and
characters, and sentiments which would best satisfy
the cravings of his own ruling fancy. The rules
of painting, sculpture, architecture, music, answer
perhaps the same purpose, whenever we find in any
of their provinces respectively what would be commonly denominated poetical composition. Men's
attending to proportion, perspective, harmony,
throughout the indulgence of emotions ever so
vehement, is like articulation in the sounds they
utter; it distinguishes our grief or joy from the
mere sensations of infants or of irrational animals.

" Thus poetry, in its metrical form as well as
in its substance, would seem to be deducible from
two great instinctive necessities of our common
nature—the same to which it was long ago referred
by Aristotle : the need of some vent for absorbing
or exciting thoughts which he calls imitation or

expression; and the need of so controlling that
expression, as that the presence of reason, sub-
duing and ordering it, shall be felt, and make
itself discernible throughout ; which in this case
becomes what he calls the instinct of harmony and
rhythm."

See also Mr. Keble's Review of Copleston's
Prælectiones. (Both papers are republished in
Mr. Keble's *Occasional Papers and Reviews.*)

APPENDIX B

TEXT OF THE 'POETICS,' EDITIONS, &c.

THE *Poetics* was not included in the edition of Aristotle which issued from the Aldine Press in 1495-98, but was first printed in Greek in 1508 in the volume of *Rhetores Græci*. The Latin version, by George Valla, had been published in 1498. The text now accepted is based upon a single 11th century MS. Aᶜ (Paris, No. 1741), which was used by Vettori (Victorius) in 1560, but the palmary importance of which has been recognised in modern times by Bekker and Ritter, and more consistently followed by Susemihl, Ueberweg, Vahlen, and others. The text, as settled by Vahlen, is that now in general use. The labours of Aristotelian scholars have done much to make particular passages more readable ; though, from the fragmentary condition of the treatise as we have it, and the disarrangement which its parts have probably suffered, the healing hand is comparatively helpless. Besides the names already

given, those of Spengel, Bernays, Bonitz—in still
later years, those of W. Christ and Bywater—may
properly be mentioned.

Much interest has attached to versions of the
Poetics in the Oriental languages preserved at
Paris and Florence; since it has seemed reasonable to hope that the translators may have used a
fuller and better Greek text than any which has
reached us.   The Arabic version (Paris, 882 A),
together with a fragment of the Syriac version
from which it was prepared, have now been
examined by the Laudian Professor of Arabic
(Professor Margoliouth); the results are given in
his *Analecta Orientalia*, which contains, besides the
Arabic text, a Latin rendering of the more signi-
ficant passages of the Arabic, and also a specimen
of the " Poetica " of Avicenna.   While nothing is
contributed towards filling up the greater gaps in
the treatise, distinct evidence is given as to many
interesting points of reading.   (See notes 14 and
36 in Appendix A.)   The simplicity of the older
translator, his ignorance of Greek, and his verbal
faithfulness, are not without their humour.   Thus
οἷον ἐν τῷ ᾿Αγάθωνος ῎Ανθει is represented by
" quemadmodum si quis unum esse bonum statuit "
(οἷον ἕν τὸ ἀγαθὸν ὃς ἂν θῇ); actors are hypo-
crites ; and the poet Carcinus becomes a common
crab !

A list of the more important editions and versions, and of works immediately based upon the
Poetics, is given in chronological order.   It has

no claim to be complete, but will serve to show the number and variety of the workers in this field. It would be out of place to suggest any order of preference, otherwise than by saying that the majority of English readers may well be content with the works of Dr. Moore and Mr. Wharton, while those who only wish to read the treatise in English will find Twining's translation, reprinted in 1887 in Cassell's National Library, excellent : the text which he followed was too faulty to allow his work to be satisfactory to scholars. Twining's notes, which have not been reprinted very lately, are delightful reading from end to end. The great importance of Bernays' work has been indicated elsewhere.

LIST OF EDITIONS, &c.

VALLA (G.), Latin translation.   Venice, 1498.

Greek text among the " Rhetores Græci."
                         Venice, Aldus, 1508.

Latin translation, with the summary of Averroes.
                 Venice, Geo. Arrivabene, 1515.

PACCIUS (Pazzi), Latin translation.
                         Venice, Aldus, 1536.

ROBORTELLIUS (Fr.), " In librum de Arte Poetica explicationes."   Flor. 1548.

SEGNI (Bern.), Italian translation. Florence, 1549.

"Vinc. Madii et Barth. Lombardi in librum
de Poetica communes explanationes : Madii
vero in eundem librum propriæ annotationes."

Ven. 1550.

"Victorii (P.) Commentationes in primum
librum Aristotelis de Arte Poetarum."

Flor. 1560.

Piccolomini (Alessandro), "Annotationi nel libro
della Poetica d'Aristotele, con la traduttione del
medesimo libro in lingua volgare."

Ven. 1575.

Castelvetro (Lodovico), "Poetica vulgarizzata e
sposta."   Bale, 1576.

Heinsius recensuit.   Lugd. Batav. 1610.

Dacier, "La Poétique traduite en Français, avec
des remarques critiques."

Paris and Amsterdam, 1692.

Goulstone (Theodore), Latin translation.

Cambridge, 1696.

Batteux, "Les quatre poétiques d'Aristote,
d'Horace, de Vida, de Despreaux, avec les
traductions et des remarques par l'Abbé
Batteux."   Paris, 1771.

Metastasio (Pietro), "Estratto dell' Arte Poetica
d' Aristotele e considerazioni su la medesima."

Paris, 1782.

TWINING (Thomas), "Aristotle's Treatise on Poetry, translated with notes on the translation and on the original, and two dissertations on poetical and musical imitation."

London, 1789.

[The Rev. Thomas Twining entered Sidney Sussex College, Cambridge, in 1755, and became a Fellow in 1760. His life was passed at Colchester: he had sole charge of the parish of Fordham from 1764, the year of his marriage, and latterly held the living of St. Mary's in Colchester till his death in 1804. See "Recreations and Studies of a Country Clergyman of the Eighteenth Century" (Murray, 1882) for a very pleasant account of his learned friendships, his driving tours in England and Wales, and his great dread of a French invasion, as recorded in his own letters.]

PYE (H. J.), "A Commentary illustrating the Poetic of Aristotle by examples taken chiefly from the modern poets. To which is prefixed a new and corrected edition of the translation of the Poetic." London, 1792.

MOOR (James, LL.D., Professor of Greek in the University of Glasgow), "On the end of Tragedy, according to Aristotle, an Essay in two parts." Glasgow, 1794.

TYRWHITT (Thomas), "De Poetica Liber. Textum

recensuit, versionem refinxit, et animadversioni-
bus illustravit Thomas Tyrwhitt." Oxon. 1794.

[This accomplished scholar was born in 1730,
and was a member of Queen's and Merton Colleges,
Oxford; he was an under-secretary of the War
Department, a clerk of the House of Commons,
and a Curator of the British Museum. The latter
years of his life were devoted to literature, English
as well as that of the ancient classics. He died
in 1786; his edition of the "Poetics" was a
posthumous work.]

HERMANN (Godfrey), Latin translation and Com-
    mentary.   Leipsic, 1802.

RITTER (Fr.), Latin translation and Commentary.
                                Cologne, 1839.

EGGER (M. E.), "Essai sur l'histoire de la
    Critique chez les Grecs, suivi de la Poétique
    d'Aristote et d'extraits de ses Problèmes, avec
    traduction française et commentaire."
                                Paris, 1849.

BERNAYS (Jacob), "Grundzüge der verlorenen
    Abhandlung des Aristoteles über Wirkung der
    Tragödie."   Breslau, 1857.

SAINT-HILAIRE (J. Barthelemy), "Poétique tra-
    duite en français et accompagnée de notes
    perpetuelles."   Paris, 1858.

STAHR (Adolf), "Aristoteles und die Wirkung
    der Tragödie."   Berlin, 1859.

STAHR (Adolf), German translation, with Introduction and Notes. Stuttgart ——

SUSEMIHL (F.), German translation, with Introduction and Notes. Leipsic, 1865 and 1874.

VAHLEN (J.), " Beiträge zu Aristoteles' Poetik."
Vienna, 1865.

VAHLEN (J.) recensuit. Berlin, 1867.

TEICHMÜLLER (Gustav), " Beiträge zur Erklärung der Poetik des Aristoteles." Halle, 1867.

UEBERWEG (F.), German translation, notes, and critical appendix. Berlin, 1869.

REINKENS (J. H.), "Aristoteles über Kunst, besonders über Tragödie." Vienna, 1870.

UEBERWEG (F.), "Ars Poetica ad fidem potissimum codicis antiquissimi Aᶜ (Parisiensis, 1741)." Berlin, 1870.

VAHLEN (J.) iterum recensuit et adnotatione critica auxit. Berlin, 1874.

MOORE (Rev. Edward, B.D.), Vahlen's text with notes. Oxford, 1875.

CHRIST (W.) recensuit. Leipsic, 1878.

BERNAYS (Jacob), "Zwei Abhandlungen über Aristotelische Theorie des Drama " (the work of 1857, with other matter). Berlin, 1880.

I

BRAUNDSCHEID (F.), Text, German translation, critical notes, and Commentary.

Wiesbaden, 1882.

WHARTON (E. R), Vahlen's text, with English translation and notes.   Oxford, 1883.

MARGOLIOUTH (D.), "Analecta Orientalia ad Poeticam Aristoteleam."   London, 1887.

THE END

Printed by R. & R. CLARK, *Edinburgh*

MACMILLAN'S CLASSICAL TRANSLATIONS.

ARISTOTLE—THE POLITICS. By Rev. J. E. C. WELL-DON, M.A. 10s. 6d.

THE RHETORIC. By the same. 7s. 6d.

THE ETHICS. By the same. [In preparation.

CICERO—SELECT LETTERS. Translated from Watson's Edition. By Rev. G. E. JEANS, M.A. 10s. 6d.

ACADEMICS. Translated by J. S. REID, M.L. 5s. 6d.

HERODOTUS—THE HISTORY. By G. C. MACAULAY. 2 vols. 18s.

HOMER—ODYSSEY. By Professor S. H. BUTCHER, M.A., and A. LANG, M.A. 6s.

ILIAD. By A. LANG, M.A., WALTER LEAF, Litt.D., and ERNEST MYERS. 12s. 6d.

THE ODYSSEY. BOOKS I.-XII. By the EARL OF CARNARVON. 8s. 6d.

HORACE. By J. LONSDALE, M.A., and S. LEE, M.A. 3s. 6d.

JUVENAL—THIRTEEN SATIRES. By A. LEEPER, M.A. 3s. 6d.

LIVY. BOOKS XXI.-XXV. By Rev. A. J. CHURCH, M.A., and W. J. BRODRIBB, M.A. 7s. 6d.

PINDAR—ODES. By ERNEST MYERS, M.A. Second Edition. 5s.

PLATO—REPUBLIC. By J. LL. DAVIES, M.A., and D. J. VAUGHAN, M.A. 4s. 6d.

EUTHYPHRO, APOLOGY, CRITO, AND PHÆDO. By F. J. CHURCH. 4s. 6d.

PHÆDRUS, LYSIS, AND PROTAGORAS. By Rev. J. WRIGHT, M.A. 4s. 6d.

POLYBIUS—THE HISTORIES. By E. S. SHUCKBURGH. 2 vols. 24s.

SALLUST—CATILINE AND JUGURTHA. By A. W. POLLARD, B.A. 6s. The Catiline, 3s.

TACITUS. By A. J. CHURCH, M.A., and W. J. BRODRIBB, M.A. History, 6s. Annals, 7s. 6d. Agricola and Germania, 4s. 6d.

THEOCRITUS, BION, AND MOSCHUS. By A. LANG, M.A. 4s. 6d.

VIRGIL. By J. LONSDALE, M.A., and S. LEE, M.A. 3s. 6d. THE ÆNEID. By J. W. MACKAIL, M.A. 7s. 6d.

XENOPHON—COMPLETE WORKS. By H. G. DAKYNS, M.A. With Introduction and Essays. 4 vols. Vol. I., containing "The Anabasis" and "The Hellenica." 10s. 6d.

[Vol. II. in the Press.

MACMILLAN AND CO., LONDON.

MACMILLAN'S CLASSICAL LIBRARY.

ÆSCHYLUS—THE "SEVEN AGAINST THEBES." (With Translation.) By A. W. VERRALL, Litt.D. 8vo. 7s. 6d.

AGAMEMNON. Edited, with Introduction, Commentary, and Translation, by A. W. VERRALL, Litt.D. 8vo. 12s.

THE SUPPLICES. (With Translation.) By T. G. TUCKER, M.A. 8vo. 10s. 6d.

BABRIUS. By W. G. RUTHERFORD, M.A., LL.D. 12s. 6d.

CICERO—ACADEMICA. By J. S. REID, M.L. 15s.

EURIPIDES—MEDEA. By A. W. VERRALL, Litt.D. 7s. 6d.

HERODOTUS. BOOKS I.-III. By Professor A. H. SAYCE. 16s.

HOMER—ILIAD. 2 vols. Vol. I. Books I.-XII. Vol. II. Books XIII.-XXIV. By WALTER LEAF, Litt.D. 14s. each.

JUVENAL—THIRTEEN SATIRES. By Professor J. E. B. MAYOR. Vol. I. Fourth Edition. 10s. 6d. Vol. II. 10s. 6d.

KTESIAS—THE FRAGMENTS OF THE PERSIKA OF KTESIAS. Edited, with Introduction and Notes, by JOHN GILMORE, M.A. 3s. 6d.

PINDAR—NEMEAN ODES. By J. B. BURY, M.A. 12s.

PLATO—PHÆDO. By R. D. ARCHER-HIND, M.A. 8s. 6d.

TIMÆUS. By the same Editor. 8vo. 16s.

PLINY—LETTERS TO TRAJAN. Edited by E. G. HARDY, M.A. 10s. 6d.

TACITUS—ANNALS. By Professor G. O. HOLBROOKE, 16s.

THE HISTORIES. Edited, with Introduction and Notes, by Rev. W. A. SPOONER, M.A. 16s.

THUCYDIDES. BOOK IV. Revised Text, Illustrating the Principal Causes of Corruption in the Manuscripts of this Author. By W. G. RUTHERFORD, M.A. 7s. 6d.

MACMILLAN AND CO., LONDON.

MACMILLAN'S CLASSICAL SERIES.

Fcap. 8vo. Cloth.

ÆSCHINES—IN CTESIPHONTA. Edited by Rev. T. Gwatkin, M.A., and E. S. Shuckburgh, M.A. 5s.

ÆSCHYLUS—PERSÆ. Edited by A. O. Prickard, M.A. With Map. 2s. 6d.

THE "SEVEN AGAINST THEBES." Edited by A. W. Verrall, Litt.D., and M. A. Bayfield, M.A. 2s. 6d.

ANDOCIDES — DE MYSTERIIS. Edited by W. J. Hickie, M.A. 2s. 6d.

ATTIC ORATORS, SELECTIONS FROM THE. Antiphon, Andocides, Lysias, Isocrates, and Isæus. Edited by R. C. Jebb, Litt.D. 5s.

CÆSAR—THE GALLIC WAR. Edited after Kraner by Rev. J. Bond, M.A., and Rev. A. S. Walpole, M.A. With Maps. 4s. 6d.

CATULLUS—SELECT POEMS. Edited by F. P. Simpson, B.A. 3s. 6d. [The Text of this Edition is carefully adapted to School use.]

CICERO—THE CATILINE ORATIONS. From the German of Karl Halm. Edited by A. S. Wilkins, Litt.D. 2s. 6d.

PRO LEGE MANILIA. Edited, after Halm, by Professor A. S. Wilkins, Litt.D. 2s. 6d.

THE SECOND PHILIPPIC ORATION. From the German of Karl Halm. Edited, with Corrections and Additions, by Professor J. E. B. Mayor. 3s. 6d.

PRO ROSCIO AMERINO. Edited, after Halm, by E. H. Donkin, M.A. 2s. 6d.

PRO P. SESTIO. Edited by Rev. H. A. Holden, M.A. 3s. 6d.

SELECT LETTERS. Edited by Professor R. Y. Tyrrell, M.A.

DEMOSTHENES—DE CORONA. Edited by B. Drake, M.A. New and revised edition. 3s. 6d.

ADVERSUS LEPTINEM. Edited by Rev. J. R. King, M.A. 2s. 6d.

THE FIRST PHILIPPIC. Edited, after C. Rehdantz, by Rev. T. Gwatkin. 2s. 6d.

EURIPIDES—HIPPOLYTUS. Edited by Professor J. P. Mahaffy and J. B. Bury. 2s. 6d.

MEDEA. Edited by A. W. Verrall, Litt.D. 2s. 6d.

IPHIGENIA IN TAURIS. Edited by E. B. England, M.A. 3s.

ION. Edited by M. A. Bayfield, M.A. 2s. 6d.

MACMILLAN AND CO., LONDON.

MACMILLAN'S CLASSICAL SERIES.

Fcap. 8vo. Cloth.

HERODOTUS. BOOK III. Edited by G. C. MACAULAY, M.A. 2s. 6d.

BOOK VI. Edited by Professor J. STRACHAN, M.A. 3s. 6d.

BOOK VII. Edited by Mrs. MONTAGU BUTLER. 3s. 6d.

HOMER—ILIAD. BOOKS I., IX., XI., XVI.-XXIV. THE STORY OF ACHILLES. Edited by J. H. PRATT, M.A., and W. LEAF, Litt.D. 5s.

ODYSSEY. BOOK IX. Edited by Professor J. E. B. MAYOR, M.A. 2s. 6d.

ODYSSEY. BOOKS XXI.-XXIV. THE TRIUMPH OF ODYSSEUS. Edited by S. G. HAMILTON, B.A. 2s. 6d.

HORACE—THE ODES. Edited by T. E. PAGE, M.A. 5s. (Books I., II., III., and IV. separately, 2s. each).

THE SATIRES. Edited by Professor A. PALMER, M.A. 5s.

THE EPISTLES AND ARS POETICA. Edited by Professor A. S. WILKINS, Litt.D. 5s.

JUVENAL—THIRTEEN SATIRES. Edited, for the use of Schools, by E. G. HARDY, M.A. 5s. [The Text of this Edition is carefully adapted to School use.]

SELECT SATIRES. Edited by Professor JOHN E. B. MAYOR. X. and XI., 3s. 6d. XII.-XVI., 4s. 6d.

LIVY. BOOKS II. and III. Edited by Rev. H. M. STEPHENSON, M.A. 3s. 6d.

BOOKS XXI. and XXII. Edited by Rev. W. W. CAPES, M.A. 4s. 6d.

BOOKS XXIII. and XXIV. Edited by G. C. MACAULAY. With Maps. 3s. 6d.

THE LAST TWO KINGS OF MACEDON. Extracts from the Fourth and Fifth Decades of Livy. Selected and Edited by F. H. RAWLINS, M.A. With Maps. 2s. 6d.

LUCRETIUS. BOOKS I.-III. Edited by J. H. WARBURTON LEE, M.A. 3s. 6d.

LYSIAS—SELECT ORATIONS. Edited by E. S. SHUCKBURGH, M.A. 5s.

MARTIAL—SELECT EPIGRAMS. Edited by Rev. H. M. STEPHENSON, M.A. 5s.

OVID—FASTI. Edited by G. H. HALLAM, M.A. With Maps. 3s. 6d.

HEROIDUM EPISTULÆ XIII. Edited by E. S. SHUCKBURGH, M.A. 3s. 6d.

METAMORPHOSES. BOOKS XIII. and XIV. Edited by C. SIMMONS, M.A. 3s. 6d.

MACMILLAN AND CO., LONDON.

MACMILLAN'S CLASSICAL SERIES.

Fcap. 8vo.   Cloth.

PLATO—THE REPUBLIC. BOOKS I.-V.   Edited by
T. H. WARREN, M.A.   5s.

LACHES.   Edited by M. T. TATHAM, M.A.   2s. 6d.

PLAUTUS—MILES GLORIOSUS.   Edited by Professor R.
Y. TYRRELL, M.A.   3s. 6d.

AMPHITRUO.   Edited by A. PALMER, M.A.   3s. 6d.

CAPTIVI.   Edited by A. RHYS-SMITH, M.A.

PLINY—LETTERS. BOOKS I. and II.   Edited by J.
COWAN, M.A.   3s.

LETTERS.   BOOK III.   Edited by Professor J. E. B.
MAYOR.   With Life of Pliny by G. H. RENDALL.   3s. 6d.

PLUTARCH—LIFE OF THEMISTOKLES.   Edited by
Rev. H. A. HOLDEN, M.A., LL.D.   3s. 6d.

LIVES OF GALBA AND OTHO.   Edited by E. G.
HARDY, M.A.   5s.

POLYBIUS.   The History of the Achæan League as contained in the remains of Polybius.   Edited by W. W.
CAPES.   5s.

PROPERTIUS—SELECT POEMS.   Edited by Professor
J. P. POSTGATE, M.A.   5s.

SALLUST—CATILINE AND JUGURTHA.   Edited by
C. MERIVALE, D.D.   3s. 6d.   Or separately, 2s. each.

BELLUM CATULINÆ.   Edited by A. M. COOK, M.A.
2s. 6d.

TACITUS—AGRICOLA AND GERMANIA.   Edited by
A. J. CHURCH, M.A., and W. J. BRODRIBB, M.A.
3s. 6d.   Or separately, 2s. each.

THE ANNALS.   BOOK VI.   By the same Editors.   2s.

THE HISTORIES.   BOOKS I. and II.   Edited by A.
D. GODLEY, M.A.   3s. 6d.

THE HISTORIES.   BOOKS III.-V.   By the same
Editor.   3s. 6d.

TERENCE—HAUTON TIMORUMENOS.   Edited by E.
S. SHUCKBURGH, M.A.   2s. 6d.   With Translation.
3s. 6d.

PHORMIO.   Edited by Rev. J. BOND, M.A., and Rev.
A. S. WALPOLE, M.A.   2s. 6d.

MACMILLAN AND CO., LONDON.

MACMILLAN'S CLASSICAL SERIES.

Fcap. 8vo. Cloth.

THUCYDIDES. BOOK II. Edited by E. C. MARCHANT, M.A.

BOOK IV. Edited by C. E. GRAVES, M.A. 3s. 6d.

BOOK V. By the same Editor.

BOOKS VI. and VII. THE SICILIAN EXPEDITION. Edited by Rev. P. FROST, M.A. With Map. 3s. 6d.

VIRGIL—ÆNEID. BOOKS II. and III. THE NARRATIVE OF ÆNEAS. Edited by E. W. HOWSON, M.A. 2s.

XENOPHON—HELLENICA. BOOKS I. and II. Edited by H. HAILSTONE, M.A. 2s. 6d.

CYROPÆDIA. BOOKS VII. and VIII. Edited by Professor A. GOODWIN, M.A. 2s. 6d.

MEMORABILIA SOCRATIS. Edited by A. R. CLUER, B.A. 5s.

THE ANABASIS. BOOKS I.-IV. Edited by Professors W. W. GOODWIN and J. W. WHITE. Adapted to Goodwin's Greek Grammar. With a Map. 3s. 6d.

HIERO. Edited by Rev. H. A. HOLDEN, M.A., LL.D. 2s. 6d.

ŒCONOMICUS. By the same Editor. With Introduction, Explanatory Notes, Critical Appendix, and Lexicon. 5s.

The following are in preparation :—

DEMOSTHENES—IN MIDIAM. Edited by Professor A. S. WILKINS, Litt.D., and HERMAN HAGER, Ph.D.

EURIPIDES — BACCHÆ. Edited by Professor R. Y. TYRRELL, M.A.

HERODOTUS. BOOK V. Edited by Professor J. STRACHAN, M.A.

ISÆOS—THE ORATIONS. Edited by Professor WILLIAM RIDGEWAY, M.A.

OVID—METAMORPHOSES. BOOKS I.-III. Edited by C. SIMMONS, M.A.

SALLUST—JUGURTHA. Edited by A. M. COOK, M.A.

TACITUS—THE ANNALS. BOOKS I. and II. Edited by J. S. REID, Litt.D.

Other Volumes will follow.

MACMILLAN AND CO., LONDON.

Sept. 1891

A Catalogue

OF

Educational Books

PUBLISHED BY

Macmillan & Co.

BEDFORD STREET, STRAND, LONDON

CONTENTS

	PAGE
CLASSICS—	
ELEMENTARY CLASSICS . . .	2
CLASSICAL SERIES	4
CLASSICAL LIBRARY ; Texts, Commentaries, Translations . .	6
GRAMMAR, COMPOSITION, AND PHILOLOGY	9
ANTIQUITIES, ANCIENT HISTORY, AND PHILOSOPHY . . .	12
MODERN LANGUAGES AND LITERATURE—	
ENGLISH	14
FRENCH	18
GERMAN	20
MODERN GREEK . . .	21
ITALIAN	21
SPANISH	21
MATHEMATICS—	
ARITHMETIC	22
BOOK-KEEPING . . .	23
ALGEBRA	23
EUCLID AND PURE GEOMETRY .	24
GEOMETRICAL DRAWING . .	25
MENSURATION . . .	25
TRIGONOMETRY . . .	25
ANALYTICAL GEOMETRY . .	26
PROBLEMS AND QUESTIONS IN MATHEMATICS . .	27
HIGHER PURE MATHEMATICS .	27
MECHANICS . . .	28

	PAGE
PHYSICS	30
ASTRONOMY . . .	32
HISTORICAL . . .	33
NATURAL SCIENCES—	
CHEMISTRY	33
PHYSICAL GEOGRAPHY, GEOLOGY, AND MINERALOGY . .	35
BIOLOGY	36
MEDICINE	38
HUMAN SCIENCES—	
MENTAL AND MORAL PHILOSOPHY	39
POLITICAL ECONOMY . .	40
LAW AND POLITICS . .	41
ANTHROPOLOGY . .	43
EDUCATION . . .	43
TECHNICAL KNOWLEDGE—	
CIVIL AND MECHANICAL ENGINEERING . . .	44
MILITARY AND NAVAL SCIENCE	44
AGRICULTURE . .	45
DOMESTIC ECONOMY . .	46
BOOK-KEEPING . .	46
COMMERCE . .	46
GEOGRAPHY .	47
HISTORY .	47
ART . .	50
DIVINITY	51

A

CLASSICS.

Elementary Classics; Classical Series; Classical Library, (1) Texts, (2) Translations; Grammar, Composition, and Philology; Antiquities, Ancient History, and Philosophy.

*ELEMENTARY CLASSICS.

18mo, Eighteenpence each.

The following contain Introductions, Notes, and **Vocabularies,** and in some cases **Exercises.**

ACCIDENCE, LATIN, AND EXERCISES ARRANGED FOR BEGINNERS.—By W. WELCH, M.A., and C. G. DUFFIELD, M.A.

AESCHYLUS.—PROMETHEUS VINCTUS. By Rev. H. M. STEPHENSON, M.A.

ARRIAN.—SELECTIONS. With Exercises. By Rev. JOHN BOND, M.A., and Rev. A. S. WALPOLE, M.A.

AULUS GELLIUS, STORIES FROM.—Adapted for Beginners. **With Exercises.** By Rev. G. H. NALL, M.A., Assistant Master at Westminster.

CÆSAR.—THE HELVETIAN WAR. Being Selections **from Book** I. of The Gallic War. Adapted for **Beginners.** With Exercises. **By** W. WELCH, M.A., and **C. G. DUFFIELD,** M.A.

THE INVASION OF BRITAIN. Being Selections from Books IV. and V. of The Gallic War. Adapted **for** Beginners. With Exercises. By W WELCH, M.A., and **C. G.** DUFFIELD, M.A.

SCENES FROM BOOKS V. AND VI. By C. COLBECK, **M.A.**

THE GALLIC WAR. BOOK I. By Rev. A. S. WALPOLE, M.A.

BOOKS II. AND III. By the Rev. **W. G.** RUTHERFORD, M.A., LL.D.

BOOK IV. By CLEMENT BRYANS, M.A., Assistant Master at Dulwich College.

BOOK V. By C. COLBECK, M.A., Assistant Master at Harrow.

BOOK VI. By the same Editor.

BOOK VII. By Rev. J. BOND, M.A., and Rev. A. S. WALPOLE, M.A.

THE CIVIL WAR. BOOK I. By M. MONTGOMERY, M.A.   *[In the Press.*

CICERO.—DE SENECTUTE. By E. S. SHUCKBURGH, M.A.

DE AMICITIA. By the same Editor.

STORIES OF ROMAN HISTORY. Adapted for Beginners. With Exercises. By Rev. G. E. JEANS, M.A., and A. V JONES, M.A.

EURIPIDES.—ALCESTIS. By Rev. M. A. BAYFIELD, M.A.

MEDEA. By A. W. VERRALL, Litt.D., and Rev M. A. BAYFIELD, M.A.   *[In the Press.*

HECUBA. By Rev. J. BOND, **M.A., and Rev.** A. S. WALPOLE, M.A.

EUTROPIUS.—Adapted for Beginners. **With** Exercises. By W. WELCH, M.A., and C. G. DUFFIELD, M.A.

HERODOTUS. TALES FROM HERODOTUS. Atticised by G. S. FARNELL, M.A.   *[In the Press.*

HOMER.—ILIAD. BOOK I. By Rev. J. BOND, M.A., and Rev. A. S. WALPOLE, M.A.

BOOK XVIII. By S. R. JAMES, M.A., Assistant Master at Eton.

ODYSSEY. BOOK I. By Rev. J. BOND, M.A., and Rev. A. S. WALPOLE, M.A.

HORACE.—ODES. BOOKS I.-IV. By T. E. PAGE, M.A., Assistant Master at the Charterhouse. Each 1s. 6d.

LIVY.—BOOK I. By H. M. STEPHENSON, M.A.
BOOK XXI. Adapted from Mr. Capes's Edition. By J. E. MELHUISH, M.A.
BOOK XXII. By the same.
THE HANNIBALIAN WAR. Being part of the XXI. and XXII. BOOKS OF LIVY adapted for Beginners. By G. C. MACAULAY, M.A.
THE SIEGE OF SYRACUSE. Being part of the XXIV. and XXV. BOOKS OF LIVY, adapted for Beginners. With Exercises. By G. RICHARDS, M.A., and Rev. A. S. WALPOLE, M.A.
LEGENDS OF ANCIENT ROME. Adapted for Beginners. With Exercises. By H. WILKINSON, M.A.

LUCIAN.—EXTRACTS FROM LUCIAN. With Exercises. By Rev. J BOND, M.A., and Rev. A. S. WALPOLE, M.A.

NEPOS.—SELECTIONS ILLUSTRATIVE OF GREEK AND ROMAN HISTORY. With Exercises. By G. S. FARNELL, M.A.

OVID.—SELECTIONS. By E. S. SHUCKBURGH, M.A.
EASY SELECTIONS FROM OVID IN ELEGIAC VERSE. With Exercises. By H. WILKINSON, M.A.
STORIES FROM THE METAMORPHOSES. With Exercises. By Rev. J. BOND, M.A., and Rev. A. S. WALPOLE, M.A.

PHÆDRUS.— SELECT FABLES. Adapted for Beginners. With Exercises. By Rev. A. S. WALPOLE, M.A.

THUCYDIDES.—THE RISE OF THE ATHENIAN EMPIRE. BOOK I. CHS. 89-117 and 228-238. With Exercises. By F. H. COLSON, M.A.

VIRGIL.—SELECTIONS. By E. S. SHUCKBURGH, M.A.
BUCOLICS. By T. E. PAGE, M.A.
GEORGICS. BOOK I. By the same Editor.
BOOK II. By Rev. J. H. SKRINE, M.A.
ÆNEID. BOOK I. By Rev. A. S. WALPOLE, M.A.
BOOK II. By T. E. PAGE, M.A.
BOOK III. By the same Editor.
BOOK IV. By Rev. H. M. STEPHENSON, M.A.
BOOK V. By Rev. A. CALVERT, M.A.
BOOK VI. By T. E. PAGE, M.A.
BOOK VII. By Rev. A. CALVERT, M.A.
BOOK VIII. By the same Editor.
BOOK IX. By Rev. H. M. STEPHENSON, M.A.
BOOK X. By S. G. OWEN, M.A.

XENOPHON.—ANABASIS. Selections, adapted for Beginners. With Exercises. By W. WELCH, M.A., and C. G. DUFFIELD, M.A.
BOOK I. With Exercises. By E. A. WELLS, M.A.
BOOK I. By Rev. A. S. WALPOLE, M.A.
BOOK II. By the same Editor.
BOOK III. By Rev. G. H. NALL, M.A.
BOOK IV. By Rev. E. D. STONE, M.A.
SELECTIONS FROM BOOK IV. With Exercises. By the same Editor.
SELECTIONS FROM THE CYROPÆDIA. With Exercises. By A. H. COOKE, M.A., Fellow and Lecturer of King's College, Cambridge.

The following contain Introductions and Notes, but no Vocabulary :—

CICERO.—SELECT LETTERS. By Rev. G. E. JEANS, M.A.

HERODOTUS.—SELECTIONS FROM BOOKS VII. AND VIII. THE EXPEDITION OF XERXES. By A. H. COOKE, M.A.

HORACE.—SELECTIONS FROM THE SATIRES AND EPISTLES. By Rev. W. J. V. BAKER, M.A.
SELECT EPODES AND ARS POETICA. By H. A. DALTON, M.A., Assistant Master at Winchester.

PLATO.—EUTHYPHRO AND MENEXENUS. By C. E. Graves, M.A.

TERENCE.—SCENES FROM THE ANDRIA. By F. W. Cornish, M.A., Assistant Master at Eton.

THE GREEK ELEGIAC POETS.—FROM CALLINUS TO CALLIMACHUS. Selected by Rev. Herbert Kynaston, D.D.

THUCYDIDES.—BOOK IV. Chs. 1-41. THE CAPTURE OF SPHACTERIA. By C. E. Graves, M.A.

CLASSICAL SERIES
FOR COLLEGES AND SCHOOLS.
Fcap. 8vo.

ÆSCHINES.—IN CTESIPHONTA. By Rev. T. Gwatkin, M.A., and E. S. Shuckburgh, M.A. 5s.

ÆSCHYLUS.—PERSÆ. By A. O. Prickard, M.A., Fellow and Tutor of New College, Oxford. With Map. 2s. 6d.

SEVEN AGAINST THEBES. SCHOOL EDITION. By A. W. Verrall, Litt.D., Fellow of Trinity College, Cambridge, and M. A. Bayfield, M.A., Headmaster of Christ's College, Brecon. 2s. 6d.

ANDOCIDES.—DE MYSTERIIS. By W. J. Hickie, M.A. 2s. 6d.

ATTIC ORATORS.—Selections from ANTIPHON, ANDOCIDES, LYSIAS, ISOCRATES, and ISAEUS. By R. C. Jebb, Litt.D., Regius Professor of Greek in the University of Cambridge. 5s.

*CÆSAR.—THE GALLIC WAR. By Rev. John Bond, M.A., and Rev. A. S. Walpole, M.A. With Maps. 4s. 6d.

CATULLUS.—SELECT POEMS. Edited by F. P. Simpson, B.A. 3s. 6d. The Text of this Edition is carefully expurgated for School use.

*CICERO.—THE CATILINE ORATIONS. By A. S. Wilkins, Litt.D., Professor of Latin in the Owens College, Victoria University, Manchester. 2s. 6d.

PRO LEGE MANILIA. By Prof. A. S. Wilkins, Litt.D. 2s. 6d.

THE SECOND PHILIPPIC ORATION. By John E. B. Mayor, M.A., Professor of Latin in the University of Cambridge. 3s. 6d.

PRO ROSCIO AMERINO. By E. H. Donkin, M.A. 2s. 6d.

PRO P. SESTIO. By Rev. H. A. Holden, Litt.D. 3s. 6d.

SELECT LETTERS. Edited by R. Y. Tyrrell, M.A. [In the Press.

DEMOSTHENES.—DE CORONA. By B. Drake, M.A. 7th Edition, revised by E. S. Shuckburgh, M.A. 3s. 6d.

ADVERSUS LEPTINEM. By Rev. J. R. King, M.A., Fellow and Tutor of Oriel College, Oxford. 2s. 6d.

THE FIRST PHILIPPIC. By Rev. T. Gwatkin, M.A. 2s. 6d.

IN MIDIAM. By Prof. A. S. Wilkins, Litt.D., and Herman Hager, Ph.D., of the Owens College, Victoria University, Manchester. [In preparation.

EURIPIDES.—HIPPOLYTUS. By Rev. J. P. Mahaffy, D.D., Fellow of Trinity College, and Professor of Ancient History in the University of Dublin, and J. B. Bury, M.A., Fellow of Trinity College, Dublin. 2s. 6d.

MEDEA. By A. W. Verrall, Litt.D., Fellow of Trinity College, Cambridge. 2s. 6d.

IPHIGENIA IN TAURIS. By E. B. England, M.A. 3s.

ION. By M. A. Bayfield, M.A., Headmaster of Christ's College, Brecon. 2s. 6d.

BACCHAE. By R. Y. Tyrrell, M.A., Regius Professor of Greek in the University of Dublin. [In preparation.

HERODOTUS.—BOOK III. By G. C. Macaulay, M.A. 2s. 6d.

BOOK V. By J. Strachan, M.A., Professor of Greek in the Owens College, Victoria University, Manchester. [In preparation.

BOOK VI. By the same. 3s. 6d.

BOOK VII. By Mrs. A. F. Butler. 3s. 6d.

HESIOD.—THE WORKS AND DAYS. By W. T. Lendrum, M.A., Assistant Master at Dulwich College. [In preparation.

HOMER.—**ILIAD.** BOOKS I., IX., XI., XVI.-XXIV. THE STORY OF ACHILLES. By the late J. H. PRATT, M.A., and WALTER LEAF, Litt.D., Fellows of Trinity College, Cambridge. 5s.

ODYSSEY. BOOK IX. By Prof. JOHN E. B. MAYOR. 2s. 6d.

ODYSSEY. BOOKS XXI.-XXIV. THE TRIUMPH OF ODYSSEUS. By S. G. HAMILTON, B.A., Fellow of Hertford College, Oxford. 2s. 6d.

HORACE.—*THE ODES. By T. E. PAGE, M.A., Assistant Master at the Charterhouse. 5s. (BOOKS I., II., III., and IV. separately, 2s. each.)

THE SATIRES. By ARTHUR PALMER, M.A., Professor of Latin in the University of Dublin. 5s.

THE EPISTLES AND ARS POETICA. By A. S. WILKINS, Litt.D., Professor of Latin in the Owens College, Victoria University, Manchester. 5s.

ISAEOS.—THE ORATIONS. By WILLIAM RIDGEWAY, M.A., Professor of Greek in Queen's College, Cork. [In preparation.

JUVENAL.—*THIRTEEN SATIRES. By E. G. HARDY, M.A. 5s. The Text is carefully expurgated for School use.

SELECT SATIRES. By Prof. JOHN E. B. MAYOR. X. and XI. 3s. 6d. XII.-XVI. 4s. 6d.

LIVY.—*BOOKS II. and III. By Rev. H. M. STEPHENSON, M.A. 3s. 6d.

*BOOKS XXI. and XXII. By Rev. W. W. CAPES, M.A. With Maps. 4s. 6d.

*BOOKS XXIII. and XXIV. By G. C. MACAULAY, M.A. With Maps. 3s. 6d.

*THE LAST TWO KINGS OF MACEDON. EXTRACTS FROM THE FOURTH AND FIFTH DECADES OF LIVY. By F. H. RAWLINS, M.A., Assistant Master at Eton. With Maps. 2s. 6d.

THE SUBJUGATION OF ITALY. SELECTIONS FROM THE FIRST DECADE. By G. E. MARINDIN, M.A. [In preparation.

LUCRETIUS.—BOOKS I.-III. By J. H. WARBURTON LEE, M.A., Assistant Master at Rossall. 3s. 6d.

LYSIAS.—SELECT ORATIONS. By E. S. SHUCKBURGH, M.A. 5s.

MARTIAL.—SELECT EPIGRAMS. By Rev. H. M. STEPHENSON, M.A. 5s.

*OVID.—FASTI. By G. H. HALLAM, M.A., Assistant Master at Harrow. With Maps. 3s. 6d.

*HEROIDUM EPISTULÆ XIII. By E. S. SHUCKBURGH, M.A. 3s. 6d.

METAMORPHOSES. BOOKS I.-III. By C. SIMMONS, M.A. [In preparation.

BOOKS XIII. and XIV. By the same Editor. 3s. 6d.

PLATO.—LACHES. By M. T. TATHAM, M.A. 2s. 6d.

THE REPUBLIC. BOOKS I.-V. By T. H. WARREN, M.A., President of Magdalen College, Oxford. 5s.

PLAUTUS.—MILES GLORIOSUS. By R. Y. TYRRELL, M.A., Regius Professor of Greek in the University of Dublin. 2d Ed., revised. 3s. 6d.

AMPHITRUO. By ARTHUR PALMER, M.A., Professor of Latin in the University of Dublin. 3s. 6d.

CAPTIVI. By A. RHYS-SMITH, M.A. [In the Press.

PLINY.—LETTERS. BOOKS I. and II. By J. COWAN, M.A., Assistant Master at the Manchester Grammar School. 3s.

LETTERS. BOOK III. By Prof. JOHN E. B. MAYOR. With Life of Pliny by G. H. RENDALL, M.A. 3s. 6d.

PLUTARCH.—LIFE OF THEMISTOKLES. By Rev. H. A. HOLDEN, Litt.D. 3s. 6d.

LIVES OF GALBA AND OTHO. By E. G. HARDY, M.A. 5s.

POLYBIUS.—THE HISTORY OF THE ACHÆAN LEAGUE AS CONTAINED IN THE REMAINS OF POLYBIUS. By W. W. CAPES, M.A. 5s.

PROPERTIUS.—SELECT POEMS. By Prof. J. P. POSTGATE, Litt.D., Fellow of Trinity College, Cambridge. 2d Ed., revised. 5s.

SALLUST.—*CATILINA and JUGURTHA. By C. MERIVALE, D.D., Dean of Ely. 3s. 6d. Or separately, 2s. each.

*BELLUM CATULINÆ. By A. M. COOK, M.A., Assistant Master at St. Paul's School. 2s. 6d.

JUGURTHA. By the same Editor. [In preparation.

TACITUS.—THE ANNALS. BOOKS I. and II. By J. S. Reid, Litt.D. [*In prep.*
  THE ANNALS. BOOK VI. By A. J. Church, M.A., and W. J. Brodribb, M.A. 2s.
  THE HISTORIES. BOOKS I. and II. By A. D. Godley, M.A., Fellow of Magdalen College, Oxford. 3s. 6d. BOOKS III.–V. By the same. 3s. 6d.
  AGRICOLA and GERMANIA. By A. J. Church, M.A., and W. J. Brodribb, M.A. 3s. 6d. Or separately, 2s. each.
TERENCE.—HAUTON TIMORUMENOS. By E. S. Shuckburgh, M.A. 2s. 6d. With Translation. 3s. 6d.
  PHORMIO. By Rev. John Bond, M.A., and Rev. A. S. Walpole, M.A. 2s. 6d.
THUCYDIDES.—BOOK I. By C. Bryans, M.A. [*In preparation.*
  BOOK II. By E. C. Marchant, M.A., Assistant Master at St. Paul's. [*In the Press.*
  BOOK III. By C. Bryans, M.A. [*In preparation.*
  BOOK IV. By C. E. Graves, M.A., Classical Lecturer at St. John's College, Cambridge. 3s. 6d.
  BOOK V. By the same Editor. [*In the Press.*
  BOOKS VI. and VII. THE SICILIAN EXPEDITION. By Rev. Percival Frost, M.A. With Map. 3s. 6d.
  BOOK VIII. By Prof. T. G. Tucker, Litt.D. [*In the Press.*
TIBULLUS.—SELECT POEMS. By Prof. J. P. Postgate, Litt.D. [*In preparation.*
VIRGIL.—ÆNEID. BOOKS II. and III. THE NARRATIVE OF ÆNEAS. By E. W. Howson, M.A., Assistant Master at Harrow. 2s.
XENOPHON.—*THE ANABASIS. BOOKS I.–IV. By Profs. W. W. Goodwin and J. W. White. Adapted to Goodwin's Greek Grammar. With Map. 3s. 6d.
  HELLENICA. BOOKS I. and II. By H. Hailstone, B.A. With Map. 2s. 6d.
  CYROPÆDIA. BOOKS VII. and VIII. By A. Goodwin, M.A., Professor of Classics in University College, London. 2s. 6d.
  MEMORABILIA SOCRATIS. By A. R. Cluer, B.A., Balliol College, Oxford. 5s.
  HIERO. By Rev. H. A. Holden, Litt.D., LL.D. 2s. 6d.
  OECONOMICUS. By the same. With Lexicon. 5s.

CLASSICAL LIBRARY.

Texts, Edited with Introductions and Notes, for the use of Advanced Students; Commentaries and Translations.

ÆSCHYLUS.—THE SUPPLICES. A Revised Text, with Translation. By T. G. Tucker, Litt.D., Professor of Classical Philology in the University of Melbourne. 8vo. 10s. 6d.
  THE SEVEN AGAINST THEBES. With Translation. By A. W. Verrall, Litt.D., Fellow of Trinity College, Cambridge. 8vo. 7s. 6d.
  AGAMEMNON. With Translation. By A. W. Verrall, Litt.D. 8vo. 12s.
  AGAMEMNON, CHOEPHOROE, AND EUMENIDES. By A. O. Prickard, M.A., Fellow and Tutor of New College, Oxford. 8vo. [*In preparation.*
  THE EUMENIDES. With Verse Translation. By Bernard Drake, M.A. 8vo. 5s.
ANTONINUS, MARCUS AURELIUS.—BOOK IV. OF THE MEDITATIONS. With Translation. By Hastings Crossley, M.A. 8vo. 6s.
ARISTOTLE.—THE METAPHYSICS. BOOK I. Translated by a Cambridge Graduate. 8vo. 5s.
  THE POLITICS. By R. D. Hicks, M.A., Fellow of Trinity College, Cambridge. 8vo. [*In the Press.*
  THE POLITICS. Translated by Rev. J. E. C. Welldon, M.A., Headmaster of Harrow. Cr. 8vo. 10s. 6d.
  THE RHETORIC. Translated by the same. Cr. 8vo. 7s. 6d.
  AN INTRODUCTION TO ARISTOTLE'S RHETORIC. With Analysis, Notes, and Appendices. By E. M. Cope, Fellow and late Tutor of Trinity College, Cambridge. 8vo. 14s.

THE ETHICS. Translated by Rev. J. E. C. WELLDON, M.A. Cr. 8vo. [*In prep.*

THE SOPHISTICI ELENCHI. With Translation. By E. POSTE, M.A., Fellow of Oriel College, Oxford. 8vo. 8s. 6d.

ON THE CONSTITUTION OF ATHENS. Edited by J. E. SANDYS, Litt.D.

ON THE CONSTITUTION OF ATHENS. Translated by E. POSTE, M.A. Cr. 8vo. 3s. 6d.

ON THE ART OF POETRY. A Lecture. By A. O. PRICKARD, M.A., Fellow and Tutor of New College, Oxford. Cr. 8vo. 3s. 6d.

ARISTOPHANES.—THE BIRDS. Translated into English Verse. By B. H. KENNEDY, D.D. Cr. 8vo. 6s. Help Notes to the Same, for the Use of Students. 1s. 6d.

ATTIC ORATORS.—FROM ANTIPHON TO ISAEOS. By R. C. JEBB, Litt.D., Regius Professor of Greek in the University of Cambridge. 2 vols. 8vo. 25s.

BABRIUS.—With Lexicon. By Rev. W. G. RUTHERFORD, M.A., LL.D., Head-master of Westminster. 8vo. 12s. 6d.

CICERO.—THE ACADEMICA. By J. S. REID, Litt.D., Fellow of Caius College, Cambridge. 8vo. 15s.

THE ACADEMICS. Translated by the same. 8vo. 5s. 6d.

SELECT LETTERS. After the Edition of ALBERT WATSON, M.A. Translated by G. E. JEANS, M.A., Fellow of Hertford College, Oxford. Cr. 8vo. 10s. 6d.

EURIPIDES.—MEDEA. Edited by A. W. VERRALL, Litt.D. 8vo. 7s. 6d.

IPHIGENEIA AT AULIS. Edited by E. B. ENGLAND, M.A. 8vo. 7s. 6d.

*INTRODUCTION TO THE STUDY OF EURIPIDES. By Professor J. P. MAHAFFY. Fcap. 8vo. 1s. 6d. (*Classical Writers.*)

HERODOTUS.—BOOKS I.-III. THE ANCIENT EMPIRES OF THE EAST. Edited by A. H. SAYCE, Deputy-Professor of Comparative Philology, Oxford. 8vo. 16s.

BOOKS IV.-IX. Edited by R. W. MACAN, M.A., Reader in Ancient History in the University of Oxford. 8vo. [*In preparation.*

THE HISTORY. Translated by G. C. MACAULAY, M.A. 2 vols. Cr. 8vo. 18s.

HOMER.—THE ILIAD. By WALTER LEAF, Litt.D. 8vo. Books I.-XII. 14s. Books XIII.-XXIV. 14s.

THE ILIAD. Translated into English Prose by ANDREW LANG, M.A., WALTER LEAF, Litt.D., and ERNEST MYERS, M.A. Cr. 8vo. 12s. 6d.

THE ODYSSEY. Done into English by S. H. BUTCHER, M.A., Professor of Greek in the University of Edinburgh, and ANDREW LANG, M.A. Cr. 8vo. 6s.

*INTRODUCTION TO THE STUDY OF HOMER. By the Right Hon. W. E. GLADSTONE. 18mo. 1s. (*Literature Primers.*)

HOMERIC DICTIONARY. Translated from the German of Dr. G. AUTENRIETH by R. P. KEEP, Ph.D. Illustrated. Cr. 8vo. 6s.

HORACE.—Translated by J. LONSDALE, M.A., and S. LEE, M.A. Gl. 8vo. 3s. 6d.

STUDIES, LITERARY AND HISTORICAL, IN THE ODES OF HORACE. By A. W. VERRALL, Litt.D. 8vo. 8s. 6d.

JUVENAL.—THIRTEEN SATIRES OF JUVENAL. By JOHN E. B. MAYOR, M.A., Professor of Latin in the University of Cambridge. Cr. 8vo. 2 vols. 10s. 6d. each. Vol. I. 10s. 6d. Vol. II. 10s. 6d.

THIRTEEN SATIRES. Translated by ALEX. LEEPER, M.A., LL.D., Warden of Trinity College, Melbourne. Cr. 8vo. 3s. 6d.

KTESIAS.—THE FRAGMENTS OF THE PERSIKA OF KTESIAS. By JOHN GILMORE, M.A. 8vo. 8s. 6d.

LIVY.—BOOKS I.-IV. Translated by Rev H. M. STEPHENSON, M.A. [*In prep.*

BOOKS XXI.-XXV. Translated by A. J. CHURCH, M.A., and W. J. BRODRIBB, M.A. Cr 8vo. 7s. 6d.

*INTRODUCTION TO THE STUDY OF LIVY. By Rev. W. W. CAPES, M.A. Fcap. 8vo. 1s. 6d. (*Classical Writers.*)

LONGINUS.—ON THE SUBLIME. Translated by H. L. HAVELL. B.A. With Introduction by ANDREW LANG. Cr. 8vo. 4s. 6d.

MARTIAL.—BOOKS I. AND II. OF THE EPIGRAMS.   By Prof. JOHN E. B.
  MAYOR, M.A. 8vo.   [In the Press.
MELEAGER.—FIFTY POEMS OF MELEAGER.   Translated by WALTER HEAD-
  LAM. Fcap. 4to. 7s. 6d.
PAUSANIAS.—DESCRIPTION OF GREECE.   Translated with Commentary
  by J. G. FRAZER, M.A., Fellow of Trinity College, Cambridge.   [In prep.
PHRYNICHUS.—THE NEW PHRYNICHUS ; being a Revised Text of the Ecloga
  of the Grammarian Phrynichus. With Introduction and Commentary by Rev.
  W. G. RUTHERFORD, M.A., LL.D., Headmaster of Westminster. 8vo. 18s.
PINDAR.—THE EXTANT ODES OF PINDAR.   Translated by ERNEST MYERS,
  M.A. Cr. 8vo. 5s.
    THE OLYMPIAN AND PYTHIAN ODES.   Edited, with an Introductory
      Essay, by BASIL GILDERSLEEVE, Professor of Greek in the Johns Hopkins
      University, U.S.A. Cr. 8vo. 7s. 6d.
    THE NEMEAN ODES. By J. B. BURY, M.A., Fellow of Trinity College,
      Dublin. 8vo. 12s.
    THE ISTHMIAN ODES. By the same Editor.   [In the Press.
PLATO.—PHÆDO. By R. D. ARCHER-HIND, M.A., Fellow of Trinity College,
  Cambridge. 8vo. 8s. 6d.
    PHÆDO. By W. D. GEDDES, LL.D., Principal of the University of Aberdeen.
      8vo. 8s. 6d.
    TIMAEUS. With Translation. By R. D. ARCHER-HIND, M.A. 8vo. 16s.
    THE REPUBLIC OF PLATO. Translated by J. LL. DAVIES, M.A., and D. J.
      VAUGHAN, M.A. 18mo. 4s. 6d.
    EUTHYPHRO, APOLOGY, CRITO, AND PHÆDO. Translated by F. J.
      CHURCH. 18mo. 4s. 6d.
    PHÆDRUS, LYSIS, AND PROTAGORAS. Translated by J. WRIGHT, M.A.
      18mo. 4s. 6d.
PLAUTUS.—THE MOSTELLARIA. By WILLIAM RAMSAY, M.A. Edited by
  G. G. RAMSAY, M.A., Professor of Humanity in the University of Glasgow.
  8vo. 14s.
PLINY.—CORRESPONDENCE WITH TRAJAN. C. Plinii Caecilii Secundi
  Epistulæ ad Traianum Imperatorem cum Eiusdem Responsis. By E. G.
  HARDY, M.A. 8vo. 10s. 6d.
POLYBIUS.—THE HISTORIES OF POLYBIUS. Translated by E. S. SHUCK-
  BURGH, M.A. 2 vols. Cr. 8vo. 24s.
SALLUST.—CATILINE AND JUGURTHA. Translated by A. W. POLLARD, B.A.
  Cr. 8vo. 6s. THE CATILINE (separately). 3s.
SOPHOCLES.—ŒDIPUS THE KING. Translated into English Verse by E. D. A.
  MORSHEAD, M.A., Assistant Master at Winchester. Fcap. 8vo. 3s. 6d.
TACITUS.—THE ANNALS. By G. O. HOLBROOKE, M.A., Professor of Latin in
  Trinity College, Hartford, U.S.A. With Maps. 8vo. 16s.
    THE ANNALS. Translated by A. J. CHURCH, M.A., and W. J. BRODRIBB, M.A.
      With Maps. Cr. 8vo. 7s. 6d.
    THE HISTORIES. By Rev. W. A. SPOONER, M.A., Fellow and Tutor of New
      College, Oxford. 8vo. 16s.
    THE HISTORY. Translated by A. J. CHURCH, M.A., and W. J. BRODRIBB,
      M.A. With Map. Cr. 8vo. 6s.
    THE AGRICOLA AND GERMANY, WITH THE DIALOGUE ON ORATORY.
      Translated by A. J. CHURCH, M.A., and W J. BRODRIBB, M.A. With Maps.
      Cr. 8vo. 4s. 6d
   *INTRODUCTION TO THE STUDY OF TACITUS. By A. J. CHURCH, M.A.,
      and W J. BRODRIBB, M.A. Fcap. 8vo. 1s. 6d. (Classical Writers.)
THEOCRITUS, BION, AND MOSCHUS. Translated by A. LANG, M.A. 18mo.
  4s. 6d. Also an Edition on Large Paper. Cr. 8vo. 9s.
THUCYDIDES.—BOOK IV. A Revision of the Text, Illustrating the Principal
  Causes of Corruption in the Manuscripts of this Author. By Rev. W. G.
  RUTHERFORD, M.A., LL.D., Headmaster of Westminster. 8vo. 7s. 6d.

BOOK VIII. By H. C. GOODHART, M.A., Fellow of Trinity College, Cambridge.
[*In the Press.*]

VIRGIL.—Translated by J. LONSDALE, M.A., and S. LEE, M.A. Gl. 8vo. 3s. 6d.

THE ÆNEID. Translated by J. W. MACKAIL, M.A., Fellow of Balliol College, Oxford. Cr. 8vo. 7s. 6d.

XENOPHON.—Translated by H. G. DAKYNS, M.A. In four vols. Cr. 8vo. Vol. I., containing "The Anabasis" and Books I. and II. of "The Hellenica." 10s. 6d. Vol. II. "Hellenica" III.-VII., and the two Polities—"Athenian" and "Laconian," the "Agesilaus," and the tract on "Revenues." With Maps and Plans. [*In the Press.*]

GRAMMAR, COMPOSITION, & PHILOLOGY.

*BELCHER.—SHORT EXERCISES IN LATIN PROSE COMPOSITION AND EXAMINATION PAPERS IN LATIN GRAMMAR. Part I. By Rev. H. BELCHER, LL.D., Rector of the High School, Dunedin, N.Z. 18mo. 1s. 6d. KEY, for Teachers only. 18mo. 3s. 6d.

*Part II., On the Syntax of Sentences, with an Appendix, including EXERCISES IN LATIN IDIOMS, etc. 18mo. 2s. KEY, for Teachers only. 18mo. 2s.

BLACKIE.—GREEK AND ENGLISH DIALOGUES FOR USE IN SCHOOLS AND COLLEGES. By JOHN STUART BLACKIE, Emeritus Professor of Greek in the University of Edinburgh. New Edition. Fcap. 8vo. 2s. 6d.

A GREEK PRIMER, COLLOQUIAL AND CONSTRUCTIVE. Cr. 8vo. 2s. 6d.

*BRYANS.—LATIN PROSE EXERCISES BASED UPON CÆSAR'S GALLIC WAR. With a Classification of Cæsar's Chief Phrases and Grammatical Notes on Cæsar's Usages. By CLEMENT BRYANS, M.A., Assistant Master at Dulwich College. Ex. fcap. 8vo. 2s. 6d. KEY, for Teachers only. 4s. 6d.

GREEK PROSE EXERCISES based upon Thucydides. By the same.
[*In preparation.*]

COOKSON.—A LATIN SYNTAX. By CHRISTOPHER COOKSON, M.A., Assistant Master at St. Paul's School. 8vo. [*In preparation.*]

CORNELL UNIVERSITY STUDIES IN CLASSICAL PHILOLOGY. Edited by I. FLAGG, W. G. HALE, and B. I. WHEELER. I. The CUM-Constructions: their History and Functions. By W. G. HALE. Part 1. Critical. 1s. 8d. net. Part 2. Constructive. 3s. 4d. net. II. Analogy and the Scope of its Application in Language. By B. I. WHEELER. 1s. 3d. net.

*EICKE.—FIRST LESSONS IN LATIN. By K. M. EICKE, B.A., Assistant Master at Oundle School. Gl. 8vo. 2s. 6d.

*ENGLAND.—EXERCISES ON LATIN SYNTAX AND IDIOM. ARRANGED WITH REFERENCE TO ROBY'S SCHOOL LATIN GRAMMAR. By E. B. ENGLAND, Assistant Lecturer at the Owens College, Victoria University, Manchester. Cr. 8vo. 2s. 6d. KEY, for Teachers only. 2s. 6d.

GILES.—A SHORT MANUAL OF PHILOLOGY FOR CLASSICAL STUDENTS By P. GILES, M.A., Reader in Comparative Philology in the University of Cambridge. Cr. 8vo. [*In the Press*]

GOODWIN.—Works by W. W. GOODWIN, LL.D., D.C.L., Professor of Greek in Harvard University, U.S.A.

SYNTAX OF THE MOODS AND TENSES OF THE GREEK VERB. New Ed., revised and enlarged. 8vo. 14s.

*A GREEK GRAMMAR. Cr. 8vo. 6s.

*A GREEK GRAMMAR FOR SCHOOLS. Cr. 8vo. 3s. 6d.

GREENWOOD.—THE ELEMENTS OF GREEK GRAMMAR. Adapted to the System of Crude Forms. By J. G. GREENWOOD, sometime Principal of the Owens College, Manchester. Cr. 8vo. 5s. 6d.

HADLEY.—ESSAYS, PHILOLOGICAL AND CRITICAL. By JAMES HADLEY, late Professor in Yale College. 8vo. 16s.

HADLEY and ALLEN.—A GREEK GRAMMAR FOR SCHOOLS AND COLLEGES. By JAMES HADLEY, late Professor in Yale College. Revised and in part rewritten by F. DE F. ALLEN, Professor in Harvard College. Cr. 8vo. 6s.

HODGSON.—MYTHOLOGY FOR LATIN VERSIFICATION. A brief sketch of the Fables of the Ancients, prepared to be rendered into Latin Verse for Schools. By F. HODGSON, B.D., late Provost of Eton. New Ed., revised by F C. HODGSON, M.A. 18mo. 3s.

*JACKSON.—FIRST STEPS TO GREEK PROSE COMPOSITION By BLOMFIELD JACKSON, M.A., Assistant Master at King's College School. 18mo. 1s. 6d. KEY, for Teachers only. 18mo. 3s. 6d.

*SECOND STEPS TO GREEK PROSE COMPOSITION, with Miscellaneous Idioms, Aids to Accentuation, and Examination Papers in Greek Scholarship. By the same. 18mo. 2s. 6d. KEY, for Teachers only. 18mo. 3s. 6d.

KYNASTON.—EXERCISES IN THE COMPOSITION OF GREEK IAMBIC VERSE by Translations from English Dramatists. By Rev. H. KYNASTON, D.D., Professor of Classics in the University of Durham. With Vocabulary. Ex. fcap. 8vo. 5s.

KEY, for Teachers only. Ex. fcap. 8vo. 4s. 6d.

LUPTON.—*AN INTRODUCTION TO LATIN ELEGIAC VERSE COMPOSI-TION. By J. H. LUPTON, Sur-Master of St. Paul's School. Gl. 8vo. 2s. 6d. KEY TO PART II. (XXV.-C.) Gl. 8vo. 3s. 6d.

*AN INTRODUCTION TO LATIN LYRIC VERSE COMPOSITION. By the same. Gl. 8vo. 3s. KEY, for Teachers only. Gl. 8vo. 4s. 6d.

MACKIE.—PARALLEL PASSAGES FOR TRANSLATION INTO GREEK AND ENGLISH. With Indexes. By Rev. ELLIS C. MACKIE, M.A., Classical Master at Heversham Grammar School. Gl. 8vo. 4s. 6d.

*MACMILLAN.—FIRST LATIN GRAMMAR. By M. C. MACMILLAN, M.A. Fcap. 8vo. 1s. 6d.

MACMILLAN'S GREEK COURSE.—Edited by Rev. W. G. RUTHERFORD, M.A., LL.D., Headmaster of Westminster. Gl. 8vo.

*FIRST GREEK GRAMMAR—ACCIDENCE. By the Editor. 2s.
*FIRST GREEK GRAMMAR—SYNTAX. By the same. 2s.
ACCIDENCE AND SYNTAX. In one volume. 3s. 6d.

*EASY EXERCISES IN GREEK ACCIDENCE. By H. G. UNDERHILL, M.A., Assistant Master at St. Paul's Preparatory School. 2s.

*A SECOND GREEK EXERCISE BOOK. By Rev. W. A. HEARD, M.A., Headmaster of Fettes College, Edinburgh. 2s. 6d.

EASY EXERCISES IN GREEK SYNTAX. By Rev. G. H. NALL, M.A., Assistant Master at Westminster School.   [In preparation.
MANUAL OF GREEK ACCIDENCE. By the Editor.   [In preparation.
MANUAL OF GREEK SYNTAX. By the Editor.   [In preparation.
ELEMENTARY GREEK COMPOSITION. By the Editor.   [In preparation.

*MACMILLAN'S GREEK READER.—STORIES AND LEGENDS. A First Greek Reader, with Notes, Vocabulary, and Exercises. By F. H. COLSON, M.A., Headmaster of Plymouth College. Gl. 8vo. 3s.

MACMILLAN'S LATIN COURSE.—By A. M. COOK, M.A., Assistant Master at St. Paul's School.

*FIRST PART. Gl. 8vo. 3s. 6d.
*SECOND PART. 2s. 6d.   [Third Part in preparation.

*MACMILLAN'S SHORTER LATIN COURSE.—By A. M. COOK, M.A. Being an abridgment of "Macmillan's Latin Course," First Part. Gl. 8vo. 1s. 6d.

*MACMILLAN'S LATIN READER.—A LATIN READER FOR THE LOWER FORMS IN SCHOOLS. By H. J. HARDY, M.A., Assistant Master at Win-chester. Gl. 8vo. 2s. 6d.

*MARSHALL.—A TABLE OF IRREGULAR GREEK VERBS, classified according to the arrangement of Curtius's Greek Grammar. By J. M. MARSHALL, M.A., Headmaster of the Grammar School, Durham. 8vo. 1s.

MAYOR.—FIRST GREEK READER. By Prof. JOHN E. B. MAYOR, M.A., Fellow of St. John's College, Cambridge. Fcap. 8vo. 4s. 6d.

MAYOR.—GREEK FOR BEGINNERS. By Rev. J. B. MAYOR, M.A., late Professor of Classical Literature in King's College, London. Part I., with Vocabulary, 1s. 6d. Parts II. and III., with Vocabulary and Index. Fcap. 8vo. 3s. 6d. **Complete** in one Vol. 4s. 6d.

NIXON.—PARALLEL EXTRACTS, Arranged for Translation into English and Latin, with Notes on Idioms. By J. E. NIXON, M.A., Fellow and Classical Lecturer, King's **College,** Cambridge. Part I.—Historical and Epistolary. Cr. 8vo. 3s. 6d.

PROSE EXTRACTS, Arranged for Translation into English and Latin, with General and Special Prefaces on Style and Idiom. By the same. I. Oratorical. II. Historical. III. Philosophical. IV. Anecdotes and Letters. 2d Ed., enlarged to 280 pp. Cr. 8vo. 4s. 6d. SELECTIONS FROM THE SAME. 3s. Translations of about 70 Extracts can be supplied to Schoolmasters (2s. 6d.), on application to the Author: and about 40 similarly of "Parallel Extracts." 1s. 6d. post free.

*PANTIN.—A FIRST LATIN VERSE BOOK. By W. E. P. PANTIN, M.A., Assistant Master at St. Paul's School. Gl. 8vo. 1s. 6d.

*PEILE.—A PRIMER OF PHILOLOGY. By J. PEILE, Litt.D., Master of Christ's College, Cambridge. 18mo. 1s.

*POSTGATE.—SERMO LATINUS. A short Guide to Latin Prose Composition. By Prof. J. P. POSTGATE, Litt.D., Fellow of Trinity College, Cambridge. Gl. 8vo. 2s. 6d. KEY to "Selected Passages." Gl. 8vo. 3s. 6d.

POSTGATE and VINCE.—A DICTIONARY OF LATIN ETYMOLOGY. By J. P. POSTGATE and C. A. VINCE. [In preparation.

POTTS.—*HINTS TOWARDS LATIN PROSE COMPOSITION. By A. W. POTTS, M.A., LL.D., late Fellow of St. John's College, Cambridge. Ex. fcap. 8vo. 3s.
*PASSAGES FOR TRANSLATION INTO LATIN PROSE. Edited with Notes and References to the above. **Ex.** fcap. 8vo. 2s. 6d. KEY, for Teachers only. 2s. 6d.

*PRESTON.—EXERCISES IN LATIN VERSE OF VARIOUS KINDS. By **Rev.** G. PRESTON. Gl. 8vo. 2s. 6d. KEY, for Teachers only. Gl. 8vo. 5s.

REID.—A GRAMMAR OF TACITUS. By J. S. REID, Litt.D., Fellow of **Caius** College, Cambridge. [In the Press.
A GRAMMAR OF VIRGIL. By the same. [In preparation.

ROBY.—Works by H. J. ROBY, M.A., late Fellow of St. John's College, Cambridge. A GRAMMAR OF THE LATIN LANGUAGE, from Plautus to Suetonius. Part I. Sounds, Inflexions, Word-formation, Appendices. Cr. **8vo. 9s.** Part II. Syntax, Prepositions, etc. 10s. 6d.
*SCHOOL LATIN GRAMMAR. Cr. **8vo. 5s.**
AN ELEMENTARY LATIN **GRAMMAR.** [In the Press.

*RUSH.—SYNTHETIC **LATIN DELECTUS.** With Notes and Vocabulary. By E. RUSH, B.A. Ex. fcap. 8vo. 2s. 6d.

*RUST.—FIRST STEPS TO LATIN PROSE COMPOSITION. By Rev. G. RUST, M.A. 18mo. 1s. 6d. KEY, for Teachers only. By W. M. YATES. 18mo. 3s. 6d.

RUTHERFORD.—Works by the Rev. W. G. RUTHERFORD, M.A., LL.D., Headmaster of Westminster.
REX LEX. A Short Digest **of** the principal Relations between **the** Latin, Greek, **and** Anglo-Saxon Sounds. 8vo. [In preparation.
THE NEW PHRYNICHUS; **being a** Revised Text of the Ecloga of the Grammarian Phrynichus. With **Introduction** and Commentary. 8vo. 18s. (See also Macmillan's Greek Course.)

SHUCKBURGH.—PASSAGES FROM LATIN AUTHORS FOR TRANSLATION INTO ENGLISH. Selected with a view to the needs of Candidates for the Cambridge Local, and Public Schools' Examinations. By E. S. SHUCKBURGH, M.A. Cr. 8vo. 2s.

*SIMPSON.—LATIN PROSE AFTER THE BEST AUTHORS: Cæsarian Prose. By F. P. SIMPSON, B.A. Ex. fcap. 8vo. 2s. 6d. KEY, for Teachers only. Ex. fcap. 8vo. 5s.

STRACHAN and WILKINS.—ANALECTA. Selected Passages for Translation. By J. S. STRACHAN, M.A., Professor of Greek, and A. S. WILKINS, Litt.D., Professor of Latin in the Owens College, Manchester. Cr. 8vo. 5s. KEY to **Latin Passages.** Cr. 8vo. **Sewed,** 6d.

THRING.—Works by the Rev. **E. THRING**, M.A., late Headmaster of Uppingham.
  A LATIN GRADUAL. A First Latin Construing Book for Beginners. With
  Coloured Sentence Maps. Fcap. 8vo. 2s. 6d.
  A MANUAL OF MOOD CONSTRUCTIONS. Fcap. 8vo. 1s. 6d.
'WELCH and DUFFIELD.—LATIN ACCIDENCE AND EXERCISES AR-
  RANGED FOR BEGINNERS. By W WELCH and C. G. DUFFIELD,
  Assistant Masters at Cranleigh School. 18mo. 1s. 6d.
WHITE.—FIRST LESSONS IN GREEK. Adapted to GOODWIN'S GREEK GRAM-
  MAR, and designed as an introduction to the ANABASIS OF XENOPHON. By
  JOHN WILLIAMS WHITE, Assistant Professor of Greek in Harvard University,
  U.S.A. Cr. 8vo. 3s. 6d.
WRIGHT.—Works by J. WRIGHT, M.A., late Headmaster of Sutton Coldfield School.
  A HELP TO LATIN GRAMMAR; or, the Form and Use of Words in Latin;
  with Progressive Exercises. Cr. 8vo. 4s. 6d.
  THE SEVEN KINGS OF ROME. An Easy Narrative, abridged from the First
  Book of Livy by the omission of Difficult Passages; being a First Latin Read-
  ing Book, with Grammatical Notes and Vocabulary. Fcap. 8vo. 3s. 6d.
  FIRST LATIN STEPS; OR, AN INTRODUCTION BY A SERIES OF
  EXAMPLES TO THE STUDY OF THE LATIN LANGUAGE. Cr. 8vo. 3s.
  ATTIC PRIMER. Arranged for the Use of Beginners. Ex. fcap. 8vo. 2s. 6d.
  A COMPLETE LATIN COURSE, comprising Rules with Examples, Exercises,
  both Latin and English, on each Rule, and Vocabularies. Cr. 8vo. 2s. 6d.

ANTIQUITIES, ANCIENT HISTORY, AND PHILOSOPHY.

ARNOLD.—A HISTORY OF THE EARLY ROMAN EMPIRE. By W T. ARNOLD,
  M.A. [In preparation.
ARNOLD.—THE SECOND PUNIC WAR. Being Chapters from THE HISTORY
  OF ROME by the late THOMAS ARNOLD, D.D., Headmaster of Rugby.
  Edited, with Notes, by W. T. ARNOLD, M.A. With 8 Maps. Cr. 8vo. 5s.
'BEESLY.—STORIES FROM THE HISTORY OF ROME. By Mrs. BEESLY.
  Fcap. 8vo. 2s. 6d.
BLACKIE.—HORÆ HELLENICÆ. By JOHN STUART BLACKIE, Emeritus Pro-
  fessor of Greek in the University of Edinburgh. 8vo. 12s.
BURN.—ROMAN LITERATURE IN RELATION TO ROMAN ART. By Rev.
  ROBERT BURN, M.A., late Fellow of Trinity College, Cambridge. Illustrated.
  Ex. cr. 8vo. 14s.
BURY.—A HISTORY OF THE LATER ROMAN EMPIRE FROM ARCADIUS
  TO IRENE, A.D. 395-800. By J. B. BURY, M.A., Fellow of Trinity College,
  Dublin. 2 vols. 8vo. 32s.
'CLASSICAL WRITERS.—Edited by JOHN RICHARD GREEN, M.A., LL.D. Fcap.
  8vo. 1s. 6d. each.
  SOPHOCLES. By Prof. L. CAMPBELL, M.A.
  EURIPIDES. By Prof. MAHAFFY, D.D.
  DEMOSTHENES. By Prof. S. H. BUTCHER, M.A.
  VIRGIL. By Prof. NETTLESHIP, M.A.
  LIVY. By Rev. W. W. CAPES, M.A.
  TACITUS. By Prof. A. J. CHURCH, M.A., and W. J. BRODRIBB, M.A.
  MILTON. By Rev. STOPFORD A. BROOKE, M.A.
DYER.—STUDIES OF THE GODS IN GREECE AT CERTAIN SANCTUARIES
  RECENTLY EXCAVATED. By LOUIS DYER, B.A. Ex. Cr. 8vo. 8s. 6d. net.
FREEMAN.—Works by EDWARD A. FREEMAN, D.C.L., LL.D., Regius Professor of
  Modern History in the University of Oxford.
  HISTORY OF ROME. (Historical Course for Schools.) 18mo. [In preparation.
  HISTORY OF GREECE. (Historical Course for Schools.) 18mo. [In preparation.
  A SCHOOL HISTORY OF ROME. Cr. 8vo. [In preparation.
  HISTORICAL ESSAYS. Second Series. [Greek and Roman History.] 8vo.
  10s. 6d.

GARDNER.—SAMOS AND SAMIAN COINS. An Essay. By PERCY GARDNER, Litt.D., Professor of Archæology in the University of Oxford. 8vo. 7s. 6d.

GEDDES.—THE PROBLEM OF THE HOMERIC POEMS. By W. D. GEDDES, Principal of the University of Aberdeen. 8vo. 14s.

GLADSTONE.—Works by the Rt. Hon. W. E. GLADSTONE, M.P.
  THE TIME AND PLACE OF HOMER. Cr. 8vo. 6s. 6d.
  LANDMARKS OF HOMERIC STUDY. Cr. 8vo. 2s. 6d.
  *A PRIMER OF HOMER. 18mo. 1s.

GOW.—A COMPANION TO SCHOOL CLASSICS. By JAMES GOW, Litt.D., Master of the High School, Nottingham. With Illustrations. 2d Ed., revised Cr. 8vo. 6s.

HARRISON and VERRALL.—MYTHOLOGY AND MONUMENTS OF ANCIENT ATHENS. Translation of a portion of the "Attica" of Pausanias. By MARGARET DE G. VERRALL. With Introductory Essay and Archæological Commentary by JANE E. HARRISON. With Illustrations and Plans. Cr. 8vo. 16s.

JEBB.—Works by R. C. JEBB, Litt.D., Professor of Greek in the University of Cambridge.
  THE ATTIC ORATORS FROM ANTIPHON TO ISAEOS. 2 vols. 8vo. 25s.
  *A PRIMER OF GREEK LITERATURE. 18mo. 1s.
                    (See also Classical Series.)

KIEPERT. — MANUAL OF ANCIENT GEOGRAPHY. By Dr. H. KIEPERT. Cr. 8vo. 5s.

LANCIANI.—ANCIENT ROME IN THE LIGHT OF RECENT DISCOVERIES. By RODOLFO LANCIANI, Professor of Archæology in the University of Rome. Illustrated. 4to. 24s.

LEAF.—INTRODUCTION TO THE ILIAD FOR ENGLISH READERS. By WALTER LEAF, Litt.D.   [In preparation.

MAHAFFY.—Works by J. P. MAHAFFY, D.D., Fellow of Trinity College, Dublin and Professor of Ancient History in the University of Dublin.
  SOCIAL LIFE IN GREECE; from Homer to Menander. Cr. 8vo. 9s.
  GREEK LIFE AND THOUGHT; from the Age of Alexander to the Roman Conquest. Cr. 8vo. 12s. 6d.
  THE GREEK WORLD UNDER ROMAN SWAY. From Plutarch to Polybius. Cr. 8vo. 10s. 6d.
  RAMBLES AND STUDIES IN GREECE. With Illustrations. With Map. Cr. 8vo. 10s. 6d.
  A HISTORY OF CLASSICAL GREEK LITERATURE. Cr. 8vo. Vol. I. In two parts. Part I. The Poets, with an Appendix on Homer by Prof. SAYCE. Part II. Dramatic Poets. Vol. II. The Prose Writers. In two parts. Part I. Herodotus to Plato. Part II. Isocrates to Aristotle. 4s. 6d. each.
  *A PRIMER OF GREEK ANTIQUITIES. With Illustrations. 18mo. 1s.
  *EURIPIDES. 18mo. 1s. 6d. (Classical Writers.)

MAYOR.—BIBLIOGRAPHICAL CLUE TO LATIN LITERATURE. Edited after HÜBNER. By Prof. JOHN E. B. MAYOR. Cr. 8vo. 10s. 6d.

NEWTON.—ESSAYS ON ART AND ARCHÆOLOGY. By Sir CHARLES NEWTON, K.C.B., D.C.L. 8vo. 12s. 6d.

PHILOLOGY.—THE JOURNAL OF PHILOLOGY. Edited by W. A. WRIGHT, M.A., I. BYWATER, M.A., and H. JACKSON, Litt.D. 4s. 6d. each (half-yearly).

SAYCE.—THE ANCIENT EMPIRES OF THE EAST. By A. H. SAYCE, M.A., Deputy-Professor of Comparative Philology, Oxford. Cr. 8vo. 6s.

SCHMIDT and WHITE. AN INTRODUCTION TO THE RHYTHMIC AND METRIC OF THE CLASSICAL LANGUAGES. By Dr. J. H. HEINRICH SCHMIDT. Translated by JOHN WILLIAMS WHITE, Ph.D. 8vo. 10s. 6d.

SHUCHHARDT.—DR. SCHLIEMANN'S EXCAVATIONS AT TROY, TIRYNS, MYCENÆ, ORCHOMENOS, ITHACA, presented in the light of recent knowledge. By Dr. CARL SHUCHHARDT. Translated by EUGENIE SELLERS. Introduction by WALTER LEAF, Litt.D. Illustrated. 8vo. 18s. net.

SHUCKBURGH.—A SCHOOL HISTORY OF ROME. By E. S. SHUCKBURGH, M.A. Cr. 8vo. [In preparation.

*STEWART.—THE TALE OF TROY. Done into English by AUBREY STEWART. Gl. 8vo. 3s. 6d.

*TOZER.—A PRIMER OF CLASSICAL GEOGRAPHY. By H. F. TOZER, M.A. 18mo. 1s.

WALDSTEIN.—CATALOGUE OF CASTS IN THE MUSEUM OF CLASSICAL ARCHÆOLOGY, CAMBRIDGE. By CHARLES WALDSTEIN, University Reader in Classical Archæology. Cr. 8vo. 1s. 6d.

₊ Also an Edition on Large Paper, small 4to. 5s.

WILKINS.—Works by Prof. WILKINS, Litt.D., LL.D.
*A PRIMER OF ROMAN ANTIQUITIES. Illustrated. 18mo. 1s.
*A PRIMER OF ROMAN LITERATURE. 18mo. 1s.

WILKINS and ARNOLD.—A MANUAL OF ROMAN ANTIQUITIES. By Prof. A. S. WILKINS, Litt.D., and W. T. ARNOLD, M.A. Cr. 8vo. Illustrated. [In preparation.

MODERN LANGUAGES AND LITERATURE.

English ; French ; German ; Modern Greek ; Italian ; Spanish.

ENGLISH.

*ABBOTT.—A SHAKESPEARIAN GRAMMAR. An Attempt to Illustrate some of the Differences between Elizabethan and Modern English. By the Rev. E. A. ABBOTT, D.D., formerly Headmaster of the City of London School. Ex. fcap. 8vo. 6s.

*BACON.—ESSAYS. With Introduction and Notes, by F. G. SELBY, M.A., Professor of Logic and Moral Philosophy, Deccan College, Poona. Gl. 8vo. 3s. ; sewed, 2s. 6d.

*BURKE.—REFLECTIONS ON THE FRENCH REVOLUTION. By the same. Gl. 8vo. 5s.

BROOKE.—*PRIMER OF ENGLISH LITERATURE. By Rev. STOPFORD A. BROOKE, M.A. 18mo. 1s.
EARLY ENGLISH LITERATURE. By the same. 2 vols. 8vo. [Vol. I. In the Press.

BUTLER.—HUDIBRAS. With Introduction and Notes, by ALFRED MILNES, M.A. Ex. fcap. 8vo. Part I. 3s. 6d. Parts II. and III. 4s. 6d.

CAMPBELL.—SELECTIONS. With Introduction and Notes, by CECIL M. BARROW, M.A., Principal of Victoria College, Palghât. Gl. 8vo. [In preparation.

COWPER.—*THE TASK : an Epistle to Joseph Hill, Esq. ; TIROCINIUM, or a Review of the Schools ; and THE HISTORY OF JOHN GILPIN. Edited, with Notes, by W. BENHAM, B.D. Gl. 8vo. 1s. (Globe Readings from Standard Authors.)
THE TASK. With Introduction and Notes, by F. J. ROWE, M.A., and W. T WEBB, M.A., Professors of English Literature, Presidency College, Calcutta. [In preparation.

*DOWDEN.—A PRIMER OF SHAKESPERE. By Prof. DOWDEN. 18mo. 1s.

DRYDEN.—SELECT PROSE WORKS. Edited, with Introduction and Notes, by Prof. C. D. YONGE. Fcap. 8vo. 2s. 6d.

*GLOBE READERS. For Standards I.-VI. Edited by A. F. MURISON. Illustrated. Gl. 8vo.

Primer I. (48 pp.)	3d.	Book III. (232 pp.)	1s. 3d.
Primer II. (48 pp.)	3d.	Book IV. (328 pp.)	1s. 9d.
Book I. (132 pp.)	6d.	Book V. (408 pp.)	2s.
Book II. (136 pp.)	9d.	Book VI. (436 pp.)	2s. 6d.

*THE SHORTER GLOBE READERS.—Illustrated. Gl. 8vo.

Primer I. (48 pp.)	3d.	Standard III. (178 pp.)	1s.
Primer II. (48 pp.)	3d.	Standard IV. (182 pp.)	1s.
Standard I. (90 pp.)	6d.	Standard V. (216 pp.)	1s. 3d.
Standard II. (124 pp.)	9d.	Standard VI. (228 pp.)	1s. 6d.

*GOLDSMITH.—THE TRAVELLER, or a Prospect of Society ; and THE DESERTED VILLAGE. With Notes, Philological and Explanatory, by J. W. HALES, M.A. Cr. 8vo. 6d.

*THE TRAVELLER AND THE DESERTED VILLAGE. With Introduction and Notes, by A. BARRETT, B.A., Professor of English Literature, Elphinstone College, Bombay. Gl. 8vo. 1s. 9d. ; sewed, 1s. 6d. The Traveller (separately), 1s., sewed.

*THE VICAR OF WAKEFIELD. With a Memoir of Goldsmith, by Prof. MASSON. Gl. 8vo. 1s. *(Globe Readings from Standard Authors.)*

SELECT ESSAYS. With Introduction and Notes, by Prof. C. D. YONGE. Fcap. 8vo. 2s. 6d.

GOSSE.—A HISTORY OF EIGHTEENTH CENTURY LITERATURE (1660-1780). By EDMUND GOSSE, M.A. Cr. 8vo. 7s. 6d.

*GRAY.—POEMS. With Introduction and Notes, by JOHN BRADSHAW, LL.D. Gl. 8vo. 1s. 9d. ; sewed, 1s. 6d.

*HALES.—LONGER ENGLISH POEMS. With Notes, Philological and Explanatory, and an Introduction on the Teaching of English, by J. W. HALES, M.A., Professor of English Literature at King's College, London. Ex. fcap. 8vo. 4s. 6d.

*HELPS.—ESSAYS WRITTEN IN THE INTERVALS OF BUSINESS. With Introduction and Notes, by F. J. ROWE, M.A., and W. T. WEBB, M.A. Gl. 8vo. 1s. 9d. ; sewed, 1s. 6d.

*JOHNSON.—LIVES OF THE POETS. The Six Chief Lives (Milton, Dryden, Swift, Addison, Pope, Gray), with Macaulay's "Life of Johnson." With Preface and Notes by MATTHEW ARNOLD. Cr. 8vo. 4s. 6d.

KELLNER.— HISTORICAL OUTLINES OF ENGLISH SYNTAX. By L. KELLNER, Ph.D. *[In the Press.*

*LAMB.—TALES FROM SHAKSPEARE. With Preface by the Rev. CANON AINGER, M.A., LL.D. Gl. 8vo. 2s. *(Globe Readings from Standard Authors.)*

*LITERATURE PRIMERS.—Edited by JOHN RICHARD GREEN, LL.D. 18mo. 1s. each.

ENGLISH GRAMMAR. By Rev. R. MORRIS, LL.D.

ENGLISH GRAMMAR EXERCISES. By R. MORRIS, LL.D., and H. C. BOWEN, M.A.

EXERCISES ON MORRIS'S PRIMER OF ENGLISH GRAMMAR. By J. WETHERELL, M.A.

ENGLISH COMPOSITION. By Professor NICHOL.

QUESTIONS AND EXERCISES ON ENGLISH COMPOSITION. By Prof. NICHOL and W. S. M'CORMICK.

ENGLISH LITERATURE. By STOPFORD BROOKE, M.A.

SHAKSPERE. By Professor DOWDEN.

THE CHILDREN'S TREASURY OF LYRICAL POETRY. Selected and arranged with Notes by FRANCIS TURNER PALGRAVE. In Two Parts. 1s. each.

PHILOLOGY. By J. PEILE, Litt.D.

ROMAN LITERATURE. By Prof. A. S. WILKINS, Litt.D.

GREEK LITERATURE. By Prof. JEBB, Litt.D.

HOMER. By the Rt. Hon. W. E. GLADSTONE, M.P.

A HISTORY OF ENGLISH LITERATURE IN FOUR VOLUMES. Cr. 8vo.

EARLY ENGLISH LITERATURE. By STOPFORD BROOKE, M.A. *[In preparation.*

ELIZABETHAN LITERATURE. (1560-1665.) By GEORGE SAINTSBURY. 7s. 6d.

EIGHTEENTH CENTURY LITERATURE. (1660-1780.) By EDMUND GOSSE, M.A. 7s. 6d.

THE MODERN PERIOD. By Prof. DOWDEN. *[In preparation.*

*MACMILLAN'S READING BOOKS.

PRIMER. 18mo. 48 pp. 2d.
BOOK I. for Standard I. 96 pp. 4d.
BOOK II. for Standard II. 144 pp. 5d.
BOOK III. for Standard III. 160 pp. 6d.

BOOK IV. for Standard IV. 176 pp. 8d.
BOOK V. for Standard V. 380 pp. 1s.
BOOK VI. for Standard VI. Cr. 8vo. 430 pp. 2s.

Book VI. is fitted for Higher Classes, and as an Introduction to English Literature.

`MACMILLAN'S COPY BOOKS.—1. Large Post 4to. Price 4d. each.   2. Post Oblong. Price 2d. each.

   1. INITIATORY EXERCISES AND SHORT LETTERS.
   2. WORDS CONSISTING OF SHORT LETTERS.
   3. LONG LETTERS. With Words containing Long Letters—Figures.
   4. WORDS CONTAINING LONG LETTERS.
   4a. PRACTISING AND REVISING COPY-BOOK. For Nos. 1 to 4.
   5. CAPITALS AND SHORT HALF-TEXT. Words beginning with a Capital.
   6. HALF-TEXT WORDS beginning with Capitals—Figures.
   7. SMALL-HAND AND HALF-TEXT. With Capitals and Figures.
   8. SMALL-HAND AND HALF-TEXT. With Capitals and Figures.
   8a. PRACTISING AND REVISING COPY-BOOK. For Nos. 5 to 8.
   9. SMALL-HAND SINGLE HEADLINES—Figures.
   10. SMALL-HAND SINGLE HEADLINES—Figures.
   11. SMALL-HAND DOUBLE HEADLINES—Figures.
   12. COMMERCIAL AND ARITHMETICAL EXAMPLES, &c.
   12a. PRACTISING AND REVISING COPY-BOOK. For Nos. 8 to 12.

   Nos. 3, 4, 5, 6, 7, 8, 9 may be had with Goodman's Patent Sliding Copies. Large Post 4to. Price 6d. each.

MARTIN.—*THE POET'S HOUR : Poetry selected and arranged for Children. By FRANCES MARTIN. 18mo. 2s. 6d.

*SPRING-TIME WITH THE POETS. By the same. 18mo. 3s. 6d.

`MILTON.—PARADISE LOST. Books I. and II. With Introduction and Notes, by MICHAEL MACMILLAN, B.A., Professor of Logic and Moral Philosophy, Elphinstone College, Bombay. Gl. 8vo. 1s. 9d. ; sewed, 1s. 6d. Or separately, 1s. 3d. ; sewed, 1s. each.

*L'ALLEGRO, IL PENSEROSO, LYCIDAS, ARCADES, SONNETS, &c. With Introduction and Notes, by W. BELL, M.A., Professor of Philosophy and Logic, Government College, Lahore. Gl. 8vo. 1s. 9d. ; sewed, 1s. 6d.

*COMUS. By the same. Gl. 8vo. 1s. 3d. ; sewed, 1s.

*SAMSON AGONISTES. By H. M. PERCIVAL, M.A., Professor of English Literature, Presidency College, Calcutta. Gl. 8vo. 2s. ; sewed, 1s. 9d.

`INTRODUCTION TO THE STUDY OF MILTON. By STOPFORD BROOKE, M.A. Fcap. 8vo. 1s. 6d. (*Classical Writers.*)

MORRIS.—Works by the Rev. R. MORRIS, LL.D.

*PRIMER OF ENGLISH GRAMMAR. 18mo. 1s.

*ELEMENTARY LESSONS IN HISTORICAL ENGLISH GRAMMAR, containing Accidence and Word-Formation. 18mo. 2s. 6d.

*HISTORICAL OUTLINES OF ENGLISH ACCIDENCE, comprising Chapters on the History and Development of the Language, and on Word-Formation. Ex. fcap. 8vo. 6s.

NICHOL and M'CORMICK.—A SHORT HISTORY OF ENGLISH LITERATURE. By Prof. JOHN NICHOL and Prof. W. S. M'CORMICK. [*In preparation.*

OLIPHANT.—THE OLD AND MIDDLE ENGLISH. By T. L. KINGTON OLIPHANT. New Ed., revised and enlarged, of "The Sources of Standard English." 2nd Ed. Gl. 8vo. 9s.

   THE NEW ENGLISH. By the same. 2 vols. Cr. 8vo. 21s.

*PALGRAVE.—THE CHILDREN'S TREASURY OF LYRICAL POETRY. Selected and arranged, with Notes, by FRANCIS T. PALGRAVE. 18mo. 2s. 6d. Also in Two Parts. 1s. each.

PATMORE.—THE CHILDREN'S GARLAND FROM THE BEST POETS. Selected and arranged by COVENTRY PATMORE. Gl. 8vo. 2s. (*Globe Readings from Standard Authors.*)

PLUTARCH.—Being a Selection from the Lives which illustrate Shakespeare. North's Translation. Edited, with Introductions, Notes, Index of Names, and Glossarial Index, by Prof. W. W. SKEAT, Litt.D. Cr. 8vo. 6s.

*RANSOME.—SHORT STUDIES OF SHAKESPEARE'S PLOTS. By CYRIL RANSOME, Professor of Modern History and Literature, Yorkshire College, Leeds. Cr. 8vo. 3s. 6d.

*RYLAND.—CHRONOLOGICAL OUTLINES OF ENGLISH LITERATURE. By F. RYLAND, M.A. Cr. 8vo. 6s.

SAINTSBURY.—A HISTORY OF ELIZABETHAN LITERATURE. 1560-1665. By GEORGE SAINTSBURY. Cr. 8vo. 7s. 6d.

SCOTT.—*LAY OF THE LAST MINSTREL, and THE LADY OF THE LAKE. Edited, with Introduction and Notes, by FRANCIS TURNER PALGRAVE. Gl. 8vo. 1s. (Globe Readings from Standard Authors.)

*THE LAY OF THE LAST MINSTREL. With Introduction and Notes, by G. H. STUART, M.A., and E. H. ELLIOT, B.A. Gl. 8vo. 2s.; sewed, 1s. 9d. Introduction and Canto I. 9d. sewed. Cantos I. to III. 1s. 3d.; sewed, 1s. Cantos IV. to VI. 1s. 3d.; sewed, 1s.

*MARMION, and THE LORD OF THE ISLES. By F. T. PALGRAVE. Gl. 8vo. 1s. (Globe Readings from Standard Authors.)

*MARMION. With Introduction and Notes, by MICHAEL MACMILLAN, B.A. Gl. 8vo. 3s.; sewed, 2s. 6d.

*THE LADY OF THE LAKE. By G. H. STUART, M.A. Gl. 8vo. 2s. 6d.; sewed, 2s.

*ROKEBY. With Introduction and Notes, by MICHAEL MACMILLAN, B.A. Gl. 8vo. 3s.; sewed, 2s. 6d.

SHAKESPEARE.—*A SHAKESPEARIAN GRAMMAR. By Rev. E. A. ABBOTT, D.D. Gl. 8vo. 6s.

A SHAKESPEARE MANUAL. By F. G. FLEAY, M.A. 2d Ed. Ex. fcap. 8vo. 4s. 6d.

*A PRIMER OF SHAKESPERE. By Prof. DOWDEN. 18mo. 1s.

*SHORT STUDIES OF SHAKESPEARE'S PLOTS. By CYRIL RANSOME, M.A. Cr. 8vo. 3s. 6d.

*THE TEMPEST. With Introduction and Notes, by K. DEIGHTON, late Principal of Agra College. Gl. 8vo. 1s. 9d.; sewed, 1s. 6d.

*MUCH ADO ABOUT NOTHING. By the same. Gl. 8vo. 1s. 9d.; sewed, 1s. 6d.

*A MIDSUMMER NIGHT'S DREAM. By the same. Gl. 8vo. 1s. 9d.; sewed, 1s. 6d.

*THE MERCHANT OF VENICE. By the same. Gl. 8vo. 1s. 9d.; sewed, 1s. 6d.

*AS YOU LIKE IT. By the same. Gl. 8vo. 1s. 9d.; sewed, 1s. 6d.

*TWELFTH NIGHT. By the same. Gl. 8vo. 1s. 9d.; sewed, 1s. 6d.

*THE WINTER'S TALE. By the same. Gl. 8vo. 2s.; sewed, 1s. 9d.

*KING JOHN. By the same. Gl. 8vo. 1s. 9d.; sewed, 1s. 6d.

*RICHARD II. By the same. Gl. 8vo. 1s. 9d.; sewed, 1s. 6d.

*HENRY V. By the same. Gl. 8vo. 1s. 9d.; sewed, 1s. 6d.

*RICHARD III. By C. H. TAWNEY, M.A., Principal and Professor of English Literature, Presidency College, Calcutta. Gl. 8vo. 2s. 6d.; sewed, 2s.

*CORIOLANUS. By K. DEIGHTON. Gl. 8vo. 2s. 6d.; sewed, 2s.

*JULIUS CÆSAR. By the same. Gl. 8vo. 1s. 9d.; sewed, 1s. 6d

*MACBETH. By the same. Gl. 8vo. 1s. 9d.; sewed, 1s. 6d.

*HAMLET By the same. Gl. 8vo. 2s. 6d.; sewed, 2s.

*KING LEAR. By the same. Gl. 8vo. 1s. 9d.; sewed, 1s. 6d.

*OTHELLO. By the same. Gl. 8vo. 2s.; sewed, 1s. 9d.

*ANTONY AND CLEOPATRA. By the same. Gl. 8vo. 2s. 6d.; sewed, 2s.

*CYMBELINE. By the same. Gl. 8vo. 2s. 6d.; sewed, 2s.

*SONNENSCHEIN and MEIKLEJOHN.—THE ENGLISH METHOD OF TEACHING TO READ. By A. SONNENSCHEIN and J. M. D. MEIKLEJOHN, M.A. Fcap. 8vo.

THE NURSERY BOOK, containing all the Two-Letter Words in the Language. 1d. (Also in Large Type on Sheets for School Walls. 5s.)

THE FIRST COURSE, consisting of Short Vowels with Single Consonants. 7d.

THE SECOND COURSE, with Combinations and Bridges, consisting of Short Vowels with Double Consonants. 7d.

THE THIRD AND FOURTH COURSES, consisting of Long Vowels, and all the Double Vowels in the Language. 7d.

*SOUTHEY.—LIFE OF NELSON. With Introduction and Notes, by MICHAEL MACMILLAN, B.A. Gl. 8vo. 3s. ; sewed, 2s. 6d.

SPENSER.—FAIRY QUEEN. Book I. With Introduction and Notes, by H. M. PERCIVAL, M.A. [In the Press.

TAYLOR.—WORDS AND PLACES; or, Etymological Illustrations of History, Ethnology, and Geography. By Rev. ISAAC TAYLOR, Litt.D. With Maps. Gl. 8vo. 6s.

TENNYSON.—THE COLLECTED WORKS OF LORD TENNYSON. An Edition for Schools. In Four Parts. Cr. 8vo. 2s. 6d. each.

TENNYSON FOR THE YOUNG. Edited, with Notes for the Use of Schools, by the Rev. ALFRED AINGER, LL.D., Canon of Bristol. 18mo. 1s. net. [In the Press.

*SELECTIONS FROM TENNYSON. With Introduction and Notes, by F. J. ROWE, M.A., and W. T. WEBB, M.A. Gl. 8vo. 3s. 6d.

This selection contains :—Recollections of the Arabian Nights, The Lady of Shalott, Œnone, The Lotos Eaters, Ulysses, Tithonus, Morte d'Arthur, Sir Galahad, Dora, Ode on the Death of the Duke of Wellington, and The Revenge.

*ENOCH ARDEN. By W. T. WEBB, M.A. Gl. 8vo. 2s.

AYLMER'S FIELD. By W. T. WEBB, M.A. [In the Press.

THE PRINCESS; A MEDLEY. By P. M. WALLACE, B.A. [In the Press.

*THE COMING OF ARTHUR, AND THE PASSING OF ARTHUR. By F. J. ROWE, M.A. Gl. 8vo. 2s.

THRING.—THE ELEMENTS OF GRAMMAR TAUGHT IN ENGLISH. By EDWARD THRING, M.A. With Questions. 4th Ed. 18mo. 2s.

*VAUGHAN.—WORDS FROM THE POETS. By C. M. VAUGHAN. 18mo. 1s.

WARD.—THE ENGLISH POETS. Selections, with Critical Introductions by various Writers and a General Introduction by MATTHEW ARNOLD. Edited by T. H. WARD, M.A. 4 Vols. Vol. I. CHAUCER TO DONNE.—Vol. II. BEN JONSON TO DRYDEN.—Vol. III. ADDISON TO BLAKE.—Vol. IV. WORDSWORTH TO ROSSETTI. 2d Ed. Cr. 8vo. 7s. 6d. each.

*WETHERELL.—EXERCISES ON MORRIS'S PRIMER OF ENGLISH GRAM- MAR. By JOHN WETHERELL, M.A., Headmaster of Towcester Grammar School. 18mo. 1s.

WOODS.—*A FIRST POETRY BOOK. By M. A. WOODS, Head Mistress of the Clifton High School for Girls. Fcap. 8vo. 2s. 6d.

*A SECOND POETRY BOOK. By the same. In Two Parts. 2s. 6d. each.

*A THIRD POETRY BOOK. By the same. 4s. 6d.

HYMNS FOR SCHOOL WORSHIP. By the same. 18mo. 1s. 6d.

WORDSWORTH.—SELECTIONS. With Introduction and Notes, by F. J. ROWE, M.A., and W. T. WEBB, M.A. Gl. 8vo. [In preparation.

YONGE.—*A BOOK OF GOLDEN DEEDS. By CHARLOTTE M. YONGE. Gl. 8vo. 2s.

*THE ABRIDGED BOOK OF GOLDEN DEEDS. 18mo. 1s.

FRENCH.

BEAUMARCHAIS.—LE BARBIER DE SEVILLE. With Introduction and Notes. By L. P. BLOUET. Fcap. 8vo. 3s. 6d.

*BOWEN.—FIRST LESSONS IN FRENCH. By H. COURTHOPE BOWEN, M.A. Ex. fcap. 8vo. 1s.

BREYMANN.—Works by HERMANN BREYMANN, Ph.D., Professor of Philology in the University of Munich.

FIRST FRENCH EXERCISE BOOK. Ex. fcap. 8vo. 4s. 6d.

SECOND FRENCH EXERCISE BOOK. Ex. fcap. 8vo. 2s. 6d.

FASNACHT.—Works by G. E. FASNACHT, late Assistant Master at Westminster.

THE ORGANIC METHOD OF STUDYING LANGUAGES. Ex. fcap. 8vo. I. French. 3s. 6d.

A SYNTHETIC FRENCH GRAMMAR FOR SCHOOLS. Cr. 8vo. 3s. 6d.

GRAMMAR AND GLOSSARY OF THE FRENCH LANGUAGE OF THE SEVENTEENTH CENTURY. Cr. 8vo. [In preparation.

MACMILLAN'S PRIMARY SERIES OF FRENCH READING BOOKS.—Edited by G. E. Fasnacht. With Illustrations, Notes, Vocabularies, and Exercises. Gl. 8vo.

*FRENCH READINGS FOR CHILDREN. By G. E. Fasnacht. 1s. 6d.

*CORNAZ—NOS ENFANTS ET LEURS AMIS. By Edith Harvey. 1s. 6d.

*DE MAISTRE—LA JEUNE SIBÉRIENNE ET LE LÉPREUX DE LA CITÉ D'AOSTE. By Stephane Barlet, B.Sc. etc. 1s. 6d.

*FLORIAN—FABLES. By Rev. Charles Yeld, M.A., Headmaster of University School, Nottingham. 1s. 6d.

*LA FONTAINE—A SELECTION OF FABLES. By L. M. Moriarty, B.A., Assistant Master at Harrow. 2s. 6d.

*MOLESWORTH—FRENCH LIFE IN LETTERS. By Mrs. Molesworth. 1s. 6d.

*PERRAULT—CONTES DE FÉES. By G. E. Fasnacht. 1s. 6d.

MACMILLAN'S PROGRESSIVE FRENCH COURSE.—By G. E. Fasnacht. Ex. fcap. 8vo.

*First Year, containing Easy Lessons on the Regular Accidence. 1s.

*Second Year, containing an Elementary Grammar with copious Exercises, Notes, and Vocabularies. 2s.

*Third Year, containing a Systematic Syntax, and Lessons in Composition. 2s. 6d.

THE TEACHER'S COMPANION TO MACMILLAN'S PROGRESSIVE FRENCH COURSE. With Copious Notes, Hints for Different Renderings, Synonyms, Philological Remarks, etc. By G. E. Fasnacht. Ex. fcap. 8vo. Each Year 4s. 6d.

*MACMILLAN'S FRENCH COMPOSITION.—By G. E. Fasnacht. Ex. fcap. 8vo. Part I. Elementary. 2s. 6d. Part II. Advanced. [In the Press.

THE TEACHER'S COMPANION TO MACMILLAN'S COURSE OF FRENCH COMPOSITION By G. E. Fasnacht. Part I. Ex. fcap. 8vo. 4s. 6d.

MACMILLAN'S PROGRESSIVE FRENCH READERS. By G. E. Fasnacht. Ex. fcap. 8vo.

*First Year, containing Tales, Historical Extracts, Letters, Dialogues, Ballads, Nursery Songs, etc., with Two Vocabularies: (1) in the order of subjects; (2) in alphabetical order. With Imitative Exercises. 2s. 6d.

*Second Year, containing Fiction in Prose and Verse, Historical and Descriptive Extracts, Essays, Letters, Dialogues, etc. With Imitative Exercises. 2s. 6d.

MACMILLAN'S FOREIGN SCHOOL CLASSICS. Edited by G. E. Fasnacht. 18mo.

*CORNEILLE—LE CID. By G. E. Fasnacht. 1s.

*DUMAS—LES DEMOISELLES DE ST. CYR. By Victor Ogen, Lecturer at University College, Liverpool. 1s. 6d.

LA FONTAINE'S FABLES. Books I.-VI. By L. M. Moriarty, B.A., Assistant Master at Harrow. [In preparation.

*MOLIÈRE—L'AVARE. By the same. 1s.

*MOLIÈRE—LE BOURGEOIS GENTILHOMME. By the same. 1s. 6d.

*MOLIÈRE—LES FEMMES SAVANTES. By G. E. Fasnacht. 1s.

*MOLIÈRE—LE MISANTHROPE. By the same. 1s.

*MOLIÈRE—LE MÉDECIN MALGRÉ LUI. By the same. 1s.

*MOLIÈRE—LES PRÉCIEUSES RIDICULES. By the same. 1s.

*RACINE—BRITANNICUS. By E. Pellissier, M.A. 2s.

*FRENCH READINGS FROM ROMAN HISTORY Selected from various Authors, by C. Colbeck, M.A., Assistant Master at Harrow. 4s. 6d.

*SAND, GEORGE—LA MARE AU DIABLE. By W. E. Russell, M.A., Assistant Master at Haileybury. 1s.

*SANDEAU, JULES—MADEMOISELLE DE LA SEIGLIÈRE.   By H. C. STEEL, Assistant Master at Winchester. 1s. 6d.

*VOLTAIRE—CHARLES XII. By G. E. FASNACHT. 3s. 6d.

*MASSON.—A COMPENDIOUS DICTIONARY OF THE FRENCH LANGUAGE. Adapted from the Dictionaries of Professor A. ELWALL. By GUSTAVE MASSON. Cr. 8vo. 3s. 6d.

MOLIÈRE.—LE MALADE IMAGINAIRE. With Introduction and **Notes, by F.** TARVER, M.A., Assistant Master at Eton. Fcap. 8vo. 2s. 6d.

*PELLISSIER.—FRENCH ROOTS AND **THEIR FAMILIES. A** Synthetic Vocabulary, based upon Derivations. **By E.** PELLISSIER, M.A., Assistant Master at Clifton College. Gl. 8vo. **6s.**

GERMAN.

BEHAGEL.—THE GERMAN LANGUAGE. **By Dr.** OTTO BEHAGEL. Translated by EMIL TRECHMANN, B.A., Ph.D., **Lecturer in** Modern Literature in the University of Sydney, N.S.W. Gl. 8vo.   [*Nearly Ready.*

HUSS.—A SYSTEM OF ORAL INSTRUCTION IN GERMAN, by means **of** Progressive Illustrations and Applications of the leading Rules of Grammar. By H. C. O. HUSS, Ph.D. Cr. 8vo. 5s.

MACMILLAN'S PRIMARY SERIES OF GERMAN READING BOOKS. Edited by G. E. FASNACHT. With Notes, Vocabularies, and Exercises. Gl. 8vo.

*GRIMM—KINDER UND HAUSMÄRCHEN. By G. E. FASNACHT. 2s. 6d.

*HAUFF—DIE KARAVANE. By HERMAN HAGER, Ph.D., Lecturer in the Owens College, Manchester. 3s.

*SCHMID, CHR. VON—H. VON EICHENFELS. **By G. E.** FASNACHT. 2s. 6d.

MACMILLAN'S PROGRESSIVE GERMAN **COURSE. By G. E.** FASNACHT. Ex. fcap. 8vo.

*FIRST YEAR. Easy lessons and **Rules on** the Regular Accidence. 1s. 6d.

*SECOND YEAR. Conversational Lessons in Systematic Accidence and Elementary **Syntax.** With Philological Illustrations and Etymological Vocabulary 3s. 6d.

THIRD YEAR.   [*In the Press.*

TEACHER'S COMPANION TO MACMILLAN'S PROGRESSIVE GERMAN COURSE. With copious Notes, Hints for Different Renderings, Synonyms, Philological Remarks, etc. By G. **E.** FASNACHT. Ex. fcap. 8vo. FIRST YEAR. 4s. 6d. SECOND YEAR. 4s. 6d.

MACMILLAN'S GERMAN COMPOSITION. By G. E. FASNACHT. Ex. fcap. 8vo.

*I. FIRST COURSE. Parallel German-English Extracts and Parallel English-German Syntax. 2s. 6d.

TEACHER'S COMPANION TO MACMILLAN'S GERMAN **COMPOSITION.** By G. E. FASNACHT. FIRST COURSE. Gl. 8vo. 4s. 6d.

MACMILLAN'S PROGRESSIVE GERMAN READERS. By G. E. FASNACHT. Ex. fcap. 8vo.

*FIRST YEAR, **containing an Introduction to the German order of Words, with** Copious Examples, **extracts from German Authors in Prose and Poetry ;** Notes, and Vocabularies. 2s. 6d.

MACMILLAN'S FOREIGN SCHOOL CLASSICS.—Edited by G. E. FASNACHT. 18mo.

FREYTAG (G.)—DOKTOR LUTHER. By F. STORR, M.A., Headmaster of the Modern Side, Merchant Taylors' School.   [*In preparation.*

*GOETHE—GÖTZ VON BERLICHINGEN. **By H. A.** BULL, M.A., Assistant Master at Wellington. 2s.

*GOETHE—FAUST. PART I., followed by an Appendix on PART **II.** By JANE LEE, Lecturer in German Literature at Newnham College, Cambridge. 4s. 6d.

*HEINE—SELECTIONS FROM THE REISEBILDER AND OTHER PROSE WORKS. By C. COLBECK, M.A., Assistant Master at Harrow. 2s. 6d.

LESSING—MINNA VON BARNHELM. By JAMES SIME, M.A. [*In preparation.*

*SCHILLER—SELECTIONS FROM **SCHILLER'S** LYRICAL **POEMS.** With a Memoir of Schiller. By E. J. TURNER, B.A., and E. D. A. MORSHEAD, M.A., Assistant Masters at Winchester. 2s. 6d.

*SCHILLER—DIE JUNGFRAU VON ORLEANS. By JOSEPH GOSTWICK. 2s. 6d.

*SCHILLER—MARIA STUART. By C. SHELDON, D.Litt., of the Royal Academical Institution, Belfast. 2s. 6d.

*SCHILLER—WILHELM TELL. By **G. E.** FASNACHT. 2s. 6d.

*SCHILLER—WALLENSTEIN. Part I. DAS LAGER. By H. B. **COTTERILL,** M.A. 2s.

*UHLAND—SELECT **BALLADS.** Adapted as a First Easy Reading Book for **Beginners. With** Vocabulary. By G. E. FASNACHT. 1s.

***PYLODET.**—NEW GUIDE TO GERMAN CONVERSATION : **containing an Alphabetical List of nearly 800** Familiar Words ; followed by Exercises, **Vocabulary of Words** in frequent **use,** Familiar Phrases and Dialogues, a Sketch of German Literature, Idiomatic Expressions, etc. By L. PYLODET. 18mo. **2s.** 6d.

SMITH.—COMMERCIAL GERMAN. By F. C. SMITH, M.A. [*In the Press.*

WHITNEY.—A COMPENDIOUS GERMAN GRAMMAR. By W. D. WHITNEY, Professor of Sanskrit and Instructor in Modern Languages in Yale College. Cr. 8vo. 4s. 6d.

A GERMAN READER IN PROSE **AND VERSE.** By the same. With Notes and Vocabulary. Cr. 8vo. 5s.

*WHITNEY and EDGREN.—A COMPENDIOUS GERMAN AND ENGLISH DICTIONARY, with Notation of Correspondences and Brief Etymologies. By Prof. W. D. WHITNEY, assisted by A. H. EDGREN. Cr. 8vo. 7s. 6d.

THE GERMAN-ENGLISH PART, separately, **5s.**

MODERN GREEK.

VINCENT and DICKSON.—HANDBOOK TO MODERN GREEK. By Sir EDGAR VINCENT, K.C.M.G., and T. G. DICKSON, M.A. With Appendix on the relation of Modern and Classical Greek by Prof. JEBB. Cr. 8vo. 6s.

ITALIAN.

DANTE.—THE INFERNO **OF DANTE. With** Translation and Notes, by A. J. BUTLER, M.A. Cr. 8vo. [*In the Press.*

THE PURGATORIO OF DANTE. With Translations and Notes, by the same. Cr. 8vo. 12s. 6d.

THE PARADISO OF DANTE. **With Translation** and Notes, **by** the same. 2d. Ed. Cr. 8vo. 12s. 6d.

READINGS ON THE PURGATORIO OF DANTE. Chiefly based on the Commentary of Benvenuto Da Imola. By the Hon. W. WARREN VERNON, M.A. With an Introduction by the Very Rev. the DEAN **OF** ST. PAUL'S. 2 vols. Cr. 8vo. 24s.

SPANISH.

CALDERON.—FOUR **PLAYS** OF CALDERON. **With** Introduction and Notes. By NORMAN MACCOLL, M.A. **Cr.** 8vo. 14s.

The four plays here given are *El Principe Constante,* **La** *Vida es Sueno, El Alcalde de Zalamea,* and *El Escondido* **y** *La Tapada.*

MATHEMATICS.

Arithmetic, Book-keeping, Algebra, **Euclid and Pure Geometry, Geometrical** Drawing, Mensuration, Trigonometry, **Analytical** Geometry (Plane and Solid), Problems and Questions **in** Mathematics, Higher Pure Mathematics, Mechanics (Statics, Dynamics, Hydrostatics, Hydrodynamics: see also Physics), Physics (Sound, Light, Heat, Electricity, Elasticity, Attractions, &c.), Astronomy, Historical.

ARITHMETIC.

*ALDIS.—THE GREAT GIANT ARITHMOS. A most Elementary Arithmetic for Children. By MARY STEADMAN ALDIS. Illustrated. Gl. 8vo. 2s. 6d.

ARMY PRELIMINARY EXAMINATION, SPECIMENS OF PAPERS SET AT THE, 1882-89.—With Answers to the Mathematical Questions. Subjects: Arithmetic, Algebra, Euclid, Geometrical Drawing, Geography, French, English Dictation. Cr. 8vo. 3s. 6d.

*BRADSHAW.—A COURSE OF EASY ARITHMETICAL EXAMPLES FOR BEGINNERS. By J. G. BRADSHAW, B.A., Assistant Master at Clifton College. Gl. 8vo. 2s. With Answers, 2s. 6d.

*BROOKSMITH.—ARITHMETIC IN THEORY AND **PRACTICE.** By J. BROOKSMITH, M.A. Cr. 8vo. 4s. 6d. KEY. Crown 8vo. 10s. 6d.

*BROOKSMITH.—ARITHMETIC FOR BEGINNERS. By J. and E. J. BROOKSMITH. Gl. 8vo. 1s. 6d.

CANDLER.—HELP TO ARITHMETIC. Designed for the use of Schools. By H. CANDLER, Mathematical Master of Uppingham School. 2d Ed. Ex. fcap. 8vo. 2s. 6d.

*DALTON.—RULES AND EXAMPLES IN **ARITHMETIC.** By the Rev. T. DALTON, M.A., Senior Mathematical Master at **Eton. New Ed., with Answers.** 18mo. 2s. 6d.

*GOYEN.—HIGHER ARITHMETIC AND ELEMENTARY MENSURATION. By P. GOYEN, Inspector of Schools, Dunedin, New Zealand. Cr. 8vo. 5s.

*HALL and KNIGHT.—ARITHMETICAL EXERCISES AND EXAMINATION PAPERS. With an Appendix containing Questions in LOGARITHMS and MENSURATION. By H. S. HALL, M.A., Master of the Military and Engineering Side, Clifton College, and S. R. KNIGHT, B.A. Gl. 8vo. 2s. 6d.

LOCK.—Works by Rev. J. B. LOCK, M.A., Senior Fellow and Bursar of Gonville and Caius College, Cambridge.

*ARITHMETIC FOR SCHOOLS. With Answers and 1000 additional Examples for Exercise. 3d Ed., revised. Gl. 8vo. 4s. 6d. Or, Part I. 2s. Part II. 3s. KEY. Cr. 8vo. 10s. 6d.

*ARITHMETIC FOR BEGINNERS. A School Class-Book of Commercial Arithmetic. Gl. 8vo. 2s. 6d. KEY. Cr. 8vo. 8s. 6d.

*A SHILLING BOOK OF ARITHMETIC, FOR ELEMENTARY SCHOOLS. 18mo. 1s. With Answers. 1s. 6d.

*PEDLEY.—EXERCISES IN ARITHMETIC for the Use of Schools. Containing more than 7000 original Examples. By SAMUEL PEDLEY. Cr. 8vo. 5s. Also in Two Parts, 2s. 6d. each.

SMITH.—Works by Rev. BARNARD SMITH, M.A., late Fellow and Senior Bursar of St. Peter's College, Cambridge.

ARITHMETIC AND ALGEBRA, in their Principles and Application; with numerous systematically arranged Examples taken from the Cambridge Examination Papers, with especial reference to the Ordinary Examination for the B.A. Degree. New Ed., carefully revised. Cr. 8vo. 10s. 6d.

*ARITHMETIC FOR SCHOOLS. Cr. 8vo. 4s. 6d. KEY. Cr. 8vo. 8s. 6d. New Edition. Revised by Prof W. H. HUDSON. [In preparation.

EXERCISES IN ARITHMETIC. Cr. 8vo. **2s.** With Answers, 2s. 6d. Answers separately, 6d.

SCHOOL CLASS-BOOK OF ARITHMETIC. 18mo. **3s.** Or separately, in Three Parts, 1s. each. KEYS. Parts I., II., and III., 2s. 6d. each.

SHILLING BOOK OF ARITHMETIC. 18mo. Or separately, Part I., 2d.; Part II., 3d.; Part III., 7d. Answers, 6d. KEY. 18mo. 4s. 6d.

*THE SAME, with Answers. 18mo, cloth. 1s. **6d.**

EXAMINATION PAPERS IN ARITHMETIC. 18mo. **1s.** 6d. **The Same,** with Answers. 18mo. 2s. Answers, 6d. KEY. 18mo. 4s. 6d.

THE METRIC SYSTEM OF ARITHMETIC, ITS PRINCIPLES AND APPLI-CATIONS, with Numerous Examples. 18mo. 3d.

A CHART OF THE METRIC SYSTEM, on a Sheet, size 42 in. by 34 in. on Roller. 3s. 6d. Also a Small Chart on a Card. **Price 1d.**

EASY LESSONS IN ARITHMETIC, combining Exercises in Reading, Writing, Spelling, and Dictation. Part I. Cr. 8vo. 9d.

EXAMINATION CARDS IN ARITHMETIC. With Answers and Hints. Standards I. and II., in box, 1s. Standards III., IV., and V., in boxes, 1s. each. Standard VI. in Two Parts, in boxes, 1s. each.

A and B papers, of nearly the same difficulty, are given so as to prevent copying, and the colours of the A and B papers differ in each Standard, and from those of every other Standard, so that a master or mistress can **see** at a glance whether the children have the proper papers.

BOOK-KEEPING.

*THORNTON.—FIRST LESSONS IN BOOK-KEEPING. By J. THORNTON. Cr. 8vo. 2s. 6d. KEY. Oblong 4to. 10s. 6d.

*PRIMER OF BOOK-KEEPING. 18mo. 1s. KEY. Demy 8vo. 2s. 6d.

ALGEBRA.

*DALTON.—RULES AND EXAMPLES IN ALGEBRA. By Rev. T. DALTON, Senior Mathematical Master at Eton. Part I. 18mo. 2s. KEY. Cr. 8vo. 7s. 6d. Part II. 18mo. **2s.** 6d.

HALL and KNIGHT.—Works by H. S. HALL, M.A., Master of the Military and Engineering Side, Clifton College, and S. R. KNIGHT, B.A.

*ELEMENTARY ALGEBRA FOR SCHOOLS. 6th Ed., revised and corrected. Gl. 8vo, bound in maroon coloured cloth, 3s. 6d.; with Answers, bound in green coloured cloth, 4s. 6d. KEY. 8s. 6d.

*ALGEBRAICAL EXERCISES AND EXAMINATION PAPERS. To accompany ELEMENTARY ALGEBRA. 2d Ed., revised. Gl. 8vo. 2s. 6d.

*HIGHER ALGEBRA. 3d Ed. Cr. 8vo. 7s. 6d. KEY. Cr. 8vo. 10s. 6d.

*JONES and CHEYNE.—ALGEBRAICAL EXERCISES. Progressively Arranged. By Rev. C. A. JONES and C. H. CHEYNE, M.A., late Mathematical Masters at Westminster School. 18mo. 2s. 6d.

KEY. By Rev. W. FAILES, M.A., Mathematical Master at Westminster School. Cr. 8vo. 7s. 6d.

SMITH.—ARITHMETIC AND ALGEBRA, in their Principles and Application; with numerous systematically arranged Examples taken from the Cambridge Examination Papers, with especial reference to the Ordinary Examination for the B.A. Degree. By Rev. BARNARD SMITH, M.A. New Edition, carefully revised. Cr. 8vo. 10s. 6d.

SMITH.—Works by CHARLES SMITH, M.A., Master of Sidney Sussex College, Cambridge.

*ELEMENTARY ALGEBRA. 2d Ed., revised. Gl. 8vo. 4s. 6d. KEY. By A. G. CRACKNELL, B.A. Cr. 8vo. 10. 6d.

*A TREATISE ON ALGEBRA. 2d Ed. Cr. 8vo. 7s. 6d. KEY. Cr. 8vo. 10s. 6d.

TODHUNTER.—Works by ISAAC TODHUNTER, F.R.S.

*ALGEBRA FOR BEGINNERS. 18mo. 2s. 6d. KEY. Cr. 8vo. 6s. 6d.

ALGEBRA FOR COLLEGES AND SCHOOLS. By Isaac Todhunter, F.R.S. Cr. 8vo. 7s. 6d. KEY. Cr. 8vo. 10s. 6d.

EUCLID AND PURE GEOMETRY.

COCKSHOTT and WALTERS.—A TREATISE ON GEOMETRICAL CONICS. In accordance with the Syllabus of the Association for the Improvement of Geometrical Teaching. By A. Cockshott, M.A., Assistant Master at Eton, and Rev. F. B. Walters, M.A., Principal of King William's College, Isle of Man. Cr. 8vo. 5s.

CONSTABLE.—GEOMETRICAL EXERCISES FOR BEGINNERS. By Samuel Constable. Cr. 8vo. 3s. 6d.

CUTHBERTSON.—EUCLIDIAN GEOMETRY. By Francis Cuthbertson, M.A., LL.D. Ex. fcap. 8vo. 4s. 6d.

DAY.—PROPERTIES OF CONIC SECTIONS PROVED GEOMETRICALLY. By Rev. H. G. Day, M.A. Part I. The Ellipse, with an ample collection of Problems. Cr. 8vo. 3s. 6d.

DEAKIN.—RIDER PAPERS ON EUCLID. BOOKS I. AND II. By Rupert Deakin, M.A. 18mo. 1s.

DODGSON.—Works by Charles L. Dodgson, M.A., Student and late Mathematical Lecturer, Christ Church, Oxford.
  EUCLID, BOOKS I. AND II. 6th Ed., with words substituted for the Algebraical Symbols used in the 1st Ed. Cr. 8vo. 2s.
  EUCLID AND HIS MODERN RIVALS. 2d Ed. Cr. 8vo. 6s.
  CURIOSA MATHEMATICA. Part I. A New Theory of Parallels. 3d Ed. Cr. 8vo. 2s.

DREW.—GEOMETRICAL TREATISE ON CONIC SECTIONS. By W. H. Drew, M.A. New Ed., enlarged. Cr. 8vo. 5s.

DUPUIS.—ELEMENTARY SYNTHETIC GEOMETRY OF THE POINT, LINE AND CIRCLE IN THE PLANE. By N F. Dupuis, M.A., Professor of Pure Mathematics in the University of Queen's College, Kingston, Canada. Gl. 8vo. 4s. 6d.

HALL and STEVENS.—A TEXT-BOOK OF EUCLID'S ELEMENTS. Including Alternative Proofs, together with additional Theorems and Exercises, classified and arranged. By H. S. Hall, M.A., and F. H. Stevens, M.A., Masters of the Military and Engineering Side, Clifton College. Gl. 8vo. Book I., 1s.; Books I. and II., 1s. 6d.; Books I.-IV., 3s.; Books III.-IV., 2s.; Books III.-VI., 3s.; Books V.-VI. and XI., 2s. 6d.; Books I.-VI. and XI., 4s. 6d.; Book XI., 1s. [KEY. In preparation.

HALSTED.—THE ELEMENTS OF GEOMETRY By G. B. Halsted, Professor of Pure and Applied Mathematics in the University of Texas. 8vo. 12s. 6d.

HAYWARD.—THE ELEMENTS OF SOLID GEOMETRY. By R. B. Hayward, M.A., F.R.S. Gl. 8vo. 3s.

LOCK.—EUCLID FOR BEGINNERS. Being an Introduction to existing Text-Books. By Rev. J. B. Lock, M.A. [In the Press.

MILNE and DAVIS.—GEOMETRICAL CONICS. Part I. The Parabola. By Rev. J. J. Milne, M.A., and R. F. Davis, M.A. Cr. 8vo. 2s.

RICHARDSON.—THE PROGRESSIVE EUCLID. Books I. and II. With Notes, Exercises, and Deductions. Edited by A. T. Richardson, M.A., Senior Mathematical Master at the Isle of Wight College. Gl. 8vo. 2s. 6d.

SYLLABUS OF PLANE GEOMETRY (corresponding to Euclid, Books I.-VI.)—Prepared by the Association for the Improvement of Geometrical Teaching. Cr. 8vo. Sewed, 1s.

SYLLABUS OF MODERN PLANE GEOMETRY.—Prepared by the Association for the Improvement of Geometrical Teaching. Cr. 8vo. Sewed. 1s.

*TODHUNTER.—THE ELEMENTS OF EUCLID. By I. Todhunter, F.R.S. 18mo. 3s. 6d. *Books I. and II. 1s. KEY. Cr. 8vo. 6s. 6d.

WILSON.—Works by Ven. Archdeacon Wilson, M.A., formerly Headmaster of Clifton College.
  ELEMENTARY GEOMETRY. BOOKS I.-V. Containing the Subjects of Euclid's first Six Books. Following the Syllabus of the Geometrical Association. Ex. fcap. 8vo. 4s. 6d.

WILSON.—Works by Ven. Archdeacon WILSON—*continued.*
  SOLID GEOMETRY AND CONIC SECTIONS. With Appendices on Trans-
  versals and Harmonic Division. Ex. fcap. 8vo. 3s. 6d.

GEOMETRICAL DRAWING.

EAGLES.—CONSTRUCTIVE GEOMETRY OF PLANE CURVES. By T. H.
  EAGLES, M.A., Instructor in Geometrical Drawing and Lecturer in Architecture
  at the Royal Indian Engineering College, Cooper's Hill. Cr. 8vo. 12s.
EDGAR and PRITCHARD. — NOTE-BOOK ON PRACTICAL SOLID OR
  DESCRIPTIVE GEOMETRY. Containing Problems with help for Solutions.
  By J. H. EDGAR and G. S. PRITCHARD. 4th Ed., revised by A. MEEZE. Gl.
  8vo. 4s. 6d.
KITCHENER.—A GEOMETRICAL NOTE-BOOK. Containing Easy Problems in
  Geometrical Drawing preparatory to the Study of Geometry. For the Use of
  Schools. By F. E. KITCHENER, M.A., Headmaster of the Newcastle-under-
  Lyme High School. 4to. 2s.
MILLAR.—ELEMENTS OF DESCRIPTIVE GEOMETRY. By J. B. MILLAR,
  Civil Engineer, Lecturer on Engineering in the Victoria University, Manchester.
  2d Ed. Cr. 8vo. 6s.
PLANT.—PRACTICAL PLANE AND DESCRIPTIVE GEOMETRY. By E. C.
  PLANT. Globe 8vo.   [*In preparation.*

MENSURATION.

STEVENS.—ELEMENTARY MENSURATION. With Exercises on the Mensura-
  tion of Plane and Solid Figures. By F. H. STEVENS, M.A. Gl. 8vo.
                                                             [*In preparation.*
TEBAY.—ELEMENTARY MENSURATION FOR SCHOOLS. By S. TEBAY.
  Ex. fcap. 8vo. 3s. 6d.
TODHUNTER.—MENSURATION FOR BEGINNERS. By ISAAC TODHUNTER,
  F.R.S. 18mo. 2s. 6d. KEY. By Rev. FR. L. MCCARTHY. Cr. 8vo. 7s. 6d.

TRIGONOMETRY.

BEASLEY.—AN ELEMENTARY TREATISE ON PLANE TRIGONOMETRY.
  With Examples. By R. D. BEASLEY, M.A. 9th Ed., revised and enlarged.
  Cr. 8vo. 3s. 6d.
BOTTOMLEY.—FOUR-FIGURE MATHEMATICAL TABLES. Comprising Log-
  arithmic and Trigonometrical Tables, and Tables of Squares, Square Roots,
  and Reciprocals. By J. T. BOTTOMLEY, M.A., Lecturer in Natural Philosophy
  in the University of Glasgow. 8vo. 2s. 6d.
HAYWARD.—THE ALGEBRA OF CO-PLANAR VECTORS AND TRIGONO-
  METRY. By R. B. HAYWARD, M.A., F.R.S., Assistant Master at Harrow
                                                             [*In preparation.*
JOHNSON.—A TREATISE ON TRIGONOMETRY. By W. E. JOHNSON, M.A.,
  late Scholar and Assistant Mathematical Lecturer at King's College, Cam-
  bridge. Cr. 8vo. 8s. 6d.
LEVETT and DAVISON.—ELEMENTS OF TRIGONOMETRY. By RAWDON
  LEVETT and A. F. DAVISON, Assistant Masters at King Edward's School,
  Birmingham.   [*In the Press.*
LOCK.—Works by Rev. J. B. LOCK, M.A., Senior Fellow and Bursar of Gonville
  and Caius College, Cambridge.
  THE TRIGONOMETRY OF ONE ANGLE. Gl. 8vo. 2s. 6d.
  TRIGONOMETRY FOR BEGINNERS, as far as the Solution of Triangles. 3d
  Ed. Gl. 8vo. 2s. 6d. KEY. Cr. 8vo. 6s. 6d.
  ELEMENTARY TRIGONOMETRY 6th Ed. (in this edition the chapter on
  logarithms has been carefully revised). Gl. 8vo. 4s. 6d. KEY Cr. 8vo. 8s. 6d.

HIGHER TRIGONOMETRY. 5th Ed. **Gl.** 8vo. 4s. 6d. **Both Parts complete** in One Volume. Gl. 8vo. 7s. 6d.

M'CLELLAND and PRESTON. — A TREATISE ON SPHERICAL TRIGONO- METRY. With applications to Spherical Geometry and numerous Examples. By W. J. M'CLELLAND, M.A., Principal of the Incorporated Society's School, Santry, Dublin, and T. PRESTON, M.A. Cr. 8vo. 8s. 6d., or : Part I. To the End of Solution of Triangles, **4s.** 6d. Part II., 5s.

MATTHEWS.—MANUAL OF LOGARITHMS. **By G.** F. MATTHEWS, B.A. 8vo. 5s. net.

PALMER.—**TEXT-BOOK OF** PRACTICAL **LOGARITHMS** AND TRIGONO- METRY. **By J.** H. **PALMER,** Headmaster, R.N., H.M.S. *Cambridge,* Devon- port. Gl. 8vo. 4s. 6d.

SNOWBALL.—THE ELEMENTS **OF PLANE AND** SPHERICAL TRIGONO- METRY. **By J.** C. SNOWBALL. **14th Ed.** Cr. 8vo. **7s.** 6d.

TODHUNTER.—Works by ISAAC TODHUNTER, F.R.S.

*TRIGONOMETRY FOR BEGINNERS. 18mo. 2s. 6d. KEY. Cr. 8vo. 8s. 6d.

PLANE TRIGONOMETRY. Cr. 8vo. **5s.** A New Edition, revised **by R.** W. HOGG, M.A. Cr. 8vo. 5s. KEY. Cr. 8vo. 10s. 6d.

A TREATISE ON SPHERICAL TRIGONOMETRY. Cr. 8vo. **4s. 6d.**

WOLSTENHOLME.—EXAMPLES FOR PRACTICE IN THE USE OF SEVEN- FIGURE LOGARITHMS. By JOSEPH WOLSTENHOLME, D.Sc., late Professor of Mathematics in the Royal Indian Engineering Coll., Cooper's Hill. 8vo. 5s.

ANALYTICAL GEOMETRY (Plane and Solid).

DYER.—EXERCISES IN ANALYTICAL GEOMETRY. By **J.** M. DYER, M.A., Assistant Master at Eton. Illustrated. **Cr. 8vo.** 4s. 6d.

FERRERS.—AN ELEMENTARY **TREATISE ON** TRILINEAR CO-ORDIN- ATES, the Method of Reciprocal **Polars, and the** Theory of Projectors. By the Rev. N. M. FERRERS, D.D., **F.R.S.,** Master of Gonville and Caius College, Cambridge. 4th Ed., revised. **Cr. 8vo.** 6s. 6d.

FROST.—Works by PERCIVAL FROST, D.Sc., **F.R.S., Fellow and** Mathematical Lecturer at King's College, Cambridge.

AN ELEMENTARY TREATISE ON CURVE TRACING. **8vo. 12s.**

SOLID GEOMETRY. 3d Ed. Demy 8vo. 16s.

HINTS FOR THE SOLUTION OF PROBLEMS in the Third Edition of SOLID GEOMETRY. 8vo. 8s. 6d.

JOHNSON.—CURVE TRACING IN CARTESIAN CO-ORDINATES. By W. WOOLSEY JOHNSON, Professor of Mathematics at the U.S. Naval Academy, Annapolis, Maryland. Cr. **8vo.** 4s. 6d.

M'CLELLAND.—THE GEOMETRY OF THE **CIRCLE.** By W. J. M'CLELLAND, M.A. Cr. 8vo. [*In the Press.*

PUCKLE.—AN ELEMENTARY TREATISE ON CONIC SECTIONS AND AL- GEBRAIC GEOMETRY With Numerous Examples and Hints for their Solu- tion. By G. H. PUCKLE, M.A. 5th Ed., revised and enlarged. Cr. 8vo. 7s. 6d.

SMITH.—Works **by** CHARLES **SMITH, M.A., Master of Sidney** Sussex College, Cambridge.

CONIC SECTIONS. 7th Ed. Cr. 8vo. **7s. 6d.**

SOLUTIONS TO CONIC SECTIONS. **Cr. 8vo. 10s. 6d.**

AN ELEMENTARY TREATISE ON **SOLID GEOMETRY.** 2d Ed. Cr. 8vo. 9s. 6d.

TODHUNTER.—Works by ISAAC TODHUNTER, F.R.S.

PLANE CO-ORDINATE GEOMETRY, as applied to the Straight Line and the Conic Sections. Cr. 8vo. 7s. 6d.

KEY. By C. W BOURNE, M.A., Headmaster of King's College School. Cr. 8vo. 10s. 6d.

TODHUNTER.—Works by Isaac Todhunter, F.R.S.—*continued*.
EXAMPLES OF ANALYTICAL GEOMETRY OF THREE DIMENSIONS.
New Ed., revised. Cr. 8vo. 4s.

PROBLEMS AND QUESTIONS IN MATHEMATICS.

ARMY PRELIMINARY EXAMINATION, 1882-1890, Specimens of Papers set at the. With Answers to the Mathematical Questions. Subjects: Arithmetic, Algebra, Euclid, Geometrical Drawing, Geography, French, English Dictation. Cr. 8vo. 3s. 6d.

CAMBRIDGE SENATE-HOUSE PROBLEMS AND RIDERS, WITH SOLUTIONS:—
1875—PROBLEMS AND RIDERS. By A. G. Greenhill, F.R.S. Cr. 8vo. 8s. 6d.
1878—SOLUTIONS OF SENATE-HOUSE PROBLEMS. By the Mathematical Moderators and Examiners. Edited by J. W. L. Glaisher, F.R.S., Fellow of Trinity College, Cambridge. 12s.

CHRISTIE.—A COLLECTION OF ELEMENTARY TEST-QUESTIONS IN PURE AND MIXED MATHEMATICS; with Answers and Appendices on Synthetic Division, and on the Solution of Numerical Equations by Horner's Method. By James R. Christie, F.R.S. Cr. 8vo. 8s. 6d.

CLIFFORD.—MATHEMATICAL PAPERS. By W. K. Clifford. Edited by R. Tucker. With an Introduction by H. J. Stephen Smith, M.A. 8vo. 30s.

MILNE.—Works by Rev. John J. Milne, Private Tutor.
WEEKLY PROBLEM PAPERS. With Notes intended for the use of Students preparing for Mathematical Scholarships, and for Junior Members of the Universities who are reading for Mathematical Honours. Pott 8vo. 4s. 6d.
SOLUTIONS TO WEEKLY PROBLEM PAPERS. Cr. 8vo. 10s. 6d.
COMPANION TO WEEKLY PROBLEM PAPERS. Cr. 8vo. 10s. 6d.

RICHARDSON.—MISCELLANEOUS MATHEMATICAL PAPERS. Elementary and Advanced. By A. T. Richardson, M.A., Senior Mathematical Master at the Isle of Wight College. [*In the Press.*

SANDHURST MATHEMATICAL PAPERS, for admission into the Royal Military College, 1881-1889. Edited by E. J. Brooksmith, B.A., Instructor in Mathematics at the Royal Military Academy, Woolwich. Cr. 8vo. 3s. 6d.

WOOLWICH MATHEMATICAL PAPERS, for Admission into the Royal Military Academy, Woolwich, 1880-1888 inclusive. By the same Editor. Cr. 8vo. 6s.

WOLSTENHOLME.—Works by Joseph Wolstenholme, D.Sc., late Professor of Mathematics in the Royal Engineering Coll., Cooper's Hill.
MATHEMATICAL PROBLEMS, on Subjects included in the First and Second Divisions of the Schedule of Subjects for the Cambridge Mathematical Tripos Examination. New Ed., greatly enlarged. 8vo. 18s.
EXAMPLES FOR PRACTICE IN THE USE OF SEVEN-FIGURE LOGARITHMS. 8vo. 5s.

HIGHER PURE MATHEMATICS.

AIRY.—Works by Sir G. B. Airy, K.C.B., formerly Astronomer-Royal.
ELEMENTARY TREATISE ON PARTIAL DIFFERENTIAL EQUATIONS. With Diagrams. 2d Ed. Cr. 8vo. 5s. 6d.
ON THE ALGEBRAICAL AND NUMERICAL THEORY OF ERRORS OF OBSERVATIONS AND THE COMBINATION OF OBSERVATIONS. 2d Ed., revised. Cr. 8vo. 6s. 6d.

BOOLE.—THE CALCULUS OF FINITE DIFFERENCES. By G. Boole. 3d Ed., revised by J. F. Moulton, Q.C. Cr. 8vo. 10s. 6d.

EDWARDS.—THE DIFFERENTIAL CALCULUS. By Joseph Edwards, M.A. With Applications and numerous Examples. Cr. 8vo. 10s. 6d.

FERRERS.—AN ELEMENTARY TREATISE ON SPHERICAL HARMONICS, AND SUBJECTS CONNECTED WITH THEM. By Rev. N. M. Ferrers, D.D. F.R.S., Master of Gonville and Caius College, Cambridge. Cr. 8vo. 7s. 6d.

FORSYTH.—A TREATISE ON DIFFERENTIAL EQUATIONS. By ANDREW RUSSELL FORSYTH, F.R.S., Fellow and Assistant Tutor of Trinity College, Cambridge. 2d Ed. 8vo. 14s.

FROST.—AN ELEMENTARY TREATISE ON CURVE TRACING. By PERCIVAL FROST, M.A., D.Sc. 8vo. 12s.

GRAHAM.—GEOMETRY OF POSITION. By R. H. GRAHAM. Cr. 8vo. 7s. 6d

GREENHILL.—DIFFERENTIAL AND INTEGRAL CALCULUS. By A. G. GREENHILL, Professor of Mathematics to the Senior Class of Artillery Officers, Woolwich. New Ed. Cr. 8vo. 10s. 6d.

APPLICATIONS OF ELLIPTIC FUNCTIONS. By the same. [In the Press.

JOHNSON.—Works by WILLIAM WOOLSEY JOHNSON, Professor of Mathematics at the U.S. Naval Academy, Annapolis, Maryland.

INTEGRAL CALCULUS, an Elementary Treatise on the. Founded on the Method of Rates or Fluxions. 8vo. 9s.

CURVE TRACING IN CARTESIAN CO-ORDINATES. Cr. 8vo. 4s. 6d.

A TREATISE ON ORDINARY AND DIFFERENTIAL EQUATIONS. Ex. cr. 8vo. 15s.

KELLAND and TAIT.—INTRODUCTION TO QUATERNIONS, with numerous examples. By P. KELLAND and P. G. TAIT, Professors in the Department of Mathematics in the University of Edinburgh. 2d Ed. Cr. 8vo. 7s. 6d.

KEMPE.—HOW TO DRAW A STRAIGHT LINE: a Lecture on Linkages. By A. B. KEMPE. Illustrated. Cr. 8vo. 1s. 6d.

KNOX.—DIFFERENTIAL CALCULUS FOR BEGINNERS. By ALEXANDER KNOX. Fcap. 8vo. 3s. 6d.

MUIR.—THE THEORY OF DETERMINANTS IN THE HISTORICAL ORDER OF ITS DEVELOPMENT. Part I. Determinants in General. Leibnitz (1693) to Cayley (1841). By THOS. MUIR, Mathematical Master in the High School of Glasgow. 8vo. 10s. 6d.

RICE and JOHNSON.—AN ELEMENTARY TREATISE ON THE DIFFEREN-TIAL CALCULUS. Founded on the Method of Rates or Fluxions. By J. M. RICE, Professor of Mathematics in the United States Navy, and W. W. JOHN-SON, Professor of Mathematics at the United States Naval Academy. 3d Ed., revised and corrected. 8vo. 18s. Abridged Ed. 9s.

TODHUNTER.—Works by ISAAC TODHUNTER, F.R.S.

AN ELEMENTARY TREATISE ON THE THEORY OF EQUATIONS. Cr. 8vo. 7s. 6d.

A TREATISE ON THE DIFFERENTIAL CALCULUS. Cr. 8vo. 10s. 6d. KEY. Cr. 8vo. 10s. 6d.

A TREATISE ON THE INTEGRAL CALCULUS AND ITS APPLICATIONS. Cr. 8vo. 10s. 6d. KEY. Cr. 8vo. 10s. 6d.

A HISTORY OF THE MATHEMATICAL THEORY OF PROBABILITY, from the time of Pascal to that of Laplace. 8vo. 18s.

AN ELEMENTARY TREATISE ON LAPLACE'S, LAME'S, AND BESSEL'S FUNCTIONS. Cr. 8vo. 10s. 6d.

MECHANICS: Statics, Dynamics, Hydrostatics, Hydrodynamics. (See also Physics.)

ALEXANDER and THOMSON.—ELEMENTARY APPLIED MECHANICS. By Prof. T. ALEXANDER and A. W. THOMSON. Part II. Transverse Stress. Cr. 8vo. 10s. 6d.

BALL.—EXPERIMENTAL MECHANICS. A Course of Lectures delivered at the Royal College of Science for Ireland. By Sir R. S. BALL, F.R.S. 2d Ed. Illustrated. Cr. 8vo. 6s.

CLIFFORD.—THE ELEMENTS OF DYNAMIC. An Introduction to the Study of Motion and Rest in Solid and Fluid Bodies. By W. K. CLIFFORD. Part I.—Kinematic. Cr. 8vo. Books I.–III. 7s. 6d. ; Book IV. and Appendix, 6s.

COTTERILL.—APPLIED MECHANICS: An Elementary General Introduction to the Theory of Structures and Machines. By J. H. COTTERILL, F.R.S., Professor of Applied Mechanics in the Royal Naval College, Greenwich. 8vo. 18s.

COTTERILL and SLADE.—LESSONS IN APPLIED MECHANICS. By Prof. J. H. COTTERILL and J. H. SLADE. Fcap. 8vo. 5s. 6d.

DYNAMICS, SYLLABUS OF ELEMENTARY. Part I. Linear Dynamics. With an Appendix on the Meanings of the Symbols in Physical Equations. Prepared by the Association for the Improvement of Geometrical Teaching. 4to. 1s.

GANGUILLET and KUTTER.—A GENERAL FORMULA FOR THE UNIFORM FLOW OF WATER IN RIVERS AND OTHER CHANNELS. By E. GANGUILLET and W. R. KUTTER. Translated, with Additions, including Tables and Diagrams, and the Elements of over 1200 Gaugings of Rivers, Small Channels, and Pipes in English Measure, by R. HERING, Assoc. Am. Soc., C.E., M. Inst. C.E., and J. C. TRAUTWINE Jun., Assoc. Am. Soc. C.E., Assoc. Inst. C.E. 8vo. 17s.

GRAHAM.—GEOMETRY OF POSITION. By R. H. GRAHAM. Cr. 8vo. 7s. 6d.

GREAVES.—Works by JOHN GREAVES, M.A., Fellow and Mathematical Lecturer at Christ's College, Cambridge.

*STATICS FOR BEGINNERS. Gl. 8vo. 3s. 6d.

A TREATISE ON ELEMENTARY STATICS. 2d Ed. Cr. 8vo. 6s. 6d.

GREENHILL.—HYDROSTATICS. By A. G. GREENHILL, Professor of Mathematics to the Senior Class of Artillery Officers, Woolwich. Cr. 8vo. [In preparation.

*HICKS.—ELEMENTARY DYNAMICS OF PARTICLES AND SOLIDS. By W. M. HICKS, D.Sc., Principal and Professor of Mathematics and Physics, Firth College, Sheffield. Cr. 8vo. 6s. 6d.

JELLETT.—A TREATISE ON THE THEORY OF FRICTION. By JOHN H. JELLETT, B.D., late Provost of Trinity College, Dublin. 8vo. 8s. 6d.

KENNEDY.—THE MECHANICS OF MACHINERY. By A. B. W. KENNEDY, F.R.S. Illustrated. Cr. 8vo. 12s. 6d.

LOCK.—Works by Rev. J. B. LOCK, M.A.

*ELEMENTARY STATICS. 2d Ed. Gl. 8vo. 4s. 6d.

*ELEMENTARY DYNAMICS. 3d Ed. Gl. 8vo. 4s. 6d.

ELEMENTARY HYDROSTATICS. Gl. 8vo. [In preparation.

MECHANICS FOR BEGINNERS. Gl. 8vo. Part I. MECHANICS OF SOLIDS. [In the Press. Part II. MECHANICS OF FLUIDS. [In preparation.

MACGREGOR.—KINEMATICS AND DYNAMICS. An Elementary Treatise. By J. G. MACGREGOR, D.Sc., Munro Professor of Physics in Dalhousie College, Halifax, Nova Scotia. Illustrated. Cr. 8vo. 10s. 6d.

PARKINSON.—AN ELEMENTARY TREATISE ON MECHANICS. By S. PARKINSON, D.D., F.R.S., late Tutor and Prælector of St. John's College, Cambridge. 6th Ed., revised. Cr. 8vo. 9s. 6d.

PIRIE.—LESSONS ON RIGID DYNAMICS. By Rev. G. PIRIE, M.A., Professor of Mathematics in the University of Aberdeen. Cr. 8vo. 6s.

ROUTH.—Works by EDWARD JOHN ROUTH, D.Sc., LL.D., F.R.S., Hon. Fellow of St. Peter's College, Cambridge.

A TREATISE ON THE DYNAMICS OF THE SYSTEM OF RIGID BODIES. With numerous Examples. Two Vols. 8vo. Vol. I.—Elementary Parts. 5th Ed. 14s. Vol. II.—The Advanced Parts. 4th Ed. 14s.

STABILITY OF A GIVEN STATE OF MOTION, PARTICULARLY STEADY MOTION. Adams Prize Essay for 1877. 8vo. 8s. 6d.

*SANDERSON.—HYDROSTATICS FOR BEGINNERS. By F. W. SANDERSON, M.A., Assistant Master at Dulwich College. Gl. 8vo. 4s. 6d.

TAIT and STEELE.—A TREATISE ON DYNAMICS OF A PARTICLE. By Professor TAIT, M.A., and W. J. STEELE, B.A. 6th Ed., revised. Cr. 8vo. 12s.

TODHUNTER.—Works by ISAAC TODHUNTER, F.R.S.

*MECHANICS FOR BEGINNERS. 18mo. 4s. 6d. KEY. Cr. 8vo. 6s. 6d.

A TREATISE ON ANALYTICAL STATICS. 5th Ed. Edited by Prof. J. D. EVERETT, F.R.S. Cr. 8vo. 10s. 6d.

PHYSICS: Sound, Light, Heat, Electricity, Elasticity, Attractions, etc. (See also Mechanics.)

AIRY.—Works by Sir G. B. AIRY, K.C.B., formerly Astronomer-Royal.
> ON SOUND AND ATMOSPHERIC VIBRATIONS. With the Mathematical Elements of Music. 2d Ed., revised and enlarged. Cr. 8vo. 9s.
> GRAVITATION: An Elementary Explanation of the Principal Perturbations in the Solar System. 2d Ed. Cr. 8vo. 7s. 6d.

CLAUSIUS.—MECHANICAL THEORY OF HEAT. By R. CLAUSIUS. Translated by W. R. BROWNE, M.A. Cr. 8vo. 10s. 6d.

CUMMING.—AN INTRODUCTION TO THE THEORY OF ELECTRICITY. By LINNÆUS CUMMING, M.A., Assistant Master at Rugby. Illustrated. Cr. 8vo. 8s. 6d.

DANIELL.—A TEXT-BOOK OF THE PRINCIPLES OF PHYSICS. By ALFRED DANIELL, D.Sc. Illustrated. 2d Ed., revised and enlarged. 8vo. 21s.

DAY.—ELECTRIC LIGHT ARITHMETIC. By R. E. DAY, Evening Lecturer in Experimental Physics at King's College, London. Pott 8vo. 2s.

EVERETT.—ILLUSTRATIONS OF THE C. G. S. SYSTEM OF UNITS WITH TABLES OF PHYSICAL CONSTANTS. By J D. EVERETT, F R.S., Professor of Natural Philosophy, Queen's College, Belfast. New Ed. Ex. fcap. 8vo. 5s.

FERRERS.—AN ELEMENTARY TREATISE ON SPHERICAL HARMONICS, and Subjects connected with them. By Rev. N. M. FERRERS, D.D., F.R.S., Master of Gonville and Caius College, Cambridge. Cr. 8vo. 7s. 6d.

FESSENDEN.—PHYSICS FOR PUBLIC SCHOOLS. By C. FESSENDEN. Illustrated. Fcap. 8vo. [In the Press.

GRAY.—THE THEORY AND PRACTICE OF ABSOLUTE MEASUREMENTS IN ELECTRICITY AND MAGNETISM. By A. GRAY, F.R.S.E., Professor of Physics in the University College of North Wales. Two Vols. Cr. 8vo. Vol. I. 12s. 6d. [Vol. II. In the Press.
> ABSOLUTE MEASUREMENTS IN ELECTRICITY AND MAGNETISM. 2d Ed., revised and greatly enlarged. Fcap. 8vo. 5s. 6d.

IBBETSON.—THE MATHEMATICAL THEORY OF PERFECTLY ELASTIC SOLIDS, with a Short Account of Viscous Fluids. By W. J. IBBETSON, late Senior Scholar of Clare College, Cambridge. 8vo. 21s.

'**JONES.**—EXAMPLES IN PHYSICS. Containing over 1000 Problems with Answers and numerous solved Examples. Suitable for candidates preparing for the Intermediate, Science, Preliminary, Scientific, and other Examinations of the University of London. By D. E. JONES, B.Sc., Professor of Physics in the University College of Wales, Aberystwyth. Fcap. 8vo. 3s. 6d.
> ʼELEMENTARY LESSONS IN HEAT, LIGHT, AND SOUND. By the same. Gl. 8vo. 2s. 6d.

LOCKYER.—CONTRIBUTIONS TO SOLAR PHYSICS. By J. NORMAN LOCKYER, F.R.S. With Illustrations. Royal 8vo. 31s. 6d.

LODGE.—MODERN VIEWS OF ELECTRICITY. By OLIVER J. LODGE, F.R.S., Professor of Experimental Physics in University College, Liverpool. Illustrated. Cr. 8vo. 6s. 6d.

LOEWY.—ʼQUESTIONS AND EXAMPLES ON EXPERIMENTAL PHYSICS: Sound, Light, Heat, Electricity, and Magnetism. By B. LOEWY, Examiner in Experimental Physics to the College of Preceptors. Fcap. 8vo. 2s.
> ʼA GRADUATED COURSE OF NATURAL SCIENCE FOR ELEMENTARY AND TECHNICAL SCHOOLS AND COLLEGES. By the same. In Three Parts. Part I. FIRST YEAR'S COURSE. Gl. 8vo. 2s. Part II. [In preparation.

LUPTON.—NUMERICAL TABLES AND CONSTANTS IN ELEMENTARY SCIENCE. By S. LUPTON, M.A., late Assistant Master at Harrow. Ex. fcap. 8vo. 2s. 6d.

MACFARLANE.—PHYSICAL ARITHMETIC. By A. MACFARLANE, D.Sc., late Examiner in Mathematics at the University of Edinburgh. Cr. 8vo. 7s. 6d.

*MAYER.—SOUND: **A Series** of Simple, Entertaining, and Inexpensive Experiments in the Phenomena of Sound. By A. M. MAYER, Professor of Physics in the Stevens Institute of Technology. Illustrated. Cr. 8vo. 3s. 6d.

*MAYER and BARNARD.—LIGHT: **A Series** of Simple, Entertaining, and Inexpensive Experiments in the Phenomena of Light. By A. M. MAYER and C. BARNARD. Illustrated. Cr. 8vo. **2s.** 6d.

MOLLOY.—GLEANINGS IN SCIENCE: Popular Lectures on Scientific Subjects. By the Rev. GERALD MOLLOY, D.Sc., Rector of the Catholic University of Ireland. 8vo. **7s.** 6d.

NEWTON.—PRINCIPIA. Edited by Prof. Sir W. THOMSON, P.R.S., and Prof. BLACKBURNE. 4to. **31s.** 6d.

THE FIRST THREE SECTIONS OF NEWTON'S PRINCIPIA. With Notes and Illustrations. Also a Collection of **Problems,** principally intended as Examples of Newton's Methods. By P. FROST, **M.A.**, D.Sc. 3d Ed. 8vo. 12s.

PARKINSON.—A TREATISE ON OPTICS. By S. PARKINSON, D.D., F.R.S., late Tutor and Prælector of St. John's College, Cambridge. 4th Ed., revised and enlarged. Cr. 8vo. 10s. 6d.

PEABODY.—THERMODYNAMICS OF THE STEAM-ENGINE AND OTHER HEAT-ENGINES. By CECIL H. PEABODY, Associate Professor of Steam Engineering, Massachusetts Institute of Technology. 8vo. 21s.

PERRY. — STEAM: An Elementary Treatise. By JOHN PERRY, Professor of Mechanical Engineering and Applied Mechanics at the Technical College, Finsbury. 18mo. 4s. 6d.

PICKERING.—ELEMENTS OF PHYSICAL MANIPULATION. By Prof. EDWARD C. PICKERING. Medium 8vo. Part I., 12s. 6d. Part II., 14s.

PRESTON.—THE THEORY OF LIGHT. By THOMAS PRESTON, M.A. Illustrated. 8vo. 12s. 6d.

THE THEORY OF HEAT. By the same Author. 8vo. [In preparation.

RAYLEIGH.—THE THEORY OF SOUND. By Lord RAYLEIGH, F.R.S. 8vo. Vol. I., 12s. 6d. Vol. II., 12s. 6d. [Vol. III. In the Press.

SHANN.—AN ELEMENTARY TREATISE ON HEAT, IN RELATION TO STEAM AND THE STEAM-ENGINE. By G. SHANN, M.A. Illustrated. Cr. 8vo. 4s. 6d.

SPOTTISWOODE.—POLARISATION OF LIGHT. By the late W. SPOTTISWOODE, F.R.S. Illustrated. Cr. 8vo. 3s. 6d.

STEWART.—Works by BALFOUR STEWART, F.R.S., late Langworthy Professor of Physics in the Owens College, Victoria University, Manchester.

*PRIMER OF PHYSICS. Illustrated. With Questions. 18mo. 1s.

*LESSONS IN ELEMENTARY PHYSICS. Illustrated. Fcap. 8vo. 4s. 6d.

*QUESTIONS. By Prof. T. H. CORE. Fcap. 8vo. 2s.

STEWART and GEE.—LESSONS IN ELEMENTARY PRACTICAL PHYSICS. By BALFOUR STEWART, F.R.S., and W. W. HALDANE GEE, B.Sc. Cr. 8vo. Vol. I. GENERAL PHYSICAL PROCESSES. 6s. Vol. II. ELECTRICITY AND MAGNETISM. 7s. 6d. [Vol. III. OPTICS, HEAT, AND SOUND. In the Press.

*PRACTICAL PHYSICS FOR SCHOOLS AND THE JUNIOR STUDENTS OF COLLEGES. Gl. 8vo. Vol. I. ELECTRICITY AND MAGNETISM. 2s. 6d. [Vol. II. OPTICS, HEAT, AND SOUND. In the Press.

STOKES.—ON LIGHT. Burnett Lectures, delivered in Aberdeen in 1883-4-5. By Sir G. G. STOKES, F.R.S., Lucasian Professor of Mathematics in the University of Cambridge. First Course: ON THE NATURE OF LIGHT. Second Course: ON LIGHT AS A MEANS OF INVESTIGATION. Third Course: ON THE BENEFICIAL EFFECTS OF LIGHT. Cr. 8vo. 7s. 6d.
⁂ The 2d and 3d Courses may be had separately. Cr. 8vo. 2s. 6d. each.

STONE.—AN ELEMENTARY TREATISE ON SOUND. By W. H. STONE. Illustrated. Fcap. 8vo. 3s. 6d.

TAIT.—HEAT. By P. G. TAIT, Professor of Natural Philosophy in the University of Edinburgh. Cr. 8vo. 6s.

LECTURES ON SOME RECENT ADVANCES IN PHYSICAL SCIENCE. By the same. 3d Edition. Crown 8vo. 9s.

TAYLOR.—SOUND AND MUSIC. An Elementary Treatise on the Physical Constitution of Musical Sounds and Harmony, including the Chief Acoustical Discoveries of Professor Helmholtz. By SEDLEY TAYLOR, M.A. Illustrated. 2d Ed. Ex. cr. 8vo. 8s. 6d.

*THOMPSON. — ELEMENTARY LESSONS IN ELECTRICITY AND MAGNETISM. By SILVANUS P THOMPSON, Principal and Professor of Physics in the Technical College, Finsbury. Illustrated. New Ed., revised. Fcap. 8vo. 4s. 6d.

THOMSON.—Works by J. J. THOMSON, Professor of Experimental Physics in the University of Cambridge.

A TREATISE ON THE MOTION OF VORTEX RINGS. Adams Prize Essay 1882. 8vo. 6s.
APPLICATIONS OF DYNAMICS TO PHYSICS AND CHEMISTRY. Cr. 8vo. 7s. 6d.

THOMSON.—Works by Sir W. THOMSON, P.R.S., Professor of Natural Philosophy in the University of Glasgow.

ELECTROSTATICS AND MAGNETISM, REPRINTS OF PAPERS ON. 2d Ed. 8vo. 18s.
POPULAR LECTURES AND ADDRESSES. 3 Vols. Illustrated. Cr. 8vo. Vol. I. CONSTITUTION OF MATTER. 7s. 6d. Vol. III. NAVIGATION. 7s. 6d.

TODHUNTER.—Works by ISAAC TODHUNTER, F.R.S.

AN ELEMENTARY TREATISE ON LAPLACE'S, LAMÉ'S, AND BESSEL'S FUNCTIONS. Crown 8vo. 10s. 6d.
A HISTORY OF THE MATHEMATICAL THEORIES OF ATTRACTION, AND THE FIGURE OF THE EARTH, from the time of Newton to that of Laplace. 2 vols. 8vo. 24s.

TURNER.—A COLLECTION OF EXAMPLES ON HEAT AND ELECTRICITY. By H. H. TURNER, Fellow of Trinity College, Cambridge. Cr. 8vo. 2s. 6d.

WRIGHT.—LIGHT: A Course of Experimental Optics, chiefly with the Lantern. By LEWIS WRIGHT. Illustrated. Cr. 8vo. 7s. 6d.

ASTRONOMY.

AIRY.—Works by Sir G. B. AIRY, K.C.B., formerly Astronomer-Royal.

*POPULAR ASTRONOMY. 7th Ed. Revised by H. H. TURNER, M.A. 18mo. 4s. 6d.
GRAVITATION : An Elementary Explanation of the Principal Perturbations in the Solar System. 2d Ed. Cr. 8vo. 7s. 6d.

CHEYNE.—AN ELEMENTARY TREATISE ON THE PLANETARY THEORY. By C. H. H. CHEYNE. With Problems. 3d Ed. Edited by Rev. A. FREEMAN, M.A., F.R.A.S. Cr. 8vo. 7s. 6d.

CLARK and SADLER.—THE STAR GUIDE. By L. CLARK and H. SADLER. Roy. 8vo. 5s.

CROSSLEY, GLEDHILL, and WILSON.—A HANDBOOK OF DOUBLE STARS. By E. CROSSLEY, J. GLEDHILL, and J. M. WILSON. 8vo. 21s.
CORRECTIONS TO THE HANDBOOK OF DOUBLE STARS. 8vo. 1s.

FORBES.—TRANSIT OF VENUS. By G. FORBES, Professor of Natural Philosophy in the Andersonian University, Glasgow. Illustrated. Cr. 8vo. 3s. 6d.

GODFRAY.—Works by HUGH GODFRAY, M.A., Mathematical Lecturer at Pembroke College, Cambridge.

A TREATISE ON ASTRONOMY. 4th Ed. 8vo. 12s. 6d.
AN ELEMENTARY TREATISE ON THE LUNAR THEORY, with a brief Sketch of the Problem up to the time of Newton. 2d Ed., revised. Cr. 8vo. 5s. 6d.

LOCKYER.—Works by J. NORMAN LOCKYER, F.R.S.

*PRIMER OF ASTRONOMY. Illustrated. 18mo. 1s.
*ELEMENTARY LESSONS IN ASTRONOMY. With Spectra of the Sun, Stars, and Nebulæ, and numerous Illustrations. 36th Thousand. Revised throughout. Fcap. 8vo. 5s. 6d.

*QUESTIONS ON LOCKYER'S ELEMENTARY LESSONS IN ASTRONOMY By J. FORBES ROBERTSON. 18mo. 1s. 6d.

THE CHEMISTRY OF THE SUN. Illustrated. 8vo. **14s.**

THE METEORITIC HYPOTHESIS OF THE ORIGIN OF COSMICAL SYSTEMS. Illustrated. 8vo. 17s. net.

THE EVOLUTION OF THE HEAVENS AND THE EARTH. Cr. 8vo. Illustrated. [*In the Press.*

LOCKYER and SEABROKE.—STAR-GAZING PAST AND PRESENT. By J. NORMAN LOCKYER, F.R.S. Expanded from Shorthand Notes with the assistance of G. M. SEABROKE, F.R.A.S. Royal 8vo. 21s.

NEWCOMB.—POPULAR ASTRONOMY. By S. NEWCOMB, **LL.D.**, Professor U.S. Naval Observatory Illustrated. 2d Ed., revised. 8vo. **18s.**

HISTORICAL.

BALL.—A SHORT ACCOUNT OF THE HISTORY OF MATHEMATICS. By W. W. R. BALL, M.A. Cr. 8vo. 10s. 6d.

NATURAL SCIENCES.

Chemistry ; Physical Geography, Geology, and Mineralogy ; Biology ; Medicine.

(For MECHANICS, PHYSICS, and ASTRONOMY, see *MATHEMATICS.*)

CHEMISTRY.

ARMSTRONG.—A MANUAL OF INORGANIC CHEMISTRY. By HENRY ARMSTRONG, F.R.S., Professor of Chemistry in the City and Guilds of London Technical Institute. Cr. 8vo. [*In preparation.*

*COHEN.—THE OWENS COLLEGE COURSE OF PRACTICAL ORGANIC CHEMISTRY. By JULIUS B. COHEN, Ph.D., Assistant Lecturer on Chemistry in the Owens College, Manchester. With a Preface by Sir HENRY ROSCOE, F.R.S., and C. SCHORLEMMER, F.R.S. Fcap. 8vo. 2s. 6d.

COOKE.—ELEMENTS OF CHEMICAL PHYSICS. By JOSIAH P. COOKE, Jun., Erving Professor of Chemistry and Mineralogy in Harvard University. 4th Ed. 8vo. 21s.

FLEISCHER.—A SYSTEM OF VOLUMETRIC ANALYSIS. By EMIL FLEISCHER. Translated, with Notes and Additions, by M. M. P. MUIR, F.R.S.E. Illustrated. Cr. 8vo. 7s. 6d.

FRANKLAND.—A HANDBOOK OF AGRICULTURAL CHEMICAL ANALYSIS. By P. F. FRANKLAND, F.R.S., Professor of Chemistry in University College, Dundee. Cr. 8vo. 7s. 6d.

HARTLEY.—A COURSE OF QUANTITATIVE ANALYSIS FOR STUDENTS. By W. NOEL HARTLEY, F.R.S., Professor of Chemistry and of Applied Chemistry, Science and Art Department, Royal College of Science, Dublin. Gl. 8vo. **5s.**

HEMPEL.—METHODS OF GAS **ANALYSIS.** By Dr. WALTHER HEMPEL. Translated by Dr. L. M. DENNIS. [*In preparation.*

HIORNS.—PRACTICAL METALLURGY AND ASSAYING. A Text-Book for the use of Teachers, Students, and Assayers. By ARTHUR H. HIORNS, Principal of the School of Metallurgy, Birmingham and Midland Institute. Illustrated. Gl. 8vo. 6s.

A TEXT-BOOK OF ELEMENTARY METALLURGY FOR THE USE OF STUDENTS. To which is added an Appendix of Examination Questions, embracing the whole of the Questions set in the three stages of the subject by the Science and Art Department for the past twenty years. By the same. Gl. 8vo. 4s.

IRON AND STEEL MANUFACTURE. A Text-Book for Beginners. By the same. Illustrated. Gl. 8vo. 3s. 6d.

MIXED METALS OR METALLIC ALLOYS. By the same. Gl. 8vo. 6s.

JONES.—*THE OWENS COLLEGE JUNIOR COURSE OF PRACTICAL CHEMISTRY. By FRANCIS JONES, F.R.S.E., Chemical Master at the Grammar School, Manchester. With Preface by Sir HENRY ROSCOE, F.R.S. Illustrated. Fcap. 8vo. 2s. 6d.

*QUESTIONS ON CHEMISTRY. A Series of Problems and Exercises in Inorganic and Organic Chemistry. By the same. Fcap. 8vo. 3s.

LANDAUER.—BLOWPIPE ANALYSIS. By J. LANDAUER. Authorised English Edition by J. TAYLOR and W. E. KAY, of Owens College, Manchester.

[New Edition in the Press.

LOCKYER.—THE CHEMISTRY OF THE SUN. By J. NORMAN LOCKYER, F.R.S. Illustrated. 8vo. 14s.

LUPTON.—CHEMICAL ARITHMETIC. With 1200 Problems. By S. LUPTON, M.A. 2d Ed., revised and abridged. Fcap. 8vo. 4s. 6d.

MANSFIELD.—A THEORY OF SALTS. By C. B. MANSFIELD. Crown 8vo. 14s.

MELDOLA.—THE CHEMISTRY OF PHOTOGRAPHY. By RAPHAEL MELDOLA, F.R.S., Professor of Chemistry in the Technical College, Finsbury. Cr. 8vo. 6s.

MEYER.—HISTORY OF CHEMISTRY FROM THE EARLIEST TIMES TO THE PRESENT DAY. By ERNST VON MEYER, Ph.D. Translated by GEORGE McGOWAN, Ph.D. 8vo. 14s. net.

MIXTER.—AN ELEMENTARY TEXT-BOOK OF CHEMISTRY. By WILLIAM G. MIXTER, Professor of Chemistry in the Sheffield Scientific School of Yale College. 2d and revised Ed. Cr. 8vo. 7s. 6d.

MUIR.—PRACTICAL CHEMISTRY FOR MEDICAL STUDENTS. Specially arranged for the first M.B. Course. By M. M. P. MUIR, F.R.S.E., Fellow and Prælector in Chemistry at Gonville and Caius College, Cambridge. Fcap. 8vo. 1s. 6d.

MUIR and WILSON.—THE ELEMENTS OF THERMAL CHEMISTRY. By M. M. P. MUIR, F.R.S.E.; assisted by D. M. WILSON. 8vo. 12s. 6d.

OSTWALD. — OUTLINES OF GENERAL CHEMISTRY (PHYSICAL AND THEORETICAL). By Prof. W. OSTWALD. Translated by JAMES WALKER, D.Sc., Ph.D. 8vo. 10s. net.

RAMSAY.—EXPERIMENTAL PROOFS OF CHEMICAL THEORY FOR BEGINNERS. By WILLIAM RAMSAY, F.R.S., Professor of Chemistry in University College, London. Pott 8vo. 2s. 6d.

REMSEN.—Works by IRA REMSEN, Professor of Chemistry in the Johns Hopkins University, U.S.A.

COMPOUNDS OF CARBON: or, Organic Chemistry, an Introduction to the Study of. Cr. 8vo. 6s. 6d.

AN INTRODUCTION TO THE STUDY OF CHEMISTRY (INORGANIC CHEMISTRY). Cr. 8vo. 6s. 6d.

*THE ELEMENTS OF CHEMISTRY. A Text-Book for Beginners. Fcap. 8vo. 2s. 6d.

A TEXT-BOOK OF INORGANIC CHEMISTRY. 8vo. 16s.

ROSCOE.—Works by Sir HENRY E. ROSCOE, F.R.S., formerly Professor of Chemistry in the Owens College, Victoria University, Manchester.

*PRIMER OF CHEMISTRY. Illustrated. With Questions. 18mo. 1s.

*LESSONS IN ELEMENTARY CHEMISTRY, INORGANIC AND ORGANIC. With Illustrations and Chromolitho of the Solar Spectrum, and of the Alkalies and Alkaline Earths. Fcap. 8vo. 4s. 6d.

ROSCOE and SCHORLEMMER.—INORGANIC AND ORGANIC CHEMISTRY. A Complete Treatise on Inorganic and Organic Chemistry. By Sir HENRY E. ROSCOE, F.R.S., and Prof. C. SCHORLEMMER, F.R.S. Illustrated. 8vo.

Vols. I. and II. INORGANIC CHEMISTRY. Vol. I.—The Non-Metallic Elements. 2d Ed. 21s. Vol. II. Part I.—Metals. 18s. Part II.—Metals. 18s.

Vol. III.—ORGANIC CHEMISTRY. THE CHEMISTRY OF THE HYDROCARBONS and their Derivatives. Five Parts. Parts I., II., and IV. 21s. Parts III. and V. 18s. each.

ROSCOE **and** SCHUSTER.—SPECTRUM ANALYSIS. Lectures delivered in 1868. By Sir HENRY ROSCOE, F.R.S. 4th Ed., revised and considerably enlarged by the Author and by A. SCHUSTER, F.R.S., Ph.D., Professor of Applied Mathematics in the Owens College, Victoria University. With Appendices, Illustrations, and Plates. 8vo. 21s.

*THORPE.—A SERIES OF CHEMICAL PROBLEMS. With Key. For use in Colleges and Schools. By T. E. THORPE, B.Sc. (Vic.), Ph.D., F.R.S. Revised and Enlarged by W. TATE, Assoc.N.S.S. With Preface by Sir H. E. ROSCOE, F.R.S. New Ed. Fcap. 8vo. 2s.

THORPE **and** RÜCKER.—A TREATISE ON CHEMICAL PHYSICS. By Prof. T. E. THORPE, F.R.S., and Prof. A. W RÜCKER, F.R.S. Illustrated. 8vo.
[In preparation.

WURTZ.—A HISTORY OF CHEMICAL **THEORY.** By AD. WURTZ. Translated by HENRY WATTS, F.R.S. Crown 8vo. **6s.**

PHYSICAL GEOGRAPHY, GEOLOGY, AND MINERALOGY.

BLANFORD.—THE RUDIMENTS **OF** PHYSICAL GEOGRAPHY FOR THE USE OF INDIAN SCHOOLS; with a Glossary of Technical Terms employed. By H. F. BLANFORD, F.G.S. Illustrated. Cr. 8vo. 2s. 6d.

FERREL.—A POPULAR TREATISE ON **THE WINDS.** Comprising the General Motions of the Atmosphere, Monsoons, **Cyclones,** Tornadoes, Waterspouts, Hailstorms, etc. By WILLIAM FERREL, M.A., **Member** of the American National Academy of Sciences. 8vo. 18s.

FISHER.—PHYSICS OF THE EARTH'S CRUST. By the Rev. OSMOND FISHER, M.A., F.G.S., Hon. Fellow of King's College, London. 2d Ed., altered and enlarged. 8vo. 12s.

GEIKIE.—Works by Sir **ARCHIBALD GEIKIE, F.R.S.,** Director-General of the Geological Survey of the United Kingdom.

*PRIMER OF PHYSICAL GEOGRAPHY. Illustrated. With Questions. 18mo. 1s.

*ELEMENTARY LESSONS IN PHYSICAL GEOGRAPHY. Illustrated. **Fcap.** 8vo. 4s. 6d. *QUESTIONS ON THE SAME. 1s. 6d.

*PRIMER OF GEOLOGY. Illustrated. 18mo. **1s.**

*CLASS-BOOK **OF** GEOLOGY. Illustrated. New and Cheaper Ed. Cr. 8vo. **4s. 6d.**

TEXT-BOOK OF GEOLOGY. Illustrated. **2d Ed., 7th** Thousand, revised and enlarged. 8vo. 28s.

OUTLINES OF FIELD GEOLOGY. **Illustrated.** New Ed., revised and enlarged. Gl. 8vo. 3s. 6d.

THE SCENERY AND GEOLOGY **OF** SCOTLAND, VIEWED IN CONNEXION WITH ITS PHYSICAL GEOLOGY. Illustrated. Cr. 8vo. 12s. 6d.

HUXLEY.—PHYSIOGRAPHY. **An** Introduction to the Study of Nature. By T. H. HUXLEY, F R.S. Illustrated. New and Cheaper Edition. Cr. 8vo. 6s.

LOCKYER.—OUTLINES OF PHYSIOGRAPHY—THE MOVEMENTS OF THE EARTH. By J. NORMAN LOCKYER, F.R.S., Examiner in Physiography for the Science and Art Department. Illustrated. Cr. 8vo. Sewed, 1s. 6d.

MIERS.—A TREATISE **ON** MINERALOGY. By H. A. MIERS, of the British Museum. 8vo. *[In preparation.*

PHILLIPS. A TREATISE ON **ORE DEPOSITS.** By J. ARTHUR PHILLIPS, F.R.S. Illustrated. 8vo. 25s.

ROSENBUSCH **and** IDDINGS.—MICROSCOPICAL PHYSIOGRAPHY OF THE ROCK-MAKING MINERALS: AN AID TO THE MICROSCOPICAL STUDY OF ROCKS. By H. ROSENBUSCH. Translated and Abridged by J. P. IDDINGS. Illustrated. 8vo. 24s.

WILLIAMS.—ELEMENTS OF CRYSTALLOGRAPHY FOR STUDENTS OF CHEMISTRY, PHYSICS, AND MINERALOGY. By G. H. WILLIAMS, Ph.D., Cr. 8vo. **6s.**

BIOLOGY.

ALLEN.—ON THE COLOURS OF FLOWERS, as Illustrated in the British Flora. By GRANT ALLEN. Illustrated. Cr. 8vo. 3s. 6d.

BALFOUR.—A TREATISE ON COMPARATIVE EMBRYOLOGY. By F. M. BALFOUR, F.R.S., Fellow and Lecturer of Trinity College, Cambridge. Illustrated. 2d Ed., reprinted without alteration from the 1st Ed. 2 vols. 8vo. Vol. I. 18s. Vol. II. 21s.

BALFOUR and WARD.—A GENERAL TEXT-BOOK OF BOTANY. By ISAAC BAYLEY BALFOUR, F.R.S., Professor of Botany in the University of Edinburgh, and H. MARSHALL WARD, F.R.S., Professor of Botany in the Royal Indian Engineering College, Cooper's Hill. 8vo. [In preparation.

*BETTANY.—FIRST LESSONS IN PRACTICAL BOTANY. By G. T. BETTANY. 18mo. 1s.

*BOWER.—A COURSE OF PRACTICAL INSTRUCTION IN BOTANY. By F. O. BOWER, D.Sc., F.R.S., Regius Professor of Botany in the University of Glasgow. New Ed., revised. Cr. 8vo. 10s. 6d. Abridged Ed. [In preparation.

BUCKTON.—MONOGRAPH OF THE BRITISH CICADÆ, OR TETTIGIDÆ. By G. B. BUCKTON. In 8 parts, Quarterly. Part I. January, 1890. 8vo. Parts I.-VI. ready. 8s. each, net. Vol. I. 33s. 6d. net.

CHURCH and SCOTT.—MANUAL OF VEGETABLE PHYSIOLOGY. By Professor A. H. CHURCH, and D. H. SCOTT, D.Sc., Lecturer in the Normal School of Science. Illustrated. Cr. 8vo. [In preparation.

COPE.—THE ORIGIN OF THE FITTEST. Essays on Evolution. By E. D COPE, M.A., Ph.D. 8vo. 12s. 6d.

COUES.—HANDBOOK OF FIELD AND GENERAL ORNITHOLOGY. By Prof. ELLIOTT COUES, M.A. Illustrated. 8vo. 10s. net.

DARWIN.—MEMORIAL NOTICES OF CHARLES DARWIN, F.R.S., etc. By T. H. HUXLEY, F.R.S., G. J. ROMANES, F.R.S., ARCHIBALD GEIKIE, F.R.S., and W. THISELTON DYER, F.R.S. Reprinted from *Nature*. With a Portrait. Cr 8vo. 2s. 6d.

EIMER.—ORGANIC EVOLUTION AS THE RESULT OF THE INHERITANCE OF ACQUIRED CHARACTERS ACCORDING TO THE LAWS OF ORGANIC GROWTH. By Dr. G. H. THEODOR EIMER. Translated by J. T. CUNNINGHAM, F.R.S.E., late Fellow of University College, Oxford. 8vo. 12s. 6d.

FEARNLEY.—A MANUAL OF ELEMENTARY PRACTICAL HISTOLOGY. By WILLIAM FEARNLEY. Illustrated. Cr. 8vo. 7s. 6d.

FLOWER and GADOW.—AN INTRODUCTION TO THE OSTEOLOGY OF THE MAMMALIA. By W. H. FLOWER, F.R.S., Director of the Natural History Departments of the British Museum. Illustrated. 3d Ed. Revised with the assistance of HANS GADOW, Ph.D., Lecturer on the Advanced Morphology of Vertebrates in the University of Cambridge. Cr. 8vo. 10s. 6d.

FOSTER.—Works by MICHAEL FOSTER, M.D., F.R.S., Professor of Physiology in the University of Cambridge.

*PRIMER OF PHYSIOLOGY. Illustrated. 18mo. 1s.

A TEXT-BOOK OF PHYSIOLOGY. Illustrated. 5th Ed., largely revised. 8vo. Part I., comprising Book I. Blood—The Tissues of Movement, The Vascular Mechanism. 10s. 6d. Part II., comprising Book II. The Tissues of Chemical Action, with their Respective Mechanisms—Nutrition. 10s. 6d. Part III. The Central Nervous System. 7s. 6d.

FOSTER and BALFOUR.—THE ELEMENTS OF EMBRYOLOGY. By Prof. MICHAEL FOSTER, M.D., F.R.S., and the late F. M. BALFOUR, F.R.S., Professor of Animal Morphology in the University of Cambridge. 2d Ed., revised. Edited by A. SEDGWICK, M.A., Fellow and Assistant Lecturer of Trinity College, Cambridge, and W. HEAPE, M.A., late Demonstrator in the Morphological Laboratory of the University of Cambridge. Illustrated. Cr. 8vo. 10s. 6d.

FOSTER and LANGLEY.—A COURSE OF ELEMENTARY PRACTICAL PHYSIOLOGY AND HISTOLOGY. By Prof. MICHAEL FOSTER, M.D., F.R.S., and J. N. LANGLEY, F.R.S., Fellow of Trinity College, Cambridge. 6th Ed. Cr. 8vo. 7s. 6d.

GAMGEE.—A TEXT-BOOK OF THE PHYSIOLOGICAL CHEMISTRY OF THE ANIMAL BODY. Including an Account of the Chemical Changes occurring in Disease. By A. GAMGEE, M.D., F.R.S. Illustrated. 8vo. Vol. I. 18s.

GOODALE.—PHYSIOLOGICAL BOTANY. I. Outlines of the Histology of Phænogamous Plants. II. Vegetable Physiology. By GEORGE LINCOLN GOODALE, M.A., M.D., Professor of Botany in Harvard University. 8vo. 10s. 6d.

GRAY.—STRUCTURAL BOTANY, OR ORGANOGRAPHY ON THE BASIS OF MORPHOLOGY. To which are added the Principles of Taxonomy and Phytography, and a Glossary of Botanical Terms. By Prof. ASA GRAY, LL.D. 8vo. 10s. 6d.

THE SCIENTIFIC PAPERS OF ASA GRAY. Selected by C. SPRAGUE SARGENT. 2 vols. Vol. I. Reviews of Works on Botany and Related Subjects, 1834-1887. Vol. II. Essays, Biographical Sketches, 1841-1886. 8vo. 21s.

HAMILTON.—A SYSTEMATIC AND PRACTICAL TEXT-BOOK OF PATHOLOGY. By D. J. HAMILTON, F.R.S.E., Professor of Pathological Anatomy in the University of Aberdeen. Illustrated. 8vo. Vol. I. 25s.

HARTIG.—TEXT-BOOK OF THE DISEASES OF TREES. By Dr. ROBERT HARTIG. Translated by WM. SOMERVILLE, B.Sc., D.Œ., Professor of Agriculture and Forestry, Durham College of Science, Newcastle-on-Tyne. Edited, with Introduction, by Prof. H. MARSHALL WARD. 8vo. [In preparation.

HOOKER.—Works by Sir JOSEPH HOOKER, F.R.S., &c.
*PRIMER OF BOTANY. Illustrated. 18mo. 1s.
THE STUDENT'S FLORA OF THE BRITISH ISLANDS. 3d Ed., revised. Gl. 8vo. 10s. 6d.

HOWES.—AN ATLAS OF PRACTICAL ELEMENTARY BIOLOGY. By G. B. HOWES, Assistant Professor of Zoology, Normal School of Science and Royal School of Mines. With a Preface by Prof. T. H. HUXLEY, F.R.S. 4to. 14s.

HUXLEY.—Works by Prof. T. H. HUXLEY, F.R.S.
*INTRODUCTORY PRIMER OF SCIENCE. 18mo. 1s.
*LESSONS IN ELEMENTARY PHYSIOLOGY. Illustrated. Fcap. 8vo. 4s. 6d.
*QUESTIONS ON HUXLEY'S PHYSIOLOGY. By T. ALCOCK, M.D. 18mo. 1s. 6d.

HUXLEY and MARTIN.—A COURSE OF PRACTICAL INSTRUCTION IN ELEMENTARY BIOLOGY. By Prof. T. H. HUXLEY, F.R.S., assisted by H. N. MARTIN, F.R.S., Professor of Biology in the Johns Hopkins University, U.S.A. New Ed., revised and extended by G. B. HOWES and D. H. SCOTT, Ph.D., Assistant Professors, Normal School of Science and Royal School of Mines. With a Preface by T. H. HUXLEY, F.R.S. Cr. 8vo. 10s. 6d.

KLEIN.—Works by E. KLEIN, F.R.S., Lecturer on General Anatomy and Physiology in the Medical School of St. Bartholomew's Hospital, Professor of Bacteriology at the College of State Medicine, London.
MICRO-ORGANISMS AND DISEASE. An Introduction into the Study of Specific Micro-Organisms. Illustrated. 3d Ed., revised. Cr. 8vo. 6s.
THE BACTERIA IN ASIATIC CHOLERA. Cr. 8vo. 5s.

LANG.—TEXT-BOOK OF COMPARATIVE ANATOMY. By Dr. ARNOLD LANG. Professor of Zoology in the University of Zurich. Translated by H. M. BERNARD, M.A., and M BERNARD. Introduction by Prof. E. HAECKEL. 2 vols. Illustrated. 8vo. [In the Press.

LANKESTER.—Works by E. RAY LANKESTER, F.R.S., Linacre Professor of Human and Comparative Anatomy in the University of Oxford.
A TEXT-BOOK OF ZOOLOGY. 8vo. [In preparation.
THE ADVANCEMENT OF SCIENCE. Occasional Essays and Addresses. 8vo. 10s. 6d.

LUBBOCK.—Works by the Right Hon. Sir JOHN LUBBOCK, F.R.S., D.C.L.
THE ORIGIN AND METAMORPHOSES OF INSECTS. Illustrated. Cr. 8vo. 3s. 6d.
ON BRITISH WILD FLOWERS CONSIDERED IN RELATION TO INSECTS. Illustrated. Cr. 8vo. 4s. 6d.

LUBBOCK.—Works by the Right Hon. Sir JOHN LUBBOCK, F.R.S., D.C.L.—*cont.*
FLOWERS, FRUITS, AND LEAVES. Illustrated. 2d Ed. Cr. 8vo. 4s. 6d.
SCIENTIFIC LECTURES. 2d Ed. 8vo. 8s. 6d.
FIFTY YEARS OF SCIENCE. Being the Address delivered at York to the
British Association, August 1881. 5th Ed. Cr. 8vo. 2s. 6d.
MARTIN and MOALE.—ON THE DISSECTION OF VERTEBRATE ANIMALS.
By Prof. H. N MARTIN and W A. MOALE. Cr. 8vo. [*In preparation.*
MIVART.—LESSONS IN ELEMENTARY ANATOMY. By ST. GEORGE MIVART,
F.R.S., Lecturer on Comparative Anatomy at St. Mary's Hospital. Illustrated.
Fcap. 8vo. 6s. 6d.
MÜLLER.—THE FERTILISATION OF FLOWERS. By HERMANN MÜLLER.
Translated and Edited by D'ARCY W. THOMPSON, B.A., Professor of Biology in
University College, Dundee. With a Preface by C. DARWIN, F.R.S. Illus-
trated. 8vo. 21s.
OLIVER.—Works by DANIEL OLIVER, F.R.S., late Professor of Botany in Uni-
versity College, London.
'LESSONS IN ELEMENTARY BOTANY. Illustrated. Fcap. 8vo. 4s. 6d.
FIRST BOOK OF INDIAN BOTANY. Illustrated. Ex. fcap. 8vo. 6s. 6d.
PARKER.—Works by T. JEFFERY PARKER, F.R.S., Professor of Biology in the
University of Otago, New Zealand.
A COURSE OF INSTRUCTION IN ZOOTOMY (VERTEBRATA). Illustrated.
Cr. 8vo. 8s. 6d.
LESSONS IN ELEMENTARY BIOLOGY. Illustrated. Cr. 8vo. 10s. 6d.
PARKER and BETTANY.—THE MORPHOLOGY OF THE SKULL. By Prof.
W. K. PARKER, F.R.S., and G. T. BETTANY. Illustrated. Cr. 8vo. 10s. 6d.
ROMANES.—THE SCIENTIFIC EVIDENCES OF ORGANIC EVOLUTION.
By GEORGE J. ROMANES, F.R.S., Zoological Secretary of the Linnean Society.
Cr. 8vo. 2s. 6d.
SEDGWICK.—TREATISE ON EMBRYOLOGY. By ADAM SEDGWICK, F.R.S.,
Fellow and Lecturer of Trinity College, Cambridge. Illustrated. 8vo.
[*In preparation.*
SHUFELDT.—THE MYOLOGY OF THE RAVEN (*Corvus corax sinuatus*). A
Guide to the Study of the Muscular System in Birds. By R. W. SHUFELDT.
Illustrated. 8vo. 13s. net.
SMITH.—DISEASES OF FIELD AND GARDEN CROPS, CHIEFLY SUCH
AS ARE CAUSED BY FUNGI. By W. G SMITH, F.L.S. Illustrated. Fcap.
8vo. 4s. 6d.
STEWART and CORRY.—A FLORA OF THE NORTH-EAST OF IRELAND.
Including the Phanerogamia, the Cryptogamia Vascularia, and the Muscineæ.
By S. A. STEWART, Curator of the Collections in the Belfast Museum, and the
late T. H. CORRY, M.A., Lecturer on Botany in the University Medical and
Science Schools, Cambridge. Cr. 8vo. 5s. 6d.
WALLACE.—DARWINISM : An Exposition of the Theory of Natural Selection,
with some of its Applications. By ALFRED RUSSEL WALLACE, LL.D., F.R.S.
3d Ed. Cr. 8vo. 9s.
NATURAL SELECTION : AND TROPICAL NATURE. By the same. New
Ed. Cr. 8vo. 6s.
ISLAND LIFE. By the same. New Ed. Cr. 8vo. 6s.
WARD.—TIMBER AND SOME OF ITS DISEASES. By H. MARSHALL WARD,
F.R.S., Professor of Botany in the Royal Indian Engineering College, Cooper's
Hill. Illustrated. Cr. 8vo. 6s.
WIEDERSHEIM.—ELEMENTS OF THE COMPARATIVE ANATOMY OF
VERTEBRATES. By Prof. R. WIEDERSHEIM. Adapted by W. NEWTON
PARKER, Professor of Biology in the University College of South Wales and
Monmouthshire. With Additions. Illustrated. 8vo. 12s. 6d.

MEDICINE.

BLYTH.—A MANUAL OF PUBLIC HEALTH. By A. WYNTER BLYTH, M.R.C.S.
8vo. 17s. net.

BRUNTON.—Works by **T.** LAUDER BRUNTON, M.D., F.R.S., Examiner in Materia Medica in the University of London, in the Victoria University, and in the Royal College of Physicians, London.

A TEXT-BOOK OF PHARMACOLOGY, THERAPEUTICS, AND MATERIA MEDICA. Adapted to the United States Pharmacopœia by F. H. WILLIAMS, M.D., Boston, Mass. 3d Ed. Adapted to the New British Pharmacopœia, 1885, **and** additions, **1891.** 8vo. 21s. Or in 2 Vols. 22s. 6d.

TABLES OF MATERIA MEDICA: **A** Companion to the Materia Medica Museum. Illustrated. Cheaper Issue. 8vo. 5s.

ON THE CONNECTION BETWEEN CHEMICAL CONSTITUTION AND PHYSIOLOGICAL ACTION, BEING AN INTRODUCTION TO MODERN THERAPEUTICS. Croonian Lectures. 8vo. [*In the Press.*

GRIFFITHS.—LESSONS ON PRESCRIPTIONS AND **THE ART** OF PRE-SCRIBING. By W HANDSEL GRIFFITHS. Adapted to the Pharmacopœia, 1885. 18mo. **3s. 6d.**

HAMILTON.—A TEXT-BOOK OF PATHOLOGY, SYSTEMATIC **AND** PRAC-TICAL. By D. **J.** HAMILTON, F.R.S.E., Professor of Pathological Anatomy, University of Aberdeen. Illustrated. Vol. I. 8vo. 25s.

KLEIN.—Works by E. KLEIN, F.R.S., Lecturer on General Anatomy and **Physio-**logy in the Medical School of St. Bartholomew's Hospital, London.

MICRO-ORGANISMS **AND** DISEASE. **An** Introduction into the Study of Specific Micro-Organisms. Illustrated. **3d Ed.,** revised. Cr. 8vo. **6s.**

THE BACTERIA IN ASIATIC CHOLERA. Cr. 8vo. 5s.

WHITE.—A TEXT-BOOK OF GENERAL **THERAPEUTICS.** By W. HALE WHITE, M.D., Senior Assistant Physician to and Lecturer in Materia Medica at Guy's Hospital. Illustrated. Cr. 8vo. **8s. 6d.**

ZIEGLER—MACALISTER.—TEXT-BOOK OF **PATHOLOGICAL ANATOMY** AND PATHOGENESIS. By Prof. E. ZIEGLER. Translated and Edited by DONALD MACALISTER, M.A., M.D., Fellow and Medical Lecturer of St. John's College, Cambridge. Illustrated. 8vo.

Part I.—GENERAL PATHOLOGICAL **ANATOMY.** 2d Ed. 12s. 6d.

Part II.—SPECIAL PATHOLOGICAL ANATOMY. Sections I.-VIII. 2d Ed. **12s.** 6d. Sections IX.-XII. 12s. 6d.

HUMAN SCIENCES.

Mental and Moral Philosophy ; Political Economy ; Law and Politics ; Anthropology ; Education.

MENTAL AND MORAL PHILOSOPHY.

BALDWIN.—HANDBOOK OF PSYCHOLOGY: SENSES AND INTELLECT. By Prof. J. M. BALDWIN, M.A., LL.D. 2d Ed., revised. 8vo. 12s. 6d.

BOOLE.—THE MATHEMATICAL ANALYSIS OF LOGIC. Being an Essay towards a Calculus of Deductive Reasoning. **By** GEORGE BOOLE. 8vo. 5s.

CALDERWOOD.—HANDBOOK OF MORAL PHILOSOPHY. By Rev. HENRY CALDERWOOD, LL.D., Professor of Moral Philosophy in the University of Edinburgh. 14th Ed., largely rewritten. Cr. 8vo. 6s.

CLIFFORD.—SEEING AND THINKING. By the late Prof. W. K. CLIFFORD, F.R.S. With Diagrams. Cr. 8vo. 3s. 6d.

HÖFFDING.—OUTLINES OF **PSYCHOLOGY.** By Prof. H. HÖFFDING. Trans-lated by M. E. LOWNDES. Cr. 8vo. 6s.

JAMES.—THE PRINCIPLES OF PSYCHOLOGY. By WM. JAMES, Professor of Psychology in Harvard University. 2 vols. 8vo. 25s. net.

JARDINE.—THE ELEMENTS OF THE PSYCHOLOGY OF COGNITION. By Rev ROBERT JARDINE, D.Sc. 3d Ed., revised. Cr. 8vo. 6s. 6d.

JEVONS.—Works by W. STANLEY JEVONS, **F.R.S.**

PRIMER OF LOGIC. 18mo. 1s.

ELEMENTARY LESSONS IN LOGIC, Deductive and Inductive, with Copious Questions and Examples, and a Vocabulary of Logical Terms. Fcap. 8vo. 3s. 6d.

THE PRINCIPLES OF SCIENCE. A Treatise on Logic and Scientific Method. New and revised Ed. Cr. 8vo. 12s. 6d.

STUDIES IN DEDUCTIVE LOGIC. 2d **Ed.** Cr. 8vo. 6s.

PURE LOGIC: **AND** OTHER MINOR WORKS. Edited by **R. ADAMSON**, M.A., LL.D., Professor of Logic at Owens College, Manchester, **and HARRIET A.** JEVONS. With a Preface by Prof. ADAMSON. 8vo. 10s. 6d.

KANT—MAX MÜLLER.—CRITIQUE OF PURE REASON. By IMMANUEL KANT. 2 vols. 8vo. 16s. each. Vol. I. HISTORICAL INTRODUCTION, by LUDWIG NOIRÉ; Vol. II. CRITIQUE OF PURE REASON, translated by F. MAX MÜLLER.

KANT—MAHAFFY and BERNARD.—KANT'S CRITICAL PHILOSOPHY FOR ENGLISH READERS. By J. P. MAHAFFY, D.D., Professor of Ancient History in the University of Dublin, and JOHN H. BERNARD, B.D., Fellow of Trinity College, Dublin. A new and complete Edition in 2 vols. Cr. 8vo.

Vol. I. **THE KRITIK** OF PURE REASON EXPLAINED AND DEFENDED. **7s. 6d.**

Vol. II. **THE** PROLEGOMENA. Translated with Notes and Appendices. **6s.**

KEYNES.—FORMAL LOGIC, Studies and Exercises in. Including a Generalisation of Logical Processes in their application to Complex Inferences. By JOHN NEVILLE KEYNES, D.Sc. 2d Ed., revised and enlarged. Cr. 8vo. 10s. 6d.

McCOSH.—Works by JAMES MCCOSH, D.D., President of Princeton College.

PSYCHOLOGY. Cr. 8vo.

I. THE COGNITIVE POWERS. 6s. 6d.

II. THE MOTIVE POWERS. 6s. 6d.

FIRST AND FUNDAMENTAL TRUTHS: being a Treatise on Metaphysics. Ex. cr. 8vo. 9s.

THE PREVAILING TYPES OF PHILOSOPHY. CAN THEY LOGICALLY REACH REALITY? 8vo. 3s. 6d.

MAURICE.—MORAL AND METAPHYSICAL PHILOSOPHY. By F. D. MAURICE, M.A., late Professor of Moral Philosophy in the University of Cambridge. Vol. I.—Ancient Philosophy and the First to the Thirteenth Centuries. Vol. II.—Fourteenth Century and the French Revolution, with a glimpse into the Nineteenth Century. 4th Ed. 2 vols. 8vo. 16s.

RAY.—A TEXT-BOOK OF DEDUCTIVE LOGIC FOR THE USE OF STUDENTS. By P. K. RAY, D.Sc., Professor of Logic and Philosophy, Presidency College, Calcutta. 4th Ed. Globe 8vo. 4s. 6d.

SIDGWICK.—Works by HENRY SIDGWICK, LL.D., D.C.L., Knightbridge Professor of Moral Philosophy in the University of Cambridge.

THE METHODS OF ETHICS. 4th Ed. 8vo. 14s. A Supplement to the 2d Ed., containing all the important Additions and Alterations in the 3d Ed. 8vo. 6s.

OUTLINES OF THE HISTORY OF ETHICS, for English Readers. 2d Ed., revised. Cr. 8vo. 3s. 6d.

VENN.—Works by JOHN VENN, F.R.S., Examiner in Moral Philosophy in the University of London.

THE LOGIC OF CHANCE. An Essay on the Foundations and Province of the Theory of Probability, with special Reference to its Logical Bearings and its Application to Moral and Social Science. 3d Ed., rewritten and greatly enlarged. Cr. 8vo. 10s. 6d.

SYMBOLIC LOGIC. Cr. 8vo. 10s. 6d.

THE PRINCIPLES OF EMPIRICAL OR INDUCTIVE LOGIC. 8vo. 18s.

POLITICAL ECONOMY.

BÖHM-BAWERK.—CAPITAL AND INTEREST. Translated by WILLIAM SMART, M.A. 8vo. 12s. net.

THE POSITIVE THEORY OF CAPITAL. By the same Author and Translator. 8vo. 12s. net.

CAIRNES.—THE CHARACTER AND **LOGICAL METHOD** OF POLITICAL ECONOMY. By J. E. CAIRNES. Cr. 8vo. 6s.
  SOME LEADING PRINCIPLES OF **POLITICAL ECONOMY** NEWLY EXPOUNDED. **By** the same. 8vo. **14s.**

COSSA.—GUIDE **TO** THE STUDY **OF** POLITICAL ECONOMY. **By** Dr. L. COSSA. Translated. With a Preface by W. S. JEVONS, F.R.S. Cr. 8vo. 4s. 6d.

ʻFAWCETT.—POLITICAL ECONOMY FOR BEGINNERS, WITH QUESTIONS. By Mrs. HENRY FAWCETT. 7th Ed. 18mo. 2s. 6d.

FAWCETT.—A MANUAL OF POLITICAL ECONOMY. By the Right Hon. HENRY FAWCETT, F.R.S. 7th Ed., revised. With a Chapter on "State Socialism and the Nationalisation of the Land," and **an** Index. Cr. 8vo. 12s. **6d.**
  AN EXPLANATORY DIGEST of the **above.** By C. A. WATERS, **B.A.** Cr. 8vo. 2s. **6d.**

GILMAN.—PROFIT-SHARING BETWEEN EMPLOYER AND EMPLOYEE. A Study in the Evolution of the Wages System. By N. P. GILMAN. Cr. 8vo. 7s. 6d.

GUNTON.—WEALTH AND PROGRESS: **A Critical Examination of the Wages** Question and its Economic Relation to **Social Reform.** By GEORGE GUNTON. Cr. 8vo. 6s.

HOWELL.—THE CONFLICTS OF CAPITAL AND LABOUR HISTORICALLY AND ECONOMICALLY CONSIDERED. Being a History and Review of the Trade Unions of Great Britain, showing their Origin, Progress, Constitution, and Objects, in their varied Political, Social, Economical, and Industrial Aspects. By GEORGE HOWELL, M.P. 2d Ed., revised. Cr. 8vo. **7s. 6d.**

JEVONS.—Works by W. STANLEY JEVONS, **F.R.S.**
  *PRIMER OF POLITICAL ECONOMY. 18mo. 1s.
  THE THEORY OF POLITICAL ECONOMY. 3d Ed., revised. 8vo. 10s. 6d.

KEYNES.—THE SCOPE AND METHOD OF POLITICAL ECONOMY. By J. N. KEYNES, D.Sc. 7s. net.

MARSHALL.—PRINCIPLES OF **ECONOMICS.** By ALFRED MARSHALL, M.A. 2 vols. 8vo. Vol. I. 2d Ed. **12s. 6d. net.**

MARSHALL.—THE ECONOMICS **OF INDUSTRY.** By A. MARSHALL, M.A., Professor **of** Political Economy **in the University of** Cambridge, and MARY P. MARSHALL. Ex. fcap. 8vo. 2s. **6d.**

PALGRAVE.—**A** DICTIONARY OF POLITICAL ECONOMY. By various Writers. Edited by R. H. INGLIS PALGRAVE, F.R.S. 3s. 6d. each, **net.** No. I. *July* 1891.

PANTALEONI.—MANUAL OF POLITICAL ECONOMY. **By** Prof. M. PANTALEONI. Translated by T. **BOSTON** BRUCE.   [*In preparation.*

SIDGWICK.—**THE** PRINCIPLES OF POLITICAL ECONOMY. By HENRY SIDGWICK, **LL.D.**, D.C.L., Knightbridge **Professor** of Moral Philosophy in the University of Cambridge. 2d Ed., revised. **8vo.** 16s.

SMART.—AN INTRODUCTION TO THE THEORY OF POLITICAL ECONOMY. By WILLIAM SMART, M.A. Crown 8vo.

WALKER.—Works by FRANCIS A. WALKER, M.A.
  FIRST LESSONS IN POLITICAL ECONOMY. Cr. 8vo. 5s.
  A BRIEF TEXT-BOOK OF POLITICAL ECONOMY. Cr. 8vo. **6s. 6d.**
  POLITICAL ECONOMY. 2d Ed., revised and enlarged. 8vo. 12s. 6d.
  THE WAGES QUESTION. Ex. Cr. **8vo.** 8s. 6d. net.
  MONEY. Ex. Cr. 8vo. 8s. 6d. net.

WICKSTEED.—ALPHABET **OF** ECONOMIC SCIENCE. By PHILIP H. WICKSTEED, M.A. Part I. Elements of the Theory of Value or Worth. Gl. 8vo. 2s. 6d.

LAW AND POLITICS.

ADAMS and CUNNINGHAM.—THE SWISS CONFEDERATION. By Sir F. O. ADAMS and C. CUNNINGHAM. 8vo. 14s.

ANGLO-SAXON LAW, ESSAYS ON.—Contents: Anglo-Saxon Law Courts, Land and Family Law, and Legal Procedure. 8vo. 18s.

BALL.—THE STUDENT'S GUIDE TO THE BAR. By WALTER W. R. BALL, M.A., Fellow and Assistant Tutor of Trinity College, Cambridge. 4th Ed., revised. **Cr. 8vo. 2s. 6d.**

BIGELOW.—HISTORY OF PROCEDURE IN ENGLAND FROM THE NORMAN CONQUEST. The Norman Period, 1066-1204. By MELVILLE M. BIGELOW, Ph.D., Harvard University. 8vo. 16s.

BOUTMY.—STUDIES IN CONSTITUTIONAL LAW. By EMILE BOUTMY. Translated by Mrs. DICEY, with Preface by Prof. A. V. DICEY. Cr. 8vo. 6s.
THE ENGLISH CONSTITUTION. By the same. Translated by Mrs. EADEN, with Introduction by Sir F. POLLOCK, Bart. Cr. 8vo. 6s.

BRYCE.—THE AMERICAN COMMONWEALTH. By JAMES BRYCE, M.P., D.C.L., Regius Professor of Civil Law in the University of Oxford. Two Volumes. Ex. cr. 8vo. 25s. Part I. The National Government. Part II. The State Governments. Part III. The Party System. Part IV. Public Opinion. Part V. Illustrations and Reflections. Part VI. Social Institutions.

BUCKLAND.—OUR NATIONAL INSTITUTIONS. A Short Sketch for Schools. By ANNA BUCKLAND. With Glossary. 18mo. 1s.

CHERRY.—LECTURES ON THE GROWTH OF CRIMINAL LAW IN ANCIENT COMMUNITIES. By R. R. CHERRY, LL.D., Reid Professor of Constitutional and Criminal Law in the University of Dublin. 8vo. 5s. net.

DICEY.—INTRODUCTION TO THE STUDY OF THE LAW OF THE CONSTITU-TION By A. V. DICEY, B.C.L., Vinerian Professor of English Law in the University of Oxford. 3d Ed. 8vo. 12s. 6d.

DILKE.—PROBLEMS OF GREATER BRITAIN. By the Right Hon. Sir CHARLES WENTWORTH DILKE. With Maps. 4th Ed. Ex. cr. 8vo. 12s. 6d.

DONISTHORPE.—INDIVIDUALISM: A System of Politics. By WORDSWORTH DONISTHORPE. 8vo. 14s.

ENGLISH CITIZEN, THE.—A Series of Short Books on his Rights and Responsi-bilities. Edited by HENRY CRAIK, LL.D. Cr. 8vo. 3s. 6d. each.
CENTRAL GOVERNMENT. By H. D. TRAILL, D.C.L.
THE ELECTORATE AND THE LEGISLATURE. By SPENCER WALPOLE.
THE POOR LAW. By Rev. T. W. FOWLE, M.A. New Ed. With Appendix.
THE NATIONAL BUDGET; THE NATIONAL DEBT; TAXES AND RATES. By A. J. WILSON.
THE STATE IN RELATION TO LABOUR. By W. STANLEY JEVONS, LL.D.
THE STATE AND THE CHURCH. By the Hon. ARTHUR ELLIOT.
FOREIGN RELATIONS. By SPENCER WALPOLE.
THE STATE IN ITS RELATION TO TRADE. By Sir T. H. FARRER, Bart.
LOCAL GOVERNMENT. By M. D. CHALMERS, M.A.
THE STATE IN ITS RELATION TO EDUCATION. By HENRY CRAIK, LL.D.
THE LAND LAWS. By Sir F. POLLOCK, Bart., Professor of Jurisprudence in the University of Oxford.
COLONIES AND DEPENDENCIES. Part I. INDIA. By J. S. COTTON, M.A. II. THE COLONIES. By E. J. PAYNE, M.A.
JUSTICE AND POLICE. By F. W. MAITLAND.
THE PUNISHMENT AND PREVENTION OF CRIME. By Colonel Sir EDMUND DU CANE, K.C.B., Chairman of Commissioners of Prisons.

FISKE.—CIVIL GOVERNMENT IN THE UNITED STATES CONSIDERED WITH SOME REFERENCE TO ITS ORIGINS. By JOHN FISKE, formerly Lecturer on Philosophy at Harvard University. Cr. 8vo. 6s. 6d.

HOLMES.—THE COMMON LAW. By O. W. HOLMES, Jun. Demy 8vo. 12s.

JENKS.—THE GOVERNMENT OF VICTORIA. By EDWARD JENKS, B.A., LL.B., Professor of Law in the University of Melbourne. [In preparation.

MAITLAND.—PLEAS OF THE CROWN FOR THE COUNTY OF GLOUCESTER BEFORE THE ABBOT OF READING AND HIS FELLOW JUSTICES ITINERANT, IN THE FIFTH YEAR OF THE REIGN OF KING HENRY THE THIRD, AND THE YEAR OF GRACE 1221. By F. W. MAITLAND. 8vo. 7s. 6d.

MUNRO.—COMMERCIAL LAW. By J. E. C. MUNRO, LL.D., Professor of Law and Political Economy in the Owens College, Manchester. [In preparation.

PATERSON.—Works by JAMES PATERSON, Barrister-at-Law.
  COMMENTARIES ON THE LIBERTY OF THE SUBJECT, AND THE LAWS OF ENGLAND RELATING TO THE SECURITY OF THE PERSON. Cheaper **Issue.** Two Vols. Cr. 8vo. 21s.
  THE LIBERTY OF **THE** PRESS, SPEECH, **AND PUBLIC WORSHIP.** Being Commentaries on the Liberty of the Subject and the Laws of England. Cr. 8vo. 12s.
PHILLIMORE.—PRIVATE LAW AMONG THE ROMANS. From the Pandects. By J. G. PHILLIMORE, Q.C. 8vo. **16s.**
POLLOCK.—**ESSAYS** IN JURISPRUDENCE AND ETHICS. By Sir FREDERICK POLLOCK, Bart., **Corpus** Christi Professor of Jurisprudence in the University of Oxford. **8vo. 10s.** 6d.
  INTRODUCTION TO THE HISTORY OF THE SCIENCE OF POLITICS. **By the** same. Cr. 8vo. 2s. 6d.
RICHEY.—THE IRISH LAND LAWS. By ALEX. G. RICHEY, Q.C., Deputy Regius Professor of Feudal English Law in the University of Dublin. Cr. 8vo. 3s. 6d.
SIDGWICK.—THE ELEMENTS OF **POLITICS.** By HENRY SIDGWICK, LL.D. 8vo. 14s. net.
STEPHEN.—Works by Sir J. FITZJAMES STEPHEN, Bart.
  A DIGEST OF THE **LAW OF EVIDENCE.** 5th Ed., revised and enlarged. Cr. 8vo. 6s.
  A DIGEST **OF THE CRIMINAL LAW : CRIMES AND PUNISHMENTS.** 4th Ed., revised. 8vo. 16s.
  A DIGEST OF THE LAW OF CRIMINAL PROCEDURE IN INDICTABLE OFFENCES. By Sir J. F. STEPHEN, Bart., and H. STEPHEN, LL.M., of the Inner Temple, Barrister-at-Law. 8vo. 12s. 6d.
  A HISTORY OF THE CRIMINAL LAW **OF ENGLAND.** Three Vols. 8vo. 48s.
  GENERAL VIEW OF THE CRIMINAL **LAW OF ENGLAND.** 8vo. 14s.

ANTHROPOLOGY.

DAWKINS.—**EARLY** MAN IN BRITAIN AND HIS PLACE IN THE TER-**TIARY PERIOD.** By Prof. W BOYD DAWKINS. Medium 8vo. 25s.
FRAZER.—THE GOLDEN BOUGH. **A Study in Comparative Religion.** By J. G. FRAZER, M.A., Fellow of Trinity College, Cambridge. 2 vols. 8vo. 28s.
M'LENNAN.—THE PATRIARCHAL THEORY. Based on the papers of the late JOHN F. M'LENNAN. Edited by DONALD M'LENNAN, M.A., Barrister-at-Law. 8vo. 14s.
  STUDIES IN ANCIENT HISTORY. By the same. Comprising a Reprint of "Primitive Marriage." An inquiry into the origin of the form of capture in Marriage Ceremonies. 8vo. **16s.**
TYLOR.—ANTHROPOLOGY. An Introduction to the Study of Man and Civilisation. By E. B. TYLOR, F.R.S. Illustrated. Cr. 8vo. 7s. 6d.
WESTERMARCK.—THE HISTORY OF HUMAN MARRIAGE. By Dr. EDWARD WESTERMARCK. With Preface by A. R. WALLACE. 8vo. 14s. net.
WILSON.—THE RIGHT HAND LEFT-HANDEDNESS. By Sir D. WILSON. Cr. 8vo. 4s. 6d.

EDUCATION.

ARNOLD.—REPORTS ON ELEMENTARY SCHOOLS. 1852-1882. By MATTHEW ARNOLD, D.C.L. Edited by the Right Hon. Sir FRANCIS SANDFORD, K.C.B. **Cheaper Issue.** Cr. 8vo. 3s. 6d.
  HIGHER **SCHOOLS AND** UNIVERSITIES IN GERMANY. By the same. Crown 8vo. **6s.**
BALL.—THE STUDENT'S GUIDE TO THE BAR. By WALTER W. R. BALL, M.A., Fellow and Assistant Tutor of Trinity College, Cambridge. 4th Ed., revised. Cr. 8vo. 2s. 6d.

*BLAKISTON.—THE TEACHER. Hints on School Management. A Handbook for Managers, Teachers' Assistants, and Pupil Teachers. By J. R. BLAKISTON. Cr 8vo. 2s. 6d. (Recommended by the London, Birmingham, and Leicester School Boards.)

CALDERWOOD.—ON TEACHING. By Prof. HENRY CALDERWOOD. New Ed. Ex. fcap. 8vo. 2s. 6d.

FEARON —SCHOOL INSPECTION. By D. R. FEARON. 6th Ed. Cr. 8vo. 2s. 6d.

FITCH.—NOTES ON AMERICAN SCHOOLS AND TRAINING COLLEGES. Reprinted from the Report of the English Education Department for 1888-89, with permission of the Controller of H.M.'s Stationery Office. By J. G. FITCH, M.A. Gl. 8vo. 2s. 6d.

GEIKIE.—THE TEACHING OF GEOGRAPHY. A Practical Handbook for the use of Teachers. By Sir ARCHIBALD GEIKIE, F R.S., Director-General of the Geological Survey of the United Kingdom. Cr. 8vo. 2s.

GLADSTONE.—SPELLING REFORM FROM A NATIONAL POINT OF VIEW. By J. H. GLADSTONE. Cr. 8vo. 1s. 6d.

HERTEL.—OVERPRESSURE IN HIGH SCHOOLS IN DENMARK. By Dr. HERTEL. Translated by C. G. SÖRENSEN. With Introduction by Sir J. CRICHTON-BROWNE, F.R.S. Cr. 8vo. 3s. 6d.

TODHUNTER.—THE CONFLICT OF STUDIES. By ISAAC TODHUNTER, F.R.S. 8vo. 10s. 6d.

TECHNICAL KNOWLEDGE.

(See also MECHANICS, LAW, and MEDICINE.)

Civil and Mechanical Engineering; Military and Naval Science; Agriculture; Domestic Economy; Book-Keeping; Commerce.

CIVIL AND MECHANICAL ENGINEERING.

ALEXANDER and THOMSON.—ELEMENTARY APPLIED MECHANICS. By T. ALEXANDER, Professor of Civil Engineering, Trinity College, Dublin, and A. W. THOMSON, Professor at College of Science, Poona, India. Part II. TRANSVERSE STRESS. Cr. 8vo. 10s. 6d.

CHALMERS.—GRAPHICAL DETERMINATION OF FORCES IN ENGINEERING STRUCTURES. By J. B. CHALMERS, C.E. Illustrated. 8vo. 24s.

COTTERILL.—APPLIED MECHANICS: An Elementary General Introduction to the Theory of Structures and Machines. By J. H. COTTERILL, F.R.S., Professor of Applied Mechanics in the Royal Naval College, Greenwich. 2d Ed. 8vo. 18s.

COTTERILL and SLADE.—LESSONS IN APPLIED MECHANICS. By Prof. J. H. COTTERILL and J. H. SLADE. Fcap. 8vo. 5s. 6d.

GRAHAM.—GEOMETRY OF POSITION. By R. H. GRAHAM. Cr. 8vo. 7s. 6d.

KENNEDY.—THE MECHANICS OF MACHINERY. By A. B. W. KENNEDY, F.R.S. Illustrated. Cr. 8vo. 12s. 6d.

WHITHAM.—STEAM-ENGINE DESIGN. For the Use of Mechanical Engineers, Students, and Draughtsmen. By J. M. WHITHAM, Professor of Engineering, Arkansas Industrial University. Illustrated. 8vo. 25s.

YOUNG.—SIMPLE PRACTICAL METHODS OF CALCULATING STRAINS ON GIRDERS, ARCHES, AND TRUSSES. With a Supplementary Essay on Economy in Suspension Bridges. By E. W. YOUNG, C.E. With Diagrams. 8vo. 7s. 6d.

MILITARY AND NAVAL SCIENCE.

AITKEN.—THE GROWTH OF THE RECRUIT AND YOUNG SOLDIER. With a view to the selection of "Growing Lads" for the Army, and a Regulated System of Training for Recruits. By Sir W. AITKEN, F.R.S., Professor of Pathology in the Army Medical School. Cr. 8vo. 8s. 6d.

ARMY PRELIMINARY EXAMINATION, 1882-1890, Specimens of Papers set at the. With Answers to the Mathematical Questions. Subjects : Arithmetic, Algebra, Euclid, Geometrical Drawing, Geography, French, English Dictation. Cr. 8vo. 3s. 6d.

MATTHEWS.—MANUAL OF LOGARITHMS. By G. F. MATTHEWS, B.A. 8vo. 5s. net.

MAURICE.—WAR. By FREDERICK MAURICE, Colonel C.B., R.A. 8vo. 5s. net.

MERCUR.—ELEMENTS OF THE ART OF WAR. Prepared for the use of Cadets of the United States Military Academy. By JAMES MERCUR, Professor of Civil Engineering at the United States Academy, West Point, New York. 2d Ed., revised and corrected. 8vo. 17s.

PALMER.—TEXT-BOOK OF PRACTICAL LOGARITHMS AND TRIGONO-METRY. By J. H. PALMER, Head Schoolmaster, R.N., H.M.S. Cambridge, Devonport. Gl. 8vo. 4s. 6d.

ROBINSON.—TREATISE ON MARINE SURVEYING. Prepared for the use of younger Naval Officers. With Questions for Examinations and Exercises principally from the Papers of the Royal Naval College. With the results. By Rev. JOHN L. ROBINSON, Chaplain and Instructor in the Royal Naval College, Greenwich. Illustrated. Cr. 8vo. 7s. 6d.

SANDHURST MATHEMATICAL PAPERS, for Admission into the Royal Military College, 1881-1889. Edited by E. J BROOKSMITH, B.A., Instructor in Mathematics at the Royal Military Academy, Woolwich. Cr. 8vo. 3s. 6d.

SHORTLAND.—NAUTICAL SURVEYING. By the late Vice-Admiral SHORTLAND, LL.D. 8vo. 21s.

THOMSON.—POPULAR LECTURES AND ADDRESSES. By Sir WILLIAM THOMSON, LL.D., P.R.S. In 3 vols. Illustrated. Cr. 8vo. Vol. III. Navigation. 7s. 6d.

WILKINSON.—THE BRAIN OF AN ARMY. A Popular Account of the German General Staff. By SPENSER WILKINSON. Cr. 8vo. 2s. 6d.

WOLSELEY.—Works by General Viscount WOLSELEY, G.C.M.G.
THE SOLDIER'S POCKET-BOOK FOR FIELD SERVICE. 5th Ed., revised and enlarged. 16mo. Roan. 5s.
FIELD POCKET-BOOK FOR THE AUXILIARY FORCES. 16mo. 1s. 6d.

WOOLWICH MATHEMATICAL PAPERS, for Admission into the Royal Military Academy, Woolwich, 1880-1888 inclusive. Edited by E. J BROOKSMITH, B.A., Instructor in Mathematics at the Royal Military Academy, Woolwich. Cr. 8vo. 6s.

AGRICULTURE.

FRANKLAND.—AGRICULTURAL CHEMICAL ANALYSIS, A Handbook of. By PERCY F. FRANKLAND, F.R.S., Professor of Chemistry, University College, Dundee. Founded upon Leitfaden für die Agriculture Chemiche Analyse, von Dr. F. KROCKER. Cr. 8vo. 7s. 6d.

HARTIG.—TEXT-BOOK OF THE DISEASES OF TREES. By Dr. ROBERT HARTIG. Translated by WM. SOMERVILLE, B.Sc., D.Œ., Professor of Agriculture and Forestry, Durham College of Science, Newcastle-on-Tyne. Edited, with Introduction, by Prof. H. MARSHALL WARD. 8vo. [In preparation.

LASLETT.—TIMBER AND TIMBER TREES, NATIVE AND FOREIGN. By THOMAS LASLETT. Cr. 8vo. 8s. 6d.

SMITH.—DISEASES OF FIELD AND GARDEN CROPS, CHIEFLY SUCH AS ARE CAUSED BY FUNGI. By WORTHINGTON G. SMITH, F.L.S. Illustrated. Fcap. 8vo. 4s. 6d.

TANNER.—*ELEMENTARY LESSONS IN THE SCIENCE OF AGRICULTURAL PRACTICE. By HENRY TANNER, F.C.S., M.R.A.C., Examiner in the Principles of Agriculture under the Government Department of Science. Fcap. 8vo. 3s. 6d.
*FIRST PRINCIPLES OF AGRICULTURE. By the same. 18mo. 1s.
THE PRINCIPLES OF AGRICULTURE. By the same. A Series of Reading Books for use in Elementary Schools. Ex. fcap. 8vo.
*I. The Alphabet of the Principles of Agriculture. 6d.
*II. Further Steps in the Principles of Agriculture. 1s.
*III. Elementary School Readings on the Principles of Agriculture for the third stage. 1s.

WARD.—TIMBER AND SOME OF ITS DISEASES. By H. MARSHALL WARD, M.A., F.L.S., F.R.S., Fellow of Christ's College, Cambridge, Professor of Botany at the Royal Indian Engineering College, Cooper's Hill. With Illustrations. Cr. 8vo. 6s.

DOMESTIC ECONOMY.

*BARKER.—FIRST LESSONS IN THE PRINCIPLES OF COOKING. By LADY BARKER. 18mo. 1s.

*BERNERS.—FIRST LESSONS ON HEALTH. By J. BERNERS. 18mo. 1s.

*COOKERY BOOK.—THE MIDDLE CLASS COOKERY BOOK. Edited by the Manchester School of Domestic Cookery. Fcap. 8vo. 1s. 6d.

CRAVEN.—A GUIDE TO DISTRICT NURSES. By Mrs. DACRE CRAVEN (née FLORENCE SARAH LEES), Hon. Associate of the Order of St. John of Jerusalem, etc. Cr. 8vo. 2s. 6d.

FREDERICK.—HINTS TO HOUSEWIVES ON SEVERAL POINTS, PARTICULARLY ON THE PREPARATION OF ECONOMICAL AND TASTEFUL DISHES. By Mrs. FREDERICK. Cr. 8vo. 1s.

*GRAND'HOMME.—CUTTING-OUT AND DRESSMAKING. From the French of Mdlle. E. GRAND'HOMME. With Diagrams. 18mo. 1s.

JEX-BLAKE.—THE CARE OF INFANTS. A Manual for Mothers and Nurses. By SOPHIA JEX-BLAKE, M.D., Lecturer on Hygiene at the London School of Medicine for Women. 18mo. 1s.

RATHBONE.—THE HISTORY AND PROGRESS OF DISTRICT NURSING FROM ITS COMMENCEMENT IN THE YEAR 1859 TO THE PRESENT DATE, including the foundation by the Queen of the Queen Victoria Jubilee Institute for Nursing the Poor in their own Homes. By WILLIAM RATHBONE, M.P. Cr. 8vo. 2s. 6d.

*TEGETMEIER.—HOUSEHOLD MANAGEMENT AND COOKERY. With an Appendix of Recipes used by the Teachers of the National School of Cookery. By W. B. TEGETMEIER. Compiled at the request of the School Board for London. 18mo. 1s.

*WRIGHT.—THE SCHOOL COOKERY-BOOK. Compiled and Edited by C. E. GUTHRIE WRIGHT, Hon. Sec. to the Edinburgh School of Cookery. 18mo. 1s.

BOOK-KEEPING.

*THORNTON.—FIRST LESSONS IN BOOK-KEEPING. By J. THORNTON. Cr. 8vo. 2s. 6d. KEY. Oblong 4to. 10s. 6d.

*PRIMER OF BOOK-KEEPING. By the same. 18mo. 1s. KEY. 8vo. 2s. 6d.

COMMERCE.

MACMILLAN'S ELEMENTARY COMMERCIAL CLASS BOOKS. Edited by JAMES GOW, Litt.D., Headmaster of Nottingham School. Globe 8vo.

The following volumes are arranged for :—

*THE HISTORY OF COMMERCE IN EUROPE. By H. DE B. GIBBINS, M.A. 3s. 6d. [Ready.

COMMERCIAL GERMAN. By F. C. SMITH, B.A., formerly scholar of Magdalene College, Cambridge. [In the Press.

COMMERCIAL GEOGRAPHY. By E. C. K. GONNER, M.A., Professor of Political Economy in University College, Liverpool. [In preparation.

COMMERCIAL FRENCH.

COMMERCIAL ARITHMETIC. By A. W. SUNDERLAND, M.A., late Scholar of Trinity College, Cambridge; Fellow of the Institute of Actuaries. [In prep.

COMMERCIAL LAW. By J. E. C. MUNRO, LL.D., Professor of Law and Political Economy in the Owens College, Manchester.

GEOGRAPHY.

(See also PHYSICAL GEOGRAPHY.)

BARTHOLOMEW.—*THE ELEMENTARY SCHOOL ATLAS. By John Bar-
THOLOMEW, F.R.G.S. 4to. 1s.

*MACMILLAN'S SCHOOL ATLAS, PHYSICAL AND POLITICAL. Consisting
of 80 Maps and complete Index. By the same. Prepared for the use of
Senior Pupils. Royal 4to. 8s. 6d. Half-morocco. 10s. 6d.

THE LIBRARY REFERENCE ATLAS OF THE WORLD. By the same.
A Complete Series of 84 Modern Maps. With Geographical Index to 100,000
places. Half-morocco. Gilt edges. Folio. £2:12:6 net. Also issued in
parts, 5s. each net. Geographical Index, 7s. 6d. net. Part I., April 1891.

*CLARKE.—CLASS-BOOK OF GEOGRAPHY. By C. B. CLARKE, F.R.S. New
Ed., revised 1889, with 18 Maps. Fcap. 8vo. 3s. Sewed, 2s. 6d.

GEIKIE.—Works by Sir ARCHIBALD GEIKIE, F.R.S., Director-General of the Geological Survey of the United Kingdom.

*THE TEACHING OF GEOGRAPHY. A Practical Handbook for the use of
Teachers. Cr. 8vo. 2s.

*GEOGRAPHY OF THE BRITISH ISLES. 18mo. 1s.

*GREEN.—A SHORT GEOGRAPHY OF THE BRITISH ISLANDS. By John
RICHARD GREEN and A. S. GREEN. With Maps. Fcap. 8vo. 3s. 6d.

*GROVE.—A PRIMER OF GEOGRAPHY. By Sir GEORGE GROVE, D.C.L.
Illustrated. 18mo. 1s.

KIEPERT.—A MANUAL OF ANCIENT GEOGRAPHY. By Dr. H. KIEPERT.
Cr. 8vo. 5s.

MACMILLAN'S GEOGRAPHICAL SERIES.— Edited by Sir ARCHIBALD GEIKIE,
F.R.S., Director-General of the Geological Survey of the United Kingdom.

*THE TEACHING OF GEOGRAPHY. A Practical Handbook for the Use of
Teachers. By Sir ARCHIBALD GEIKIE, F.R.S. Cr. 8vo. 2s.

*MAPS AND MAP-DRAWING. By W. A. ELDERTON. 18mo. 1s.

*GEOGRAPHY OF THE BRITISH ISLES. By Sir A. GEIKIE, F.R.S. 18mo. 1s.

*AN ELEMENTARY CLASS-BOOK OF GENERAL GEOGRAPHY. By H. R.
MILL, D.Sc., Lecturer on Physiography and on Commercial Geography in
the Heriot-Watt College, Edinburgh. Illustrated. Cr. 8vo. 3s. 6d.

*GEOGRAPHY OF EUROPE. By J. SIME, M.A. Illustrated. Gl. 8vo. 3s.

*ELEMENTARY GEOGRAPHY OF INDIA, BURMA, AND CEYLON. By H.
F. BLANFORD, F.G.S. Gl. 8vo. 2s. 6d.

GEOGRAPHY OF NORTH AMERICA. By Prof. N. S. SHALER. [In preparation.

GEOGRAPHY OF THE BRITISH COLONIES. By G. M. DAWSON and A.
SUTHERLAND. [In the Press.

STRACHEY.—LECTURES ON GEOGRAPHY. By General RICHARD STRACHEY,
R.E. Cr. 8vo. 4s. 6d.

*TOZER.—A PRIMER OF CLASSICAL GEOGRAPHY. By H. F. TOZER, M.A.
18mo. 1s.

HISTORY.

ARNOLD.—THE SECOND PUNIC WAR. Being Chapters from THE HISTORY
OF ROME, by the late THOMAS ARNOLD, D.D., Headmaster of Rugby. Edited,
with Notes, by W. T. ARNOLD, M.A. With 8 Maps. Cr. 8vo. 5s.

ARNOLD.—A HISTORY OF THE EARLY ROMAN EMPIRE. By W. T.
ARNOLD, M.A. Cr. 8vo. [In preparation.

*BEESLY.—STORIES FROM THE HISTORY OF ROME. By Mrs. BEESLY.
Fcap. 8vo. 2s. 6d.

BRYCE.—Works by JAMES BRYCE, M.P., D.C.L., Regius Professor of Civil Law
in the University of Oxford.

THE HOLY ROMAN EMPIRE. 9th Ed. **Cr.** 8vo. **7s. 6d.**
  . Also a *Library Edition.* Demy 8vo. **14s.**
THE AMERICAN COMMONWEALTH. **2 vols. Ex. cr. 8vo. 25s.** Part I.
  The National Government. Part II. The State Governments. Part III.
  The Party System. Part IV. Public Opinion. Part V. Illustrations and
  Reflections. Part VI. Social Institutions.
*BUCKLEY.—A HISTORY OF ENGLAND FOR BEGINNERS. By ARABELLA
  B. BUCKLEY. With Maps and Tables. Gl. 8vo. 3s.
BURY.—A HISTORY OF THE LATER ROMAN EMPIRE FROM ARCADIUS
  TO IRENE, A.D. 395-800. By JOHN B. BURY, M.A., Fellow of Trinity College,
  Dublin. 2 vols. 8vo. 32s.
CASSEL.—MANUAL OF JEWISH HISTORY **AND** LITERATURE. **By Dr. D.**
  CASSEL. Translated by Mrs. HENRY LUCAS. **Fcap.** 8vo. 2s. 6d.
ENGLISH STATESMEN, TWELVE. Cr. 8vo. 2s. 6d. each.
  WILLIAM THE CONQUEROR. By EDWARD A. FREEMAN, D.C.L., **LL.D.**
  HENRY II. By Mrs. J. R. GREEN.
  EDWARD I. By F. YORK POWELL. [*In preparation.*
  HENRY VII. By JAMES GAIRDNER.
  CARDINAL WOLSEY. By Bishop CREIGHTON.
  ELIZABETH. By E. S. BEESLY. [*In preparation.*
  OLIVER CROMWELL. By FREDERIC HARRISON.
  WILLIAM III. By H. D. TRAILL.
  WALPOLE. By JOHN MORLEY.
  CHATHAM. By JOHN MORLEY. [*In preparation.*
  PITT. By JOHN MORLEY. [*In preparation.*
  PEEL. By J. R. THURSFIELD.
FISKE.—Works by JOHN FISKE, formerly Lecturer on Philosophy at Harvard
  University.
  THE CRITICAL PERIOD **IN AMERICAN HISTORY,** 1783-1789. Ex. cr.
  8vo. 10s. 6d.
  THE BEGINNINGS OF NEW ENGLAND; or, The Puritan Theocracy in its
  Relations to Civil and Religious Liberty. Cr. 8vo. 7s. 6d.
  THE AMERICAN REVOLUTION. 2 vols. Cr. 8vo. 18s.
FREEMAN.—Works by EDWARD A. FREEMAN, D.C.L., Regius Professor of Modern
  History in the University of Oxford, etc.
  *OLD ENGLISH HISTORY. With Maps. Ex. fcap. 8vo. 6s.
  A SCHOOL HISTORY OF ROME. Cr. 8vo. [*In preparation.*
  METHODS OF HISTORICAL STUDY. 8vo. 10s. 6d.
  THE **CHIEF** PERIODS OF EUROPEAN HISTORY. Six Lectures. With an
  Essay on **Greek** Cities under Roman Rule. 8vo. 10s. 6d.
  HISTORICAL **ESSAYS.** First Series. 4th Ed. 8vo. 10s. 6d.
  HISTORICAL **ESSAYS.** Second Series. 3d Ed., with additional Essays. 8vo.
  10s. 6d.
  HISTORICAL **ESSAYS. Third** Series. 8vo. 12s.
  THE GROWTH OF THE ENGLISH CONSTITUTION FROM THE EARLIEST
  TIMES. 4th Ed. Cr. 8vo. 5s.
  *GENERAL SKETCH OF EUROPEAN HISTORY. Enlarged, with Maps, etc.
  18mo. 3s. 6d.
  *PRIMER OF EUROPEAN HISTORY. 18mo. 1s. (*History Primers.*)
FRIEDMANN.—ANNE BOLEYN. A Chapter of **English History,** 1527-1536. By
  PAUL FRIEDMANN. 2 vols. 8vo. 28s.
*GIBBINS.—THE HISTORY OF COMMERCE IN EUROPE. **By** H. de B.
  GIBBINS, M.A. With Maps. Globe 8vo. 3s. 6d.
GREEN.—Works by JOHN RICHARD GREEN, LL.D., late Honorary Fellow of
  Jesus College, Oxford.
  *A SHORT HISTORY OF THE ENGLISH PEOPLE. New and Revised Ed.
  With Maps, Genealogical Tables, and Chronological Annals. Cr. 8vo. 8s. 6d.
  159th Thousand.
  *Also the same in **Four** Parts. With the corresponding portion of Mr. Tait's
  "Analysis." Crown 8vo. 3s. each. Part I. 607-1265. Part II. 1204-1553.
  Part III. 1540-1689 Part IV. 1660-1873.

HISTORY OF THE ENGLISH PEOPLE. In four vols. 8vo. 16s. each.
Vol. I.—Early England, 449-1071; Foreign Kings, 1071-1214; The Charter, 1214-1291; The Parliament, 1307-1461. With 8 Maps.
Vol. II.—The Monarchy, 1461-1540; The Reformation, 1540-1603.
Vol. III.—Puritan England, 1603-1660; The Revolution, 1660-1688. With four Maps.
Vol. IV.—The Revolution, **1688-1760; Modern England, 1760-1815.** With Maps and Index.
THE MAKING OF ENGLAND. With Maps. 8vo. 16s.
THE CONQUEST OF **ENGLAND.** With Maps and Portrait. 8vo. 18s.
*ANALYSIS OF ENGLISH HISTORY, based on Green's "Short History of the English People." By C. W. A. TAIT, M.A., Assistant Master at Clifton College. Revised and Enlarged Ed. Crown 8vo. 4s. 6d.
*READINGS FROM ENGLISH HISTORY. Selected and Edited by JOHN RICHARD GREEN. Three Parts. Gl. 8vo. 1s. 6d. each. I. Hengist to Cressy. II. Cressy to Cromwell. III. Cromwell to Balaklava.
GUEST.—LECTURES ON THE **HISTORY** OF ENGLAND. **By M. J. GUEST.** With Maps. Cr. 8vo. 6s.
*HISTORICAL COURSE FOR SCHOOLS.—Edited by E. A. FREEMAN, D.C.L., Regius Professor of Modern History in the University of Oxford. 18mo.
GENERAL SKETCH OF EUROPEAN HISTORY. By E. A. FREEMAN, D.C.L. New Ed., revised and enlarged. With Chronological Table, Maps, and Index. 3s. 6d.
HISTORY OF ENGLAND. **By EDITH THOMPSON. New Ed., revised and enlarged.** With Coloured Maps. 2s. 6d.
HISTORY OF SCOTLAND. By MARGARET MACARTHUR. 2s.
HISTORY OF **ITALY.** By Rev. W. HUNT, M.A. New Ed. With Coloured Maps. 3s. 6d.
HISTORY OF GERMANY. By J. SIME, M.A. **New** Ed., revised. **3s.**
HISTORY OF AMERICA. By JOHN A. DOYLE. With Maps. 4s. 6d.
HISTORY OF EUROPEAN COLONIES. By E. J. PAYNE, M.A. **With Maps. 4s. 6d.**
HISTORY OF FRANCE. By CHARLOTTE M. YONGE. With Maps. 3s. 6d.
HISTORY OF GREECE. By EDWARD A. FREEMAN, D.C.L. [In preparation.
HISTORY OF ROME. By EDWARD A. FREEMAN, D.C.L. [In preparation.
*HISTORY PRIMERS.—Edited by JOHN RICHARD GREEN, LL.D. 18mo. 1s. each.
ROME. By Bishop CREIGHTON. Maps.
GREECE. By C. A. FYFFE, M.A., late Fellow of University College, Oxford. Maps.
EUROPE. By E. A. FREEMAN, D.C.L. Maps.
FRANCE. By CHARLOTTE M. YONGE.
GREEK ANTIQUITIES. By Rev. J. P. MAHAFFY, D.D. Illustrated.
CLASSICAL GEOGRAPHY. By H. F. TOZER, M.A.
GEOGRAPHY. By Sir G. GROVE, D.C.L. Maps.
ROMAN ANTIQUITIES. By Prof. WILKINS, Litt.D. Illustrated.

ANALYSIS OF ENGLISH HISTORY. By Prof. T. F. TOUT, M.A.
INDIAN HISTORY: ASIATIC AND EUROPEAN. By J. TALBOYS WHEELER.
HOLE.—A GENEALOGICAL STEMMA OF THE KINGS OF ENGLAND AND FRANCE. By Rev. C. HOLE. On Sheet. 1s.
JENNINGS.—CHRONOLOGICAL TABLES. A synchronistic arrangement of the events of Ancient History (with an Index). By Rev. ARTHUR C. JENNINGS. 8vo. 5s.
LABBERTON.—NEW HISTORICAL ATLAS AND GENERAL HISTORY. By R. H. LABBERTON. 4to. New Ed., revised and enlarged. 15s.
LETHBRIDGE.—A SHORT MANUAL OF THE HISTORY OF INDIA. With an Account of INDIA AS IT IS. The Soil, Climate, and Productions; the People, their Races, Religions, Public Works, and Industries; the Civil Services, and System of Administration. By Sir ROPER LETHBRIDGE, Fellow of the Calcutta University. With Maps. Cr. 8vo. 5s.

D

MAHAFFY.—GREEK LIFE AND THOUGHT FROM THE AGE OF ALEX-
ANDER TO THE ROMAN CONQUEST. By Rev. J. P. MAHAFFY, D.D.,
Fellow of Trinity College, Dublin. Cr. 8vo. 12s. 6d.
THE GREEK WORLD UNDER ROMAN SWAY. From Plutarch to Polybius.
By the same Author. Cr. 8vo. 10s. 6d.

MARRIOTT.—THE MAKERS OF MODERN ITALY: MAZZINI, CAVOUR, GARI-
BALDI. Three Lectures. By J. A. R. MARRIOTT, M.A., Lecturer in Modern
History and Political Economy, Oxford. Cr. 8vo. 1s. 6d.

MICHELET.—A SUMMARY OF MODERN HISTORY. By M. Michelet. Translated by M. C. M. SIMPSON. Gl. 8vo. 4s. 6d.

NORGATE.—ENGLAND UNDER THE ANGEVIN KINGS. By KATE NORGATE.
With Maps and Plans. 2 vols. 8vo. 32s.

OTTÉ.—SCANDINAVIAN HISTORY. By E. C. OTTÉ. With Maps. Gl. 8vo. 6s.

SEELEY.—Works by J. R. SEELEY, M.A., Regius Professor of Modern History in
the University of Cambridge.
THE EXPANSION OF ENGLAND. Crown 8vo. 4s. 6d.
OUR COLONIAL EXPANSION. Extracts from the above. Cr. 8vo. Sewed. 1s.

*TAIT.—ANALYSIS OF ENGLISH HISTORY, based on Green's "Short
History of the English People." By C. W. A. TAIT, M.A., Assistant Master
at Clifton. Revised and Enlarged Ed. Cr. 8vo. 4s. 6d.

WHEELER.—Works by J. TALBOYS WHEELER.
*A PRIMER OF INDIAN HISTORY. Asiatic and European. 18mo. 1s.
*COLLEGE HISTORY OF INDIA, ASIATIC AND EUROPEAN. With Maps.
Cr. 8vo. 3s. ; sewed, 2s. 6d.
A SHORT HISTORY OF INDIA AND OF THE FRONTIER STATES OF
AFGHANISTAN, NEPAUL, AND BURMA. With Maps. Cr. 8vo. 12s.

YONGE.—Works by CHARLOTTE M. YONGE.
CAMEOS FROM ENGLISH HISTORY. Ex. fcap. 8vo. 5s. each. (1)
FROM ROLLO TO EDWARD II. (2) THE WARS IN FRANCE. (3)
THE WARS OF THE ROSES. (4) REFORMATION TIMES. (5) ENG-
LAND AND SPAIN. (6) FORTY YEARS OF STUART RULE (1603–1643).
(7) REBELLION AND RESTORATION (1642–1678).
EUROPEAN HISTORY. Narrated in a Series of Historical Selections from the
Best Authorities. Edited and arranged by E. M. SEWELL and C. M. YONGE.
Cr. 8vo. First Series, 1003–1154. 6s. Second Series, 1088–1228. 6s.
THE VICTORIAN HALF CENTURY—A JUBILEE BOOK. With a New
Portrait of the Queen. Cr. 8vo. Paper covers, 1s. Cloth, 1s. 6d.

ART.

*ANDERSON.—LINEAR PERSPECTIVE AND MODEL DRAWING. A School
and Art Class Manual, with Questions and Exercises for Examination, and
Examples of Examination Papers. By LAURENCE ANDERSON. Illustrated.
8vo. 2s.

COLLIER.—A PRIMER OF ART. By the Hon. JOHN COLLIER. Illustrated.
18mo. 1s.

COOK.—THE NATIONAL GALLERY, A POPULAR HANDBOOK TO. By
EDWARD T. COOK, with a preface by JOHN RUSKIN, LL.D., and Selections
from his Writings. 3d Ed. Cr. 8vo. Half-morocco, 14s.
⁎ Also an Edition on large paper, limited to 250 copies. 2 vols. 8vo.

DELAMOTTE.—A BEGINNER'S DRAWING BOOK. By P. H. DELAMOTTE,
F.S.A. Progressively arranged. New Ed., improved. Cr. 8vo. 3s. 6d.

ELLIS.—SKETCHING FROM NATURE. A Handbook for Students and
Amateurs. By TRISTRAM J. ELLIS. Illustrated by H. STACY MARKS, R.A.,
and the Author. New Ed., revised and enlarged. Cr. 8vo. 3s. 6d.

GROVE.—A DICTIONARY OF MUSIC AND MUSICIANS. A.D. 1450–1889.
Edited by Sir GEORGE GROVE, D.C.L. In four vols. 8vo. Price 21s. each.
Also in Parts.
Parts I.–XIV., Parts XIX.–XXII., 3s. 6d. each. Parts XV., XVI., 7s.
Parts XVII., XVIII., 7s. Parts XXIII.–XXV. (Appendix), 9s.

A COMPLETE INDEX TO THE ABOVE. By Mrs. E. WODEHOUSE. 8vo. 7s. 6d.

HUNT.—TALKS ABOUT ART. By WILLIAM HUNT. With a Letter from Sir J. E. MILLAIS, Bart., R.A. Cr. 8vo. 3s. 6d.

MELDOLA.—THE CHEMISTRY OF PHOTOGRAPHY. By RAPHAEL MELDOLA, F.R.S., Professor of Chemistry in the Technical College, Finsbury. Cr. 8vo. 6s.

TAYLOR.—A PRIMER OF PIANOFORTE-PLAYING. By FRANKLIN TAYLOR. Edited by Sir GEORGE GROVE. 18mo. 1s.

TAYLOR.—A SYSTEM OF SIGHT-SINGING FROM THE ESTABLISHED MUSICAL NOTATION; based on the Principle of Tonic Relation, and illustrated by Extracts from the Works of the Great Masters. By SEDLEY TAYLOR. 8vo. 5s. net.

TYRWHITT.—OUR SKETCHING CLUB. Letters and Studies on Landscape Art. By Rev. R. ST. JOHN TYRWHITT. With an authorised Reproduction of the Lessons and Woodcuts in Prof. Ruskin's "Elements of Drawing." 5th Ed. Cr. 8vo. 7s. 6d.

DIVINITY.

ABBOTT.—BIBLE LESSONS. By Rev. EDWIN A. ABBOTT, D.D. Cr. 8vo. 4s. 6d.

ABBOTT—RUSHBROOKE.—THE COMMON TRADITION OF THE SYNOPTIC GOSPELS, in the Text of the Revised Version. By Rev. EDWIN A. ABBOTT, D.D., and W. G. RUSHBROOKE, M.L. Cr. 8vo. 3s. 6d.

ARNOLD.—Works by MATTHEW ARNOLD.
A BIBLE-READING FOR SCHOOLS,—THE GREAT PROPHECY OF ISRAEL'S RESTORATION (Isaiah, Chapters xl.-lxvi.) Arranged and Edited for Young Learners. 18mo. 1s.
ISAIAH XL.-LXVI. With the Shorter Prophecies allied to it. Arranged and Edited, with Notes. Cr. 8vo. 5s.
ISAIAH OF JERUSALEM, IN THE AUTHORISED ENGLISH VERSION. With Introduction, Corrections and Notes. Cr. 8vo. 4s. 6d.

BENHAM.—A COMPANION TO THE LECTIONARY. Being a Commentary on the Proper Lessons for Sundays and Holy Days. By Rev. W. BENHAM, B.D. Cr. 8vo. 4s. 6d.

CASSEL.—MANUAL OF JEWISH HISTORY AND LITERATURE; preceded by a BRIEF SUMMARY OF BIBLE HISTORY. By Dr. D. CASSEL. Translated by Mrs. H. LUCAS. Fcap. 8vo. 2s. 6d.

CHURCH.—STORIES FROM THE BIBLE. By Rev. A. J. CHURCH, M.A. Illustrated. Cr. 8vo. 5s.

*CROSS.—BIBLE READINGS SELECTED FROM THE PENTATEUCH AND THE BOOK OF JOSHUA. By Rev. JOHN A. CROSS. 2d Ed., enlarged, with Notes. Gl. 8vo. 2s. 6d.

DRUMMOND.—INTRODUCTION TO THE STUDY OF THEOLOGY. By JAMES DRUMMOND, LL.D., Professor of Theology in Manchester New College, London. Cr. 8vo. 5s.

FARRAR.—Works by the Venerable Archdeacon F. W. FARRAR, D.D., F.R.S., Archdeacon and Canon of Westminster.
THE HISTORY OF INTERPRETATION. Bampton Lectures, 1885. 8vo. 16s.
THE MESSAGES OF THE BOOKS. Being Discourses and Notes on the Books of the New Testament. 8vo. 14s.

*GASKOIN.—THE CHILDREN'S TREASURY OF BIBLE STORIES. By Mrs. HERMAN GASKOIN. Edited with Preface by Rev. G. F. MACLEAR, D.D. 18mo. 1s. each. Part I.—OLD TESTAMENT HISTORY. Part II.—NEW TESTAMENT. Part III.—THE APOSTLES: ST. JAMES THE GREAT, ST. PAUL, AND ST. JOHN THE DIVINE.

GOLDEN TREASURY PSALTER.—Students' Edition. Being an Edition of "The Psalms chronologically arranged, by Four Friends," with briefer Notes. 18mo. 3s. 6d.

GREEK TESTAMENT.—Edited, with Introduction and Appendices, by Bishop WESTCOTT and Dr. F. J. A. HORT. Two Vols. Cr. 8vo. 10s. 6d. each. Vol. I. The Text. Vol. II. Introduction and Appendix.
SCHOOL EDITION OF TEXT. 12mo. Cloth, 4s. 6d. ; Roan, red edges, 5s. 6d. 18mo. Morocco, gilt edges, 6s. 6d.
*GREEK TESTAMENT, SCHOOL READINGS IN THE. Being the outline of the life of our Lord, as given by St. Mark, with additions from the Text of the other Evangelists. Arranged and Edited, with Notes and Vocabulary, by Rev. A. CALVERT, M.A. Fcap. 8vo. 2s. 6d.
*THE GOSPEL ACCORDING TO ST. MATTHEW. Being the Greek Text as revised by Bishop WESTCOTT and Dr. HORT. With Introduction and Notes by Rev. A. SLOMAN, M.A., Headmaster of Birkenhead School. Fcap. 8vo. 2s. 6d.
THE GOSPEL ACCORDING TO ST. MARK. Being the Greek Text as revised by Bishop WESTCOTT and Dr. HORT. With Introduction and Notes by Rev. J. O. F. MURRAY, M.A., Lecturer at Emmanuel College, Cambridge. Fcap. 8vo. [In preparation.
*THE GOSPEL ACCORDING TO ST. LUKE. Being the Greek Text as revised by Bishop WESTCOTT and Dr. HORT. With Introduction and Notes by Rev. JOHN BOND, M.A. Fcap. 8vo. 2s. 6d.
*THE ACTS OF THE APOSTLES. Being the Greek Text as revised by Bishop WESTCOTT and Dr. HORT. With Explanatory Notes by T. E. PAGE, M.A., Assistant Master at the Charterhouse. Fcap. 8vo. 3s. 6d.
GWATKIN.—CHURCH HISTORY TO THE BEGINNING OF THE MIDDLE AGES. By H. M. GWATKIN, M.A. 8vo. [In preparation.
HARDWICK.—Works by Archdeacon HARDWICK.
A HISTORY OF THE CHRISTIAN CHURCH. Middle Age. From Gregory the Great to the Excommunication of Luther. Edited by W. STUBBS, D.D., Bishop of Oxford. With 4 Maps. Cr. 8vo. 10s. 6d.
A HISTORY OF THE CHRISTIAN CHURCH DURING THE REFORMA-TION. 9th Ed. Edited by Bishop STUBBS. Cr. 8vo. 10s. 6d.
HOOLE.—THE CLASSICAL ELEMENT IN THE NEW TESTAMENT. Considered as a proof of its Genuineness, with an Appendix on the Oldest Authorities used in the Formation of the Canon. By CHARLES H. HOOLE, M.A., Student of Christ Church, Oxford. 8vo. 10s. 6d.
JENNINGS and LOWE.—THE PSALMS, WITH INTRODUCTIONS AND CRITICAL NOTES. By A. C. JENNINGS, M.A. ; assisted in parts by W. H. LOWE, M.A. In 2 vols. 2d Ed., revised. Cr. 8vo. 10s. 6d. each.
KIRKPATRICK.—THE MINOR PROPHETS. Warburtonian Lectures. By Rev. Prof. KIRKPATRICK. [In preparation.
THE DIVINE LIBRARY OF THE OLD TESTAMENT. By the same. [In prep.
KUENEN.—PENTATEUCH AND BOOK OF JOSHUA : An Historico-Critical Inquiry into the Origin and Composition of the Hexateuch. By A. KUENEN Translated by P. H. WICKSTEED, M.A. 8vo. 14s.
LIGHTFOOT.—Works by the Right Rev. J. B. LIGHTFOOT, D.D., late Bishop of Durham.
ST. PAUL'S EPISTLE TO THE GALATIANS. A Revised Text, with Introduc-tion, Notes, and Dissertations. 10th Ed., revised. 8vo. 12s.
ST. PAUL'S EPISTLE TO THE PHILIPPIANS. A Revised Text, with Intro-duction, Notes, and Dissertations. 9th Ed., revised. 8vo. 12s.
ST. PAUL'S EPISTLES TO THE COLOSSIANS AND TO PHILEMON. A Revised Text, with Introductions, Notes, and Dissertations. 8th Ed., revised. 8vo. 12s.
THE APOSTOLIC FATHERS. Part I. ST. CLEMENT OF ROME. A Revised Text, with Introductions, Notes, Dissertations, and Translations. 2 vols. 8vo. 32s.
THE APOSTOLIC FATHERS. Part II. ST. IGNATIUS—ST. POLYCARP. Revised Texts, with Introductions, Notes, Dissertations, and Translations. 2d Ed. 3 vols. 8vo. 48s.
THE APOSTOLIC FATHERS. Abridged Edition. With short Introductions, Greek Text, and English Translation. 8vo. 16s.
ESSAYS ON THE WORK ENTITLED "SUPERNATURAL RELIGION." (Reprinted from the Contemporary Review.) 8vo. 10s. 6d.

MACLEAR.—Works by the Rev. G. F. MACLEAR, D.D., Warden of St. Augustine's College, Canterbury.

ELEMENTARY THEOLOGICAL CLASS-BOOKS.

*A SHILLING BOOK OF OLD TESTAMENT HISTORY. With **Map.** 18mo.

*A SHILLING BOOK OF NEW TESTAMENT HISTORY. With Map. 18mo. These works have been carefully abridged from the Author's large manuals.

*A CLASS-BOOK **OF** OLD TESTAMENT HISTORY. Maps. **18mo.** 4s. 6d.

*A CLASS-BOOK OF NEW TESTAMENT HISTORY, including the Connection **of the** Old and New Testaments. With maps. 18mo. 5s. 6d.

AN INTRODUCTION TO THE THIRTY-NINE ARTICLES. *[In the Press.*

*AN **INTRODUCTION TO** THE CREEDS. 18mo. 2s. 6d.

*A **CLASS-BOOK OF THE** CATECHISM OF THE CHURCH OF ENGLAND. 18mo. **1s.** 6d.

*A FIRST CLASS-BOOK OF THE CATECHISM **OF THE CHURCH OF** ENGLAND. With Scripture Proofs. 18mo. 6d.

*A MANUAL OF INSTRUCTION FOR CONFIRMATION AND FIRST COM- MUNION. WITH PRAYERS AND DEVOTIONS. 32mo. 2s.

MAURICE.—THE LORD'S PRAYER, **THE** CREED, AND THE COMMAND- MENTS. To which is added the **Order** of the Scriptures. By Rev. F. D. MAURICE, M.A. 18mo. 1s.

THE PENTATEUCH AND BOOK OF JOSHUA: An Historico-Critical Inquiry into the Origin and Composition of the Hexateuch. By **A.** KUENEN, Professor of Theology at **Leiden.** Translated by P. H. WICKSTEED, M.A. 8vo. 14s.

PROCTER.—**A HISTORY OF** THE BOOK OF COMMON PRAYER, with a Ration- ale of its Offices. **By** Rev. F. PROCTER. 18th Ed. Cr. 8vo. 10s. 6d.

*PROCTER and MACLEAR.—AN ELEMENTARY INTRODUCTION TO THE BOOK OF COMMON PRAYER. Rearranged and supplemented by an Ex- planation of the Morning and Evening Prayer and the Litany. By Rev. F. PROCTER and Rev. Dr. MACLEAR. New Edition, containing the Communion Service and the Confirmation and Baptismal Offices. 18mo. 2s. 6d.

THE PSALMS, CHRONOLOGICALLY ARRANGED. By Four Friends. New Ed. Cr. 8vo. 5s. net.

THE PSALMS, WITH INTRODUCTIONS AND **CRITICAL NOTES.** By A. C. JENNINGS, M.A., Jesus College, Cambridge; assisted in parts by W. H. LOWE, M.A., Hebrew Lecturer at Christ's College, **Cambridge.** In 2 vols. 2d Ed., revised. Cr. 8vo. 10s. 6d. each.

RYLE.—**AN INTRODUCTION** TO THE CANON OF THE **OLD** TESTAMENT. By Rev. H. E. RYLE, **M.A., Hulsean** Professor of Divinity in the University of Cambridge. Cr. 8vo. *[In preparation.*

SIMPSON.—AN EPITOME OF THE HISTORY OF THE CHRISTIAN CHURCH DURING THE FIRST THREE CENTURIES, AND OF THE REFORMATION IN ENGLAND. By Rev. WILLIAM SIMPSON, M.A. 7th Ed. Fcap. 8vo. 3s. 6d.

ST. JAMES' EPISTLE.—The Greek Text, with Introduction and Notes. By Rev. JOSEPH MAYOR, M.A., Professor of Moral Philosophy in King's College, London. 8vo. *[In the **Press.***

ST. JOHN'S EPISTLES.—The Greek Text, with Notes and Essays. **By Right Rev.** B. F. WESTCOTT, D.D., Bishop of Durham. 2d Ed., revised. 8vo. 12s. 6d.

ST. PAUL'S EPISTLES.—THE EPISTLE TO THE ROMANS. Edited **by the** Very Rev. C. J. VAUGHAN, D.D., Dean of Llandaff. 5th Ed. Cr. 8vo. **7s.** 6d.

THE TWO EPISTLES TO THE CORINTHIANS, A COMMENTARY ON. **By** the late Rev. W. KAY, D.D., Rector of Great Leghs, Essex. **8vo. 9s.**

THE EPISTLE TO THE GALATIANS. Edited by **the Right Rev.** J. B. LIGHTFOOT, D.D. 10th Ed. 8vo. 12s.

THE EPISTLE TO **THE** PHILIPPIANS. By the Same Editor. 9th Ed. 8vo. 12s.

THE EPISTLE TO THE PHILIPPIANS, **with** Translation, Paraphrase, and Notes for English Readers. By the Very Rev. **C. J.** VAUGHAN, D.D. Cr. 8vo. 5s.

THE EPISTLE **TO** THE COLOSSIANS AND **TO** PHILEMON. By the Right Rev. **J. B. LIGHTFOOT,** D.D. 8th Ed. 8vo. **12s.**

THE EPISTLES TO THE EPHESIANS, THE COLOSSIANS, AND PHILE-
MON; with Introductions and Notes, and an Essay on the Traces of Foreign
Elements in the Theology of these Epistles. By Rev. J. LLEWELYN DAVIES,
M.A. 8vo. 7s. 6d.

THE EPISTLE TO THE THESSALONIANS, COMMENTARY ON THE GREEK
TEXT. By JOHN EADIE, D.D. Edited by Rev. W. YOUNG, M.A., with Preface
by Prof. CAIRNS. 8vo. 12s.

THE EPISTLE TO THE HEBREWS.—In Greek and English. With Critical and
Explanatory Notes. Edited by Rev. F. RENDALL, M.A. Cr. 8vo. 6s.

THE ENGLISH TEXT, WITH COMMENTARY. By the same Editor. **Cr.**
8vo. 7s. **6d.**

THE GREEK TEXT. With **Notes** by C. J. VAUGHAN, D.D., Dean of Llandaff.
Cr. 8vo. 7s. 6d.

THE GREEK **TEXT.** With **Notes and Essays by the Right Rev. Bishop**
WESTCOTT, D.**D.** 8vo. 14s.

VAUGHAN.—THE CHURCH OF THE FIRST DAYS. Comprising the Church
of Jerusalem, the Church of the Gentiles, the Church of the World. By C. J.
VAUGHAN, D.D., Dean of Llandaff. New Ed. Cr. 8vo. 10s. 6d.

WESTCOTT.—Works by the Right Rev. BROOKE FOSS WESTCOTT, D.D., Bishop of
Durham.

A GENERAL SURVEY OF THE HISTORY OF THE CANON OF THE NEW
TESTAMENT DURING THE FIRST FOUR CENTURIES. 6th Ed. With
Preface on "Supernatural Religion." Cr. 8vo. 10s. 6d.

INTRODUCTION TO THE STUDY OF THE FOUR GOSPELS. 7th Ed.
Cr. 8vo. 10s. 6d.

THE BIBLE IN THE CHURCH. A Popular Account of the Collection and
Reception of the Holy Scriptures in the Christian Churches. 18mo. 4s. 6d.

THE EPISTLES OF ST. JOHN. **The Greek** Text, with Notes **and** Essays.
2d Ed., revised. 8vo. 12s. 6d.

THE EPISTLE TO THE HEBREWS. The Greek Text, with Notes and Essays.
8vo. 14s.

SOME THOUGHTS FROM THE ORDINAL. Cr. 8vo. 1s. 6d.

WESTCOTT and HORT.—THE NEW TESTAMENT IN THE ORIGINAL
GREEK. The Text, revised by the Right Rev. Bishop WESTCOTT and Dr.
F. **J.** A. HORT. 2 vols. Cr. 8vo. 10s. 6d. **each.** Vol. I. Text. Vol. II.
Introduction and Appendix.

SCHOOL EDITION OF TEXT. 12mo. **4s. 6d.;** Roan, red edges, 5s. 6d. Fcap.
8vo. Morocco, gilt edges, 6s. 6d.

WRIGHT.—THE COMPOSITION OF THE FOUR GOSPELS. A Critical Enquiry. By Rev. ARTHUR WRIGHT, M A., Fellow and Tutor of Queen's College,
Cambridge. Cr. **8vo.** 5s.

WRIGHT.—THE BIBLE WORD-BOOK: A Glossary of Archaic Words and
Phrases in the Authorised Version of the Bible and the Book of Common
Prayer. By W. ALDIS WRIGHT, M.A., Vice-Master of Trinity College, Cam-
bridge. 2d Ed., revised and enlarged. Cr. 8vo. 7s. 6d.

YONGE.—SCRIPTURE READINGS FOR SCHOOLS AND FAMILIES. By
CHARLOTTE M. YONGE. In Five Vols. Ex. fcap. 8vo. 1s. 6d. each. With
Comments. 3s. 6d. each.

FIRST SERIES.—GENESIS TO DEUTERONOMY. SECOND SERIES.—FROM JOSHUA TO
SOLOMON. THIRD SERIES.—THE KINGS AND THE PROPHETS. FOURTH SERIES.
—THE GOSPEL TIMES. FIFTH SERIES.—APOSTOLIC TIMES.

ZECHARIAH—THE HEBREW STUDENT'S COMMENTARY ON ZECHARIAH,
HEBREW AND LXX. With Excursus on Syllable-dividing, Metheg, Initial
Dagesh, and Siman Rapheh. By W. H. LOWE, M.A., Hebrew Lecturer at
Christ's College, Cambridge. 8vo. 10s. 6d.

The English Illustrated Magazine.

Each Volume Complete in Itself.

Volume for 1884.

Containing 792 pages, with 428 Illustrations. Price 7s. 6d.

The Volume contains the following Complete Stories and Serials :—

The Armourer's 'Prentices. By C. M. YONGE. An Unsentimental Journey through Cornwall. By Mrs. CRAIK. **Julia.** By WALTER BESANT. **How I became a War Correspondent.** By ARCHIBALD FORBES. **The Story of a Courtship.** By STANLEY J. WEYMAN, etc.

Volume for 1885.

Containing 840 pages, with nearly 500 Illustrations. Price 8s.

The Volume contains the following Complete Stories and Serials :—

A Family Affair. By HUGH CONWAY. Girl at the Gate. By WILKIE COLLINS. The Path of Duty. By HENRY JAMES. Schwartz. By D. CHRISTIE MURRAY. A Ship of '49. By BRET HARTE. That Terrible Man. By W. E. NORRIS. Interviewed by an Emperor. By ARCHIBALD FORBES. In the Lion's Den. By the Author of "John Herring," etc.

Volume for 1886.

Containing 832 pages, with nearly 500 Illustrations. Price 8s.

The Volume contains the following Complete Stories and Serials :—

Kiss and be Friends. By the Author of "John Halifax, Gentleman." **Aunt Rachel.** By D. CHRISTIE MURRAY. A Garden of Memories. By MARGARET VELEY. My Friend Jim. By W. E. NORRIS. Harry's Inheritance. By GRANT ALLEN. Captain Lackland. By CLEMENTINA BLACK. Witnessed by Two. By Mrs. MOLESWORTH. **The Poetry did It.** By WILKIE COLLINS. **Dr. Barrere.** By Mrs. OLIPHANT. **Mere Suzanne.** By KATHARINE S. MACQUOID. Days with Sir Roger de Coverley, with pictures by HUGH THOMSON, etc.

Volume for 1887.

Containing 832 pages, with nearly 500 Illustrations. Price 8s.

The Volume contains the following Complete Stories and Serials :—

Marzio's Crucifix. By F. MARION CRAWFORD. A Secret Inheritance. By B. L. FARJEON. Jacquetta. By the Author of "John Herring." Gerald. By STANLEY J. WEYMAN. An Unknown Country. By the Author of "John Halifax, Gentleman." With Illustrations by F. NOEL PATON. A Siege Baby. By J. S. WINTER. Miss Falkland. By CLEMENTINA BLACK, etc.

The English Illustrated Magazine—*continued.*

Volume for 1888.

Containing 832 pages, with nearly 500 Illustrations. Price 8s.

Among the chief Contents of the Volume are the following Complete Stories and Serials :—

Coaching **Days and** Coaching Ways. By W. O. Tristram. With Illustrations by H. Railton and Hugh Thomson. The Story of Jael. By the Author of "Mehalah." Lil : a Liverpool Child. By Agnes C. Maitland. The Patagonia. By Henry James. Family Portraits. By S. J. Weyman. The Mediation of Ralph Hardelot. By Prof. W. Minto. That Girl in Black. By Mrs. Molesworth. Glimpses of Old English Homes. By Elizabeth Balch. Pagodas, Aurioles, and Umbrellas. By C. F. Gordon Cumming. The Magic Fan. By John Strange Winter.

Volume for 1889.

Containing 900 pages, with nearly 500 Illustrations. Price 8s.

Among the chief Contents of the Volume are the following Complete Stories and Serials :—

Sant' Ilario. By F. Marion Crawford. The House of the Wolf. By Stanley J. Weyman. Glimpses of Old English Homes. By Elizabeth Balch. One Night—The Better Man. By Arthur Paterson. How the "Crayture" got on the Strength. And other Sketches. By Archibald Forbes. La Belle Americaine. By W. E. Norris. Success. By Katharine S. Macquoid. Jenny Harlowe. By W. Clark Russell.

Volume for 1890.

Containing 900 pages, with nearly 550 Illustrations. Price 8s.

Among the chief Contents of the Volume are the following Complete Stories and Serials :—

The Ring of Amasis. By the Earl of Lytton. The Glittering Plain : or, the Land of Living Men. By William Morris. The Old Brown Mare. By W. E. Norris. My Journey to Texas. By Arthur Paterson. A Glimpse of Highclere Castle—A Glimpse of Osterley Park. By Elizabeth Balch. For the Cause. By Stanley J. Weyman. Morised. By the Marchioness of Carmarthen. Overland from India. By Sir Donald Mackenzie Wallace, K.C.I.E. The Doll's House and After. By Walter Besant. La Mulette, Anno 1814. By W. Clark Russell.

Volume for 1891.

Containing 900 pages, and about 500 Illustrations. Price 8s.

Among the chief Contents of the Volume are the following Complete Stories and Serials :—

The Witch of Prague. By F. Marion Crawford. The Wisdom Tooth. By D. Christie Murray and Henry Herman. Wooden Tony. By Mrs. W. K. Clifford. Two Jealousies. By Alan Adair. Gentleman Jim. By Mary Gaunt. Harrow School. Winchester College. Fawsley Park. Ham House. Westminster Abbey. Norwich. The New Trade-Union Movement ; Russo-Jewish Immigrant. Queen's Private Garden at Osborne.

MACMILLAN AND CO., LONDON.

VI.50.9.91.